FINLA

AND

WORLD WAR II

1939-1944

Edited by

JOHN H. WUORINEN, Ph.D.

PROFESSOR OF HISTORY, COLUMBIA UNIVERSITY

THE RONALD PRESS COMPANY , NEW YORK

CONTENTS

CONTENTS

FINLAND AND
WORLD WAR II

FOREWORD

The manuscript for this book was received in the United States late in 1945. As far as I know, it is the most important document to come out of Finland since the close of the recent war. It is the first fairly extensive presentation of the Finnish side of the story of how Finland became involved in the war, how the Finns saw and attempted to deal with the baffling problems of the war, and how they finally got out of the war in September, 1944.

The original manuscript came to my attention early in 1946. It was in Finnish. A careful reading of it led to the conclusion that it should be published and made available to the American reader. Having been a student of Finnish history and affairs for over twenty years, and having made a special effort to follow the course of events in Finland since 1939—for example, while serving in the Research and Analysis Branch of the Office of the Strategic Services, in 1942-1944—I have no hesitation in saying that this book throws a flood of light upon a phase of the second World War which has hitherto been largely left to the mercies of the inexpert and the propagandist. The story here told is, as the reader will discover, a calm and unemotional recital of fact and circumstance. The manner of presentation is, in part, restrained to the point of austerity. There is every reason, as far as I know, for believing that essential facts have not been suppressed in order to present a one-sided plea on Finland's behalf. The book is not a cheap propaganda tract.

It was for these reasons that I undertook to prepare the manuscript for publication. Having thus in a sense fathered this book, parental responsibility prompts me to offer a word or two of explanation regarding authorship and the actual task of editing.

Ever since the Russian (Allied) Control Commission began to preside over Finland's destinies in the autumn of 1944, conditions in Finland have been such as to prevent the publication of serious, objective studies of Finland's part in the war. Russian sensibilities cannot be hurt or suspicions aroused. Especially questions dealing with Russia's invasion of Finland in 1939, and with the second phase of the war which began in June, 1941, must either be ignored or discussed in a manner that distorts facts and is in keeping with Russian

3

views which label Finland as a Fascist aggressor intent upon destroy-
ing the Soviet Union. A document which tries to give an objective
account therefore cannot be published without unpleasant consequences for author and publisher alike. If this were not so, this
book would no doubt have been published in Finland months ago,
and the name of the Finnish author would occupy the customary place
on the title page.

A reading of the book shows clearly that it could have been written
only by a man who had access to the necessary information dealing
with the crucial years 1939-1944. It is more than likely that the
author belongs—or belonged—among the top leaders in Finland.
There is also reason to believe that more than one pen contributed
to the manuscript. The reasons for this surmise must remain un-
stated, however, lest they defeat the purpose which anonymity is
intended to achieve.

The manner of telling the story in the Finnish manuscript does
not always lend itself readily to easy translation into English. A
deliberate attempt has been made, however, to retain, in the version
now published, the idiom of the original. It seemed best to avoid the
use of stylistic and other devices which, while no doubt adding to
readability, might easily have led to distortions of subject matter.
The text therefore corresponds to the Finnish original in all respects.
There is but one exception this rule.

The exception is the last or concluding chapter. A reading of the
original suggests that this chapter was written in considerable haste.
Whatever the reason may have been, it is not well organized and
is partly repetitious. I have therefore rearranged its content somewhat and eliminated minor parts of it. It is in this chapter, therefore,
that something like genuine editorial function has been performed.
Care has been taken, needless to say, to leave out nothing and to add
nothing important. In its present form, the last chapter thus contains
the reflections and conclusions penned by the author, although a line
by line comparison would show some differences between the original
and the chapter as it now appears in English.

In preparing the manuscript for publication, it was felt that the
American reader would welcome a somewhat more extensive—and
somewhat different—introductory statement than the one that is contained in the first chapter. The main part of the story is therefore
preceded by a brief summary, presented in this Foreword, of Finnish
economic, political and other developments before the outbreak of the
second World War. For the same reason, it was considered per-

tinent to outline, in equally brief summary form, some of the main results of the war for Finland as the third year of "peace" draws to a close, and to note the nature and implications of the peace treaty which the Allied and Associated Powers signed with Finland on February 10, 1947. A few explanatory footnotes have also been added.

II

The Finland that fell victim to Soviet invasion in 1939 was unquestionably one of the most successful democracies in Europe. Long-range historical development before the Finns achieved independence in 1917-1918 and exceptional progress during the two decades after 1918 had given the country a place in the front rank of European democratic nations.

Until the time when Jefferson served as President of the United States and Napoleon embarked upon his career of gory conquest, Finland was a part of the Swedish kingdom. For well over 600 years, Sweden and Finland constituted a single state. For some twenty generations, Swede and Finn had been equally subjects of the same crown; they had been partners, as it were, in the upbuilding of common political, religious and social institutions, and both were equally "native Swedes" as regards political and other rights. Until Finland was separated from Sweden in 1809, the Finns had been, one can say, as self-governing as the Swedes, and had the same long tradition in the arts of government, law, administration and the like.

Finland's connection with Sweden was severed by Russian conquest. The conquest occurred in 1808-1809, and was one of the side-shows of the larger international drama of the time. The inclusion of Finland in the Russian empire did not, however, reduce the country to the status of a subject province. Finland became a self-governing part—the only self-governing part—of the empire. Its constitution, laws, courts, church and religion (Lutheran), educational system and economic life were left almost wholly unchanged. Thus autonomous Finland was able to carry on, after 1809, on the basis which the preceding centuries had given to the nation. Foreign affairs were left in Russia's hands, to be sure.

Self-governing Finland experienced a great deal of change during the century before the first World War. Farming, the source of livelihood for most of the people, was gradually modernized; industry developed on an increasing scale, especially after 1870; an up-to-date primary school system was introduced, beginning in 1866; the first railroad was opened in 1862, and the railway network grew steadily thereafter; the telephone and telegraph systems expanded rapidly after the 1880's; in shipping, steamship business grew important after 1880; a separate Finnish monetary system went into effect in 1865. Meanwhile, the political emancipation of the common man had also begun, and resulted in the granting of the free right to vote to adult women as well as men in 1906. Meantime, too, the population of the country had increased from about 1,000,000 to roughly 3,250,000, and the urban population had grown from some 40,000 to well over 500,000.

Change of another kind also occurred during the period. Down to the 1890's, Finnish self-government was left intact by Russia, and in some important respects it was even expanded. After 1890, however, the Russian imperial government began to pursue a policy of Russification which threatened constitution, self-government, and the freedom of the citizen. Despite tenacious passive resistance, the Finns were gradually forced under a rule ever more destructive of the political and other freedoms and institutions of the nation. By 1914, it seemed that Russification would triumph in the foreseeable future and that Finland and the Finns would be reduced to the status which Pan-Slavists considered proper for a Russian province.

The collapse of the Tsarist regime early in 1917 gave the Finns a chance to establish the independence of their country. An independent republic was proclaimed on December 6 of that year. It is worth noting that the bolshevik government, acting in accordance with the liberal views which it embraced at the time regarding the nationalities within Russia that desired independence, was the first to recognize the existence of Finland as a sovereign state. Before independence was fully achieved, however, a short war was fought in the spring of 1918 between Finnish Reds, intent on establishing a Soviet republic and aided by Russia, and the supporters of the legal government. The latter won and the war was over by the end of May. A republican constitution was drafted and went into effect in July, 1919. It provided for a president chosen for a six-year term, a one-chamber legislature chosen by universal suffrage (both the legislature and universal suffrage dated, in fact, from 1906) and for a government responsible to the people. The time-honored rights of the citizen, such as free speech, free assembly, a free press and the like, became a solid part of the new republican order of things as they had been a part of the older order before Russian policy had endangered or destroyed them. Sovereign Finland thus meant, from the start, a Finland securely anchored to the principles and practices of democracy.

The years between 1918 and 1939 fully demonstrated the solidity of the economic foundations which had been laid while Finland was still a part of Russia, and the robust nature of Finnish democracy under a republican constitution. Industry, farming, schools of all grades, the expanding field of social legislation, the cooperatives and many other things all showed impressive progress. The general standard of living was markedly improved, and even the depression of 1929-1933 turned out to be only a temporary obstacle in the economic life of the nation.

A few figures suffice to show what these two decades of peaceful advance meant. The population of the country had been about 3,250,000 shortly before the first World War. When the decade of the 1930's ended, it was close to 4,000,000. Two out of every three Finns were still rural, but about every second Finn made his living in non-agrarian occupations. Farming still remained the most important single industry in 1939, and one of the most significant achievements of the period related to agriculture. Between 1918 and 1922, laws were enacted to deal with the problem of the landless rural population. Renters of land were enabled to become land owners on easy, liberal terms, and by 1935 well over 100,000 new holdings had been established. The tillers of the soil had become, for all practical purposes, a class of independent small farmers. Meanwhile, the increasing use of machinery and modern methods in general had increased the agricultural self-sufficiency of the nation; by the closing thirties, about eighty-five per cent of the food needed was home grown, and exports, especially of dairy products, had attained considerable dimensions.

No less conspicuous was the expansion of industry. The value of industrial production grew rapidly: from less than three billion marks in 1919 to over thirteen billion marks in 1934 (before 1939, the value of one Finnish mark was 2.2 cents); the volume more than doubled. Timber, paper and pulp industries loomed especially large in the picture, and contributed over eighty per cent of the expanding export trade of the country. This was natural in view of the fact that timber is one of the two great natural resources—water power being the other—of Finland. Forests, the basic resource, had long benefited by scientific forestry techniques which alone made possible the continual exploitation of timber without exhausting this all-important source of national wealth. The ownership of the nation's forests reflected the sound economy of the people: the state owned some thirty-seven per cent of the forest lands, municipalities accounted for two per cent, and private individuals for about fifty-one per cent. The figure for lumber companies was a fraction under ten per cent.

By no means the least significant feature of the economic life of Finland during these years was the cooperative movement. The cooperative movement had appeared at the turn of the century and had made much headway by the time Finland became independent. It registered further gains after 1918, and by 1939 it had become important in both retail and wholesale trade and a by no means negligible factor in banking and manufacturing as well. Shortly before 1939, some thirty per cent of the total retail trade in the country was handled by the cooperatives—a figure higher than that of the other Scandinavian countries—and about forty to fifty per cent of the domestic grain sold in the home market was sold by them. Nearly all exports of dairy products went through cooperatives. They ran most of the nation's dairy industry, operated credit societies and banks on a substantial scale, and were successful in several lines of manufacturing. It is no exaggeration to say that the cooperatives played a decisive part in the process which had translated, by 1939, the concept of economic democracy into a vital and functioning part of the nation's life.

Meantime, political life showed the vigor that might be expected of a small compact republic whose citizenry is literate and schooled in the business of self-government. While political developments during these years were by no means wholly tranquil and the ship of state had to weather many a squall, and while the solution of domestic problems did not satisfy all the people all the time—seemingly a sign of active democracy wherever democracy prevails—the trend was altogether toward a broadening and strengthening of self-government by free citizens. Neither the activities of the communists, whose party was labelled treasonous and was outlawed in 1930, nor the distressing experiences of the depression years from 1929 to 1933, sufficed to capsize the boat. Socialist Democrat labor—not to be confused in any way with communists—was easily the leading and largest single political party in the country, and together with Agrarians (with whom Social Democrat labor cooperated especially after 1936) and liberals controlled the majority of the seats in the Finnish Parliament. Fascist or Nazi parties never gained seats in the legislature, and the Patriotic People's Party which no doubt harbored elements with anti-democratic inclinations, never obtained more than seven per cent of the seats, and in the last elections before the recent war, held in 1939, had to be satisfied with only four per cent.

Finland's foreign policy during this first generation of independence was simple and obvious to all who followed the course of events in the republic. It was rational and purposeful in a sense that any observer could understand. Its aim was peaceful relations with all nations, scrupulous observance of international and other commitments—witness the uninterrupted payments on the debt to the United States—and, in the event that war should break out, to observe absolute neutrality. Confidence in the League of Nations and acceptance of the obligations of League membership was a basic feature of the policy, especially down to the middle thirties. Only this kind of a policy, and the objectives it reflected, was considered useful, defensible and safe. It was responsible for the fact that Finland's foreign affairs before 1939 represented a relatively uneventful chapter in the story of these years, and it alone made possible the fruitful and expanding cooperation between Finland and her Northern neighbors, Sweden, Norway and Denmark, which had assumed many forms by the time the second World War began. This policy was not only good in terms of national interests; it was good and moral also in the sense that it harmed nobody, it threatened nobody's security, and it was in complete harmony with the principles of justice and fair dealing.

Over and above and beyond such concrete indications of the life of the nation as economic or electoral statistics, party relationships or basic objectives in the field of foreign affairs, other realities existed which were not—and normally cannot be—recorded and measured in the same way as economic advance, the rise and fall of cabinets or treaty relationships with the outside world. Yet these more intangible aspects of the Finnish way of looking at things and ways of doing things were realities of utmost importance. They gave substance and meaning and direction to both the life of the individual and the nation as a whole.

Finnish politics before 1939 had many aspects that must be called cheap and shoddy. Selfish men—and women, too—did rise to prominence, and ignorance of national and international questions was not rare in Parliament or out. Shortsightedness and narrow provincialism in the handling of public business were by no means uncommon. Thus there was much room for improvement in the domain of politics—a fact frequently stressed in the Finnish press and on the rostrum during the twenties and thirties. But corruption in public office never became a problem in Finnish politics, or callous sacrifice of the nation's welfare a result of individual ambition or of party competition for power and influence. Arbitrary government ever remained foreign to the Finns. In Finland, as in all true democracies, government wielded what power it had as a result of democratic processes. Power and functions rested on and derived from law.

Ever since the Finns became articulate about such things, they have thought, written and talked about "law-bound" liberty. "Law-bound" is a literal translation of a phrase every Finn knows; it is probably more familiar to him than is "liberty under the law" to the average American. It means that fixed rules, formulated by a democratically chosen legislature, determine what government can do and cannot do. It can tax and coerce only within the rules. It has no right to arbitrary action. What is right today is right tomorrow, and what was within the law yesterday or is within the law today will be within the law next week or until a new law, properly enacted, provides otherwise.

The acceptance of and devotion to liberty under law was deeply imbedded among the Finns. It is an interesting fact that the literature of freedom and liberty in the abstract does not loom large in Finnish culture. This does not mean that the concepts or practices of freedom have been ignored. What it means is that freedom, liberty and government under law have been taken for granted. National freedom and the liberty of the Finnish citizen and Finnish cultural independence—these have been accented more than the general ideal of human liberty. Man's search for freedom has not been the important concern; the Finns' own desire to be free, to escape foreign domination, to be masters in their own house, has been the inspiration. In a sense, this reflects provincialism and narrowness, no doubt, but the provincialism it discloses violated nobody's interests and was free from the notion that Finnish freedom could be or must be achieved and maintained at the expense of someone else's enslavement.

The Finns' culture and civilization lacks the depth and grandeur illustrated in many other lands. But it is largely free from offensive pretense or cheap pomp. It has not been purchased by the suffering of other people; it has developed from the toil and perseverance of the Finns themselves. They have long drawn freely on the common fund of western civilization which the West has accumulated in the course of many centuries. Church, education, concepts of justice, political institutions and the like especially bear this out. The result was that by 1939 the Finns could claim that by any test yet devised, their body politic, social and economic, well served the needs of a democratic people, that social equality and justice, equal economic opportunity, and equality in the domain of things political were theirs to a greater degree than was the case in some of the larger vaunted democracies in Europe. They loved their civilization and labored to make it better. They were pulling their full weight in the cause of democracy and in the complicated tasks of providing a better and richer existence for the "forgotten man."

It is a commonplace that every nation needs—the historian would perhaps say "seems to need"—as a part of its existence stirring symbols in order to progress. The Finns had their share of stirring symbols. They have no glorious and recent monarchical tradition and institutions—what monarchical tradition they had had, ended in 1809, and had become meaningless and remote by 1918 when an independent Finland appeared. The trappings of the military likewise never became a part of the Finnish "system of homages." The symbols that they revere, that quicken their hearts, appeal to their loyalties and command their love, have to do with the life and work of men who helped them to achieve the miraculous thing they had desired most, their freedom and independence. The roster of Finland's honored men is headed by poets, pedagogues, scholars and other patriots who never donned a uniform or fired a gun. While it includes men who fought for independence in 1918 and later—it includes, for example, a hero-child of twelve who died in the war of 1918, and Marshal Mannerheim who served his country as a soldier in 1918 and again in 1939-1944—it is composed overwhelmingly of men of the pen and not of the sword. This, too, is in keeping with the basic features of society and culture in Finland.

Among the basic features, perhaps the most conspicuous is the absence of a rigid class society. For the past two generations in particular, social democracy has been especially marked—evolution up and down. No "first families" monopolize public emoluments or dominate the nation. There is no aristocracy. Sons of farmers and laborers today occupy the highest posts in the state, while many a scion of yesterday's wealth and prominence now belongs in the lower strata of society. It is no accident that the majority of men and women in Finland's public life in the 1930's were either self-made successes who had risen from the anonymity of the masses to prominence in the service of the state, school, church or in the professions, or were the sons or daughters of energetic and able parents who had successfully climbed the ladder leading from the masses to the classes.

Such, in brief, was the Finland that the Finns of the twenties and thirties loved, and for which they fought after Russia proceeded to invade the country in November, 1939. They loved it not because it was richer than other countries—which it was not, and not because life was easier or men basically better than in other countries. They loved it because it was their place of birth, their homeland. Group kinship was strong and attachment to nation likewise strong. Finland's small size in itself gave the people an aspect of internal unity which citizens of larger states are often denied. They loved it because it was a free man's country; because social cleavages were not marked and economic opportunity was not in the keeping of entrenched privilege; because social and economic maladjustments were being righted by a substantial and expanding body of social legislation; because educational advance was not blocked by a system of caste; and because political and other rights were denied to nobody willing to accept the code and morality of a common man's republic founded on the rule of law and the concept that the rights of the citizen take precedence over the claims of the state. And they loved it because of its beauty. To them it was a lovely land—a land of white and blue and deep green of spruce and pine in winter, and in summer a land of silvery lake, sparkling sea and verdant field ringed by forests in the softer greens of the days when the sun stands high in the heavens and hardly sets for weeks on end. Not a land of grandeur but of quiet, clean beauty that touches the heart and elevates the mind. To them it was a land worth fighting and dying for.

III

Within two months of the invasion of Poland in September, 1939, and the division of that unhappy land by Germany and Russia, Finland became the second European nation to fall victim to unprovoked military invasion. In the unequal battle which then began the Finns at first heroically fought alone. In the later stages of the defense of their independence and democracy—that is, after June, 1941—they became enmeshed in the larger world conflict which lasted until Germany and Japan were utterly defeated. The Finnish-Russian war had been ended by then, having been brought to a close by the Armistice and preliminary peace signed in September, 1944.

The Finns had fought in the best of causes: their democratic Republic and national existence had been at stake. When the firing ceased, they had impressively shown what even a small nation can do when stoutly defended by free men who value liberty and independence higher than life itself.

The Finns did not want war in 1939. Short of abject surrender they did everything to avoid conflict with the Soviet Union. The enlightened opinion of the world condemned Russia as guilty of aggression when she invaded Finland in November of that fateful year. If justice and right had decided the outcome of the Winter War, Finland would have emerged victorious. But it was force that dictated the verdict. The Peace of March 12, 1940, despoiled Finland of ten to fourteen per cent of her best territory and economic resources. It exposed the country to further exactions and dangers during the fifteen months that followed the Peace. "Ordeal by peace" is a fitting description of Finland's position during the months from March, 1940, to June, 1941, when Russian control of the whole nation seemed to be the goal of Soviet policy. Only the Nazi attack on Russia on June 22, 1941, brought respite to the Finns.

That respite was brief. On the very first day of the Nazi invasion of the U.S.S.R., Russia renewed military operations against Finland, and on June 25, the Finnish government declared that a state of war with Russia again existed. During the next few months the Finns succeeded in recapturing the territory which had been taken from them by the peace of March, 1940, and in pushing their military operations into Soviet Karelia. To claim that these operations had nothing to do with the Winter War, or that the Finns took up arms in 1941 because they were Nazis determined to profit at the expense of an unoffending Russia, is to ignore the basic facts in the case.

After Finnish territory had been recaptured from the Russians and other strategic objectives had been reached (this had been accomplished by the end of 1941), and as the world conflict spread and Germany's failure and defeat became more obvious, how to get out of the war became a seemingly impossible problem for Finland. In the war, Finland fought the Soviet Union as a cobelligerent of Germany. In 1939-1940, Germany had aided Russia. In 1941-1944, Germany fought Russia. Because of her war-time isolation from the rest of the world, Finland's military potential and general economy (especially food supplies) had come largely to depend on German aid. In their efforts to weaken the enemy, the United Nations repeatedly advised Finland to cease fighting. At no time, however, were any assurances given that if Finland withdrew from the war her independence and food supplies would be assured.

Under the circumstances, the Finns saw only two alternatives. The first was to continue fighting and to accept the risks it involved. The second was to throw down their arms and to surrender to Russia. This would mean, it was believed, that the country would become the battleground of the Germans and the Russians. The end result would be loss of independence and annexation by Russia. The Finns chose the first alternative.

It was not till the early spring of 1944 that specific terms were presented to Finland. They were terms of surrender. They included a reparations obligation of $600,000,000, and the undertaking to intern or oust (with Russian aid, if necessary) the German troops in Finland within a month. Both demands seemed quite impossible to meet. A reparations bill of $600,000,000 would force Finland, a nation of less than 4,000,000 people, never wealthy and already impoverished by years of war for which it was not responsible, into annihilating economic servitude. To agree to intern the Germans within one month would also mean an obligation which could only end in failure. Failure would lead to default and occupation by Soviet troops. The terms were therefore rejected. It was not until September when military reverses and a downward revision of the terms of surrender offered to Finland had changed the situation, that Finland at long last was able to get out of the war.

The Russian armistice terms of September 19, 1944, were accepted in the United States and the western world in general without much critical comment.[1] In a number of instances the terms were considered surprisingly "liberal" and in keeping with the objectives and principles for which the United Nations were fighting.

Such appraisal of the terms is unrealistic. It ignores the moral aspects of Finland's war. It likewise ignores the real meaning of the economic clauses of the armistice. It can be explained only in terms of ignorance of the basic facts, although it may also have resulted in part from the feeling, nursed by war-time propaganda, that Finland, having failed to get out of the war as early as the United Nations desired, deserved nothing better.

In violation of the Atlantic Charter, accepted by Russia as well as the other United Nations, Finland was forced to cede to the Soviet Union the territory which Russia had annexed in 1940. This cession was widely interpreted at the time as a natural and legitimate

[1] The armistice agreement is printed herein as Appendix A. See pages 189-200.

"return" of Soviet territory to its rightful owner. Nothing is further
from the truth. Russia had taken the territory in 1940 as the result
of a war begun by Russia herself. That aggression gave Russia
neither a legal nor a moral right to the territory in question. Therefore, when Russia retook these areas in 1944, nothing but undis-
guised conquest was involved.

The Petsamo area was also taken, and strategic territory at Porkkala, within ten miles of Helsinki, the capital, was "leased" for a
naval base. The loss of Petsamo meant a most serious economic and
territorial amputation. Porkkala in Russian hands means an ever-
present threat to the capital and the whole nation.

These territorial losses created special problems. The whole population of the ceded areas moved into Finland. The flight from the
provinces taken by Russia was voluntary and spontaneous. It involved well over 400,000 persons. How to care for these displaced
persons created an immense difficulty. The problem will remain
acute for years to come, for Karelia alone represented ten to fourteen
per cent of Finland's industrial and agricultural resources. How
hundreds of thousands of men, women and children could find a livelihood in a truncated Finland would have meant a frightful problem
even if no other critical difficulties existed.

But other critical difficulties did and do exist. The armistice
terms also provided for reparations of $300,000,000. Payment must
be made in goods (specified as to kind and quantity) in six annual
installments of $50,000,000 each. In October, 1945, the time of pay-
ment was extended by two years. Additional demands by Russia,
however, were also presented. They included compensation for
"damage" caused by Finnish troops in Russian territory, and for
alleged destruction and moving of property out of the areas ceded
to Russia.

In view of the original Russian demand for $600,000,000, the
reduction of reparations to $300,000,000 might suggest a reasonable
obligation that can be readily met. All available facts relating to Finland's capacity to pay incontestably show, however, that even the
sum of $300,000,000 reduces the nation to economic servitude and
threatens it with utter destruction. The reparations burden Finland
must bear is vastly greater than a superficial consideration of the
armistice terms suggests.

The Winter War of 1939-1940 probably reduced the national
wealth of Finland by twenty per cent. The war of 1941-1944 caused
vast additional loss of material values. They have not been fully

measured—probably never can be fully measured—but they unquestionably were great enough to reduce Finland's economic resources and capacities by a margin wide enough to spell decades of want even if no reparations to Russia were involved.

Because of reparations obligations, Finland must export to Russia, without receiving any equivalent, commodities of various kinds valued at $300,000,000. The prices of the commodities are fixed, at Russia's insistence, in terms of 1938 prices in gold dollars. Although price increases of ten to fifteen per cent have been allowed, such increases do not materially change the picture. In terms of 1945 or 1946 prices, therefore, the Finns are obligated to deliver goods to the actual value, in all probability, of some $600,000,000. Also, Russia has demanded certain deliveries—products of the shipbuilding and metal industries, for example—which Finnish industry normally produces only in limited quantities or not at all. Thus, certain metal industries which provided only four per cent of Finland's exports before 1939 must furnish over sixty per cent of the reparations deliveries. New plants have consequently been built, at great expense, and high-cost raw materials imported from abroad, solely for reparations deliveries. The sum of $300,000,000 therefore gives no meaningful indication of the crushing weight which reparations impose on the nation.[2]

What the problem really involves is strikingly revealed if it is assumed that Finland's economic potential and other resources of the prosperous 1930's were still intact and could now be fully used to pay the reparations bill. In the 1930's, except for the depression years 1929-1933, unemployment was unimportant or practically non-

[2] It is interesting to note that Foreign Secretary Ernest Bevin of Great Britain proposed to the Council of Foreign Ministers, meeting in Paris in June and July, 1946, that the four Powers renounce all claims to reparations from Italy, in order to aid Italian recovery and prosperity. The suggestion was not accepted because of Russian opposition. The British proposal was supported by the United States. In his report to the nation, delivered over the radio on July 15, 1946, Secretary of State James F. Byrnes stated that "we . . . were opposed to putting on [Italy] a reparations burden which would delay her economic recovery . . . We reluctantly agreed that the Soviets could receive reparations up to $100,000,000. But we required them to agree that in so far as reparations were taken from Italian production, the deliveries must be arranged so as to avoid interference with economic reconstruction." Deliveries were not to begin for two years, and "the imported materials needed by Italy to make these deliveries should be supplied by the Soviets." *The New York Times,* June 19 and July 16, 1946. The final Italian peace treaty, signed in Paris on February 10, 1947, fixed Italy's reparations at $360,000,000, Russia to receive $100,000,000 of the total. Italy, a nation of 45,000,000 people and Hitler's partner in aggression before 1939 and after, thus received almost the same reparations terms as Finland, a nation of 4,000,000 people.

existent, wages rose, industrial production reached new high levels, exports and imports grew, and foreign debts were rapidly paid off. What would the payment of the present reparations bill have meant under these exceptionally favorable circumstances?

The answer is clearly given by the following facts. During the decade before 1939, Finland's annual exports normally exceeded imports. The greatest excess of exports over imports occurred in 1934; it amounted to about $29,000,000. The average "favorable balance of trade" in 1930-1939 was roughly $17,000,000 annually.

These figures are meaningless, however, unless they are related to Finnish imports. Only purchases abroad made possible the "favorable balance of trade" mentioned. Five-eighths of Finland's imports —foods, machinery, oil, coal, fertilizers, fodder, etc.—were absolutely essential for the functioning of the general national economy which yielded the $17,000,000 export surplus during the average year before 1939. Exports for which no payment could be obtained would at once have contracted imports. Without imports Finland's industrial and agrarian economy could not produce the export surplus.

Thus the conclusion inevitably is that even in the best years before 1939 when Finland enjoyed exceptional prosperity, her economy yielded an annual exportable surplus which amounted to only a fraction of what Finland now has to turn over to Russia in reparations. Even these modest export surpluses were possible only because they could be turned into foreign commodities which sustained industry and farming in Finland. Even before 1939, therefore, to have been forced to submit to the economic bleeding of reparations would have paralyzed the nation and turned its people into paupers.[3]

If Finland's pre-1939 economy could not have delivered to Russia (without catastrophic results) the tribute now exacted, the situation today is obviously vastly more difficult. The years of war from 1939 to 1944 greatly decreased the productive capacity of Finnish industry. It was, in 1946, on an average, only two-thirds of pre-war capacity. The output of export industries which must produce the reparations was, in 1945, something like fifty per cent of the output before the war. In the all-important paper, pulp and timber indus-

[3] Further proof of the immensity of the reparations obligation lies in the following figures which reduce the sum of $300,000,000 (or, rather, $600,000,000) to understandable terms: in 1936 and 1937, all raw materials used by Finnish industry averaged about $370,000,000 annually; the net value of the whole of the nation's industrial production in 1937 was about $182,000,000; the total state revenue averaged in 1928-1937, roughly $76,000,000 yearly; the total state debt in 1932 was about $125,000,000, and in 1937, about $76,000,000; in 1937 the Finnish State Railways were valued at roughly $125,000,000.

tries, which normally accounted for some eighty per cent of Finland's exports, the production figures in 1946 appear to have ranged from forty to fifty per cent of peacetime capacity. Lack of fuel and raw materials that must be imported largely accounts for the decrease. And such imports are impossible on the scale needed because exports sufficient to pay for coal and other essentials are not possible. They are impossible because of reparations.

This is clearly shown by the following figures. During the first nine months in 1945, Finland's total exports were valued at 6,700 million marks. Of this sum, 4,846 million represented goods sent to Russia as reparations. Over two-thirds of Finland's "exports," therefore, represented tribute paid to Russia. Thus less than one-third represented bona-fide exports which could be turned into sorely needed imports. This amount, in turn, represented less than fifteen per cent of the Finnish exports in 1938. It is on as slim a margin as this that the country has to depend for essential food and raw materials without which the nation cannot exist. Finnish agriculture has never produced enough for self-sufficiency. In 1946, minimum essential bread rations required the import of about 300,000 tons of grain. How to pay for absolutely necessary food imports is a problem no less pressing than the question of how to obtain relief in the present reparations set-up. Prolonged economic servitude, the ever-present threat of default in reparations payments and additional Russian demands growing out of default, starvation— such was the prospect that eventually faced the Finnish people in the third year after the armistice concluded in September, 1944.[4]

IV

While "Finland at peace" has thus come to mean a country dominated by the paralyzing problem of reparations, other forms of servitude have also appeared. Personal freedom has become limited, free speech curtailed, freedom of association and assembly restricted and the freedom of the press non-existent in the pre-1939 sense. The right to write, publish and sell books freely has disappeared. The political police and the censor have become instrumentalities for imposing the correct creed and behavior upon all and sundry. They see

[4] The reparations provisions contain penalty clauses which impose a fine of five per cent monthly in case of failure to deliver according to schedule. Inability to deliver, therefore, may mean an increase of sixty per cent per commodity annually. These penalty clauses therefore represent a possible device for long-term extortion of tribute from Finland.

to it that public discussion, dissent and criticism—the very essence of democracy—move within the safe confines of the trivial and politically innocuous. Over the scene lies the deep shadow of the Soviet Union. Upon it move the servants large and small of Moscow.

For obvious reasons, the political situation within the country immediately after the armistice was tranquil. Finland's withdrawal from the war was not achieved by a "liberation" from German occupation. The withdrawal came because further resistance was deemed useless and the acceptance of Russia's terms, harsh as they were, preferable to a continuation of war. There was no "underground" or "front" in the ordinary sense of the term working against the government that had collaborated with Germany since 1941, or a "government-in-exile" claiming to speak for the Finnish people. All parties—except the outlawed communists, who had been officially non-existent since 1930—had served in the coalition cabinets since 1941. The war effort had been sustained by a united nation, and only toward its close had important differences of opinion risen as to when and how an armistice should be sought and accepted. It did not take long, however, before the situation changed. New tensions appeared; and in the course of a few weeks a "new order" began to emerge. It meant submission of the country to exactions that stemmed from Russia.

The armistice terms obligated Finland to apprehend and punish "persons responsible for the war." Under Russian pressure, an unconstitutional law which would give a "legal" basis for the trials called for by the armistice was enacted in September, 1945. It provided that all persons—that is, Finns—who had decisively contributed to Finland's becoming involved in the war against the Soviet Union and Britain [5] in 1941, or had prevented the reestablishment of peace during the war, should be punished.

Eight prominent leaders were brought to trial in the fall of 1945. They were headed by Mr. Risto Ryti, President of the Republic from 1940 to August, 1945. Six had served in the Cabinet during the war. Among them was one of the most prominent leaders in the Finnish political labor movement and the cooperative movement, Mr. V. Tanner. One, a former Premier, had served as Finland's Minister in Berlin during the war. Two of the eight—ex-President Ryti and ex-Foreign Minister Henrik Ramsay—were the only two Finns ever

[5] The armistice was signed by Great Britain as well as Russia, Great Britain having declared war on Finland in December, 1941. Nominally the British are therefore involved in the Finnish problem, but it is Russia that has called the tune throughout.

to be knighted by Great Britain. Both had stood, long before 1939, in the front rank among the friends of Great Britain in Finland.

After being tried by a special court (itself established contrary to well established Scandinavian legal rules), all eight were found guilty and sentenced to terms ranging from two to ten years. Ex-President Ryti was given ten years at hard labor.

These men were convicted on the basis of a law which defined as a crime acts that were not punishable according to law when they were committed. The convictions meant a deviation from a basic rule in all countries whose judicial system is worthy of the name, that retroactive legislation is prohibited. This principle, which is a device for protecting the innocent and for preventing tyranny, was openly violated. The trial of the eight was thus a travesty of justice. They had done nothing they were prohibited by law from doing, and had failed to do nothing they were in law and conscience bound to do. The evidence presented against them showed that they were guilty only of having made reasonable and understandable choices between the alternatives that seemed clear in June, 1941, and later. Whatever errors in judgment were then made were made in good faith and without evil or criminal intent.[6]

The trial is only one illustration among many of the regime which has been emerging since the fall of 1944. Civil rights accepted in orderly society are violated; democratic processes are twisted or abandoned; legal immunities are like chaff in the wind that blows from Moscow; liberty and justice within the law have been largely replaced by the arbitrary compulsions exerted by Russia and applied by Finnish communists who bask in the Eastern sun and do the work of the Kremlin. And oppressed by the ever-present problem of how to keep body and soul together, many a Finn, realizing that it is impossible to live by bleating with the Finnish sheep, probably goes through the motions of howling with the Russian wolf and thus contributes to the uncertainties that face the nation.

---

[6] This seems to be the only conclusion justified by the evidence. The course of the trial is detailed in the unofficial *Sotasyyllisyysoikeudenkäynnin Asiakirjoja*, I-III, Helsinki, 1945-1946. The trial was extensively reported in the Finnish press. During the trial no attempt was made to establish a meaningful connection between Russia's invasion of Finland in 1939 and the second phase of the war after June, 1941. This in itself suffices to show how superficial and one-sided the attempt was to assign responsibility for the war. Hj. J. Procopé, Chief Counsel of the defense and former Foreign Minister, has published an excellent survey of the trial in *Fallande dom som friar* (Stockholm, 1946); the sale of the book is forbidden in Finland. A deputy member of the Court, Dr. T. T. Kaila, has published another useful description in his *Sotasyyllisemme säätytalossa* (Helsinki, 1946).

To detail the situation further would not be appropriate in this Foreword which has already expanded beyond reasonable limits. Yet, some of its aspects compel brief mention.

A prime objective of the Finns since the close of the war has been to establish the best possible relations with the Soviet Union. In one phase of this effort, the communists have been especially prominent. They are responsible, it appears, for many of the procedures involved. Among them is the "cleansing" of textbooks and libraries of everything that might be considered "anti-Russian" or "anti-Soviet." All history textbooks, for instance, have been revised; and the literature on the 1939-1940 war, which had been published by 1944, has been proscribed. In the libraries, all books that could be interpreted to contain anything "wrong" or "misleading" about the Soviet, have been removed. These tasks have been performed under the watchful eye of the Ministry of Education which has shown notable zeal in carrying out the desires of Moscow.

Meantime the nation is being prepared for a better world in other ways. The Finnish radio, now under appropriate leadership, is an important instrument in the effort. Genuine democracy, the concepts of right and wrong as normally accepted by the nation before the war, cannot be discussed on the air any more than in books. Democracy in general—and especially Finnish democracy before 1939—should be spoken of, if mentioned at all, with a sneer or condescension. Its shortcomings must be accented and its admirable aspects ignored. The assumption on the part of the powers-that-be appears to be that if the Finns are exposed long enough to the idiom and routines of the "new freedom" which Russia represents, they will ultimately change. They will then reject, because their capacity for individual judgment is gone, the old gods of democracy and liberty and will meekly and unquestioningly worship the new idols of Moscow.[7] A people dulled and cowed is a people mute and powerless. Such a people, it appears to be assumed, can be brought into being in Finland by denying free discussion and debate; by robbing the Finns of access to the literature animated by their own historical traditions and containing sources of inspiration for times evil as well as good; by closing the door on their national past, the knowledge of which has become a part of their way of understanding the generations out of which the present has grown. And if these techniques

[7] I have gone through considerable numbers of Finnish newspapers and other material covering the period from the autumn of 1944 to the spring of 1947. Reading the censored press between the lines—and behind and around the lines—leads to these conclusions.

of corruption fail, as fail they probably will, other techniques of compulsion will no doubt emerge.

They have in fact already partly emerged. The communist-controlled political police—it is under the communist Mr. Y. Leino, Minister of the Interior—has already acquired an unenviable reputation because of arrests and unexplained detentions of thousands of citizens and the mysterious disappearances of others. Ugly rumors of concentration camps circulate. Foreign travel is under the control of the political police and thus a new, formidable obstacle—in addition to exchange regulations and the like—has been placed in the path of Finns who desire to travel abroad. Public servants are dismissed without cause and individuals willing to hold their tongue and do the bidding of the communists and fellow travellers take their place. Mass meetings arranged to foment trouble have increasingly appeared as an instrument for cowing the hesitant and sustaining the men committed to Moscow's way.

It is the communists and their friends, needless to say, who call the tune, and behind them looms the larger menace of Russia. It appears safe to say that not more than ten to fifteen per cent of the Finns would be found in the communist camp in any free election. In the only election so far held since the war ended—in March, 1945—the communists remained, despite the exceptionally favorable circumstances which then aided them, in a hopeless minority. (While the elections were nominally free, Russian pressure led to the withdrawal from the electoral contest of several tested and tried laborite and other friends of democracy, and the use of campaign literature by all but the communists was restricted.) They captured less than twenty-five per cent of the seats in the Parliament. Only Russian influence and the fear of Russian displeasure explain the fact that the communists were given four important ministerial posts in the cabinet formed after the election. Among them is the all-important Ministry of the Interior which appears to have become the main agency in the fashioning of the police state which has increasingly replaced government under law.

Whether the experts in the eradication of genuine democracy and the grafting of the new "democracy" of the Russian type will succeed, time alone can tell. The chances are that they will fail unless more ruthless methods than those so far applied become the order of the day. Be that as it may, they have so far benefited by the conditions that have prevailed since the armistice of 1944. Their position was strengthened, and their opportunities appear to have been considerably increased, by the peace treaty which officially ended the state of war between Finland and the Allied and Associated Powers.

The treaty, signed in Paris on February 10, 1947, confirmed in the main the territorial provisions originally included in the armistice of September 19, 1944. It repeats the economic exactions embodied in that document and in some respects increases them. It also contains clauses that threaten definitely to turn Finnish democracy and independence into a precarious, limited privilege that can be purchased, in the future, only by subservience to Russian compulsions.[1]

The main outlines of the treaty were drafted at the conference of the Allied foreign ministers in London in the autumn of 1945, and the document was virtually finished at the Paris conference in the summer of 1946. The final draft was accepted by the foreign ministers conference in New York in November-December, 1946.

While Finland was given an opportunity at Paris to express herself regarding the provisions of the treaty, and an official delegation headed by Premier Mauno Pekkala was present at Paris, the opportunity turned out to be meaningless. The Finns suggested that the reparations amount be reduced to $200,000,000, expressed the hope that the territorial provisions be eased somewhat, and offered some other minor suggestions. The suggestions were either flatly turned down by Russia or completely ignored. While the Italians and the representatives of the other defeated powers offered objections to the Paris treaties, fear of reprisals prevented the Finns from protesting.

The same fate met proposals for change that came from other than Finnish sources. Australia proposed the insertion in the treaty of a statement characterizing the peace as conforming "to the principles of justice." The proposal was accepted and the phrase became a part of the preamble to the treaty, but other Australian proposals which, in Australia's view, would have meant a just peace, were rejected. Senator Arthur H. Vandenberg's suggestions that reparations be fixed at $200,000,000 likewise went unheeded. As a result, the main body of the treaty was merely a repetition of the fiat of 1944.

The two new economic exactions inserted in the treaty dealt with German and United Nations nationals' property in Finland. First, all German assets and property in Finland were recognized as belonging to the Soviet Union, without providing for any compensation for

[1] The peace treaty is printed herein as Appendix B. See pages 201-223.

the destruction caused by the Germans during the months (September, 1944—April, 1945) when Finland was at war with Germany and fought the Germans in north Finland. The destruction wrought by the German troops had laid waste most of the northern third of the country, and had left an immense reconstruction and relief problem on the hands of the Finns.

Secondly, the treaty provided that Finland is responsible for the restoration and surrender of property belonging to United Nations nationals, and, in the event that restoration or surrender is not possible, for compensation of such property to the extent of two-thirds of the sum necessary (at the time of payment) to purchase similar property or to make good the loss sustained. While the assets and obligations regarding German property are likely to mean a heavy additional burden for the Finns, the second in all probability will remain purely nominal because damage to property, in Finland, belonging to the nationals of the United Nations appears to be virtually nonexistent.

However onerous the territorial clauses of the treaty are, they mean a settlement that is over and done with. The reparations provisions and other economic exactions mean obligations which, no matter how paralyzing they turn out to be, will presumably be carried out in time, and, barring new Russian demands later, Finland will perhaps be freed from them after 1952. The treaty also contains provisions, however, which impose potential servitudes of another kind. They are apparently intended to be permanent.

The permanent servitudes are imposed by Articles 6-9. They ostensibly secure, under the guise of "guaranteeing" the enjoyment of basic human rights "to all persons under Finnish jurisdiction," the right of free speech, press, assembly and the like. (These rights and freedoms have long been recognized as inviolate by the Finnish constitution, laws and practices.) In the future, no measures may be taken or laws enacted which are incompatible with the broad "rights" mentioned. Also, all organizations of "Fascist type," and all other organizations "conducting propaganda hostile to the Soviet Union or to any of the United Nations," are forbidden for all time. Finally, the door is opened to new "war guilt" trials (Art. 9) which are more than likely to mean persecution, especially of prominent defenders of Finland's independence and territorial integrity during the war years.

The intent of these provisions is clear. Not only Finnish but Russian and other communists are given full immunity by them, and may henceforth carry on their work in Finland free from any restric-

tions devised or applied by Finnish authority.[8] Russian interpretation of "Fascist," of "propaganda" and of "hostile to the Soviet
Union," will in all likelihood suffice to prevent the appearance and
functioning of any organization, no matter how commendable it may
be by ordinary definitions of propriety and legality, to combat communist effort or Russian encroachments. And merely moderately
loose construction of Article 8 will suffice to lead to the outlawing, if
need be, of the whole non-communist press in Finland and of the
non-communist political parties as well. In a word, the peace treaty
accords an international guaranty—involving the Soviet Union in
the first instance—to a design which exposes the essence of Finnish
self-rule and independence to Soviet interference and caprice.

Something of the interference and pressure of the Soviet was
clearly revealed by the manner in which the news of the signing of
the peace treaty was received in Finland in February, 1947.

Nearly seven years earlier—on March 12, 1940—the first phase
of the Russo-Finnish war had been ended by a peace treaty that
deprived Finland of some ten per cent of her territory and about
twelve to fifteen per cent of her industrial and agrarian resources.
That treaty imposed no crushing reparations on the country, and it
did not provide for direct devices permitting Russian control over
the internal affairs of the nation. Yet that treaty was considered
sufficiently burdensome and disastrous to prevent every form of
public celebration. It was accepted in silent despair as an unavoidable result of the circumstances which had forced a nation that had
fought well for its freedom to accept the terms dictated by the Soviet
aggressor. The flags were at half-mast. The whole nation was in
mourning.

On February 10, 1947, when the vastly more onerous peace that
concluded the second phase of the Russo-Finnish war was signed, the
situation was outwardly different. No signs of mourning were permitted. At the order of public authority, flags were flown throughout
the country. Special radio programs were put on the air, mass meetings were held, and in Helsinki the Government was host at a gala
occasion which was attended by Finnish, Russian and other digni-
taries. The keynote was celebration and—on the surface, at least—
rejoicing over the fact that the war had at long last been formally
ended. No critical comment on the treaty was made in public, and

---

[8] The articles reinstate to full citizenship all Finnish communists who had
fled to Russia, and scores—probably hundreds—of them have already returned to
Finland.

no direct reference to Russian aggression as a cause of the war was hazarded. The staging, the script and the performance conformed to the demands of the hour which prohibited the free expression of opinion. In the face of the compulsions that were unmistakably present, the press was platitudinous and evasive, and official pronouncements either non-committal or obsequious. Satisfaction and rejoicing were limited to the communists.[9]

There is nothing in the peace treaty itself, or in the nature of its reception among the Finnish communists and fellow-travellers who repudiate western democracy and what it stands for, to remove the fears and uncertainties that have prevailed in Finland since the autumn of 1944. Some of the consequences of the fears and uncertainties stand out in bold relief. The people have as yet had no real chance to satisfy the desire, natural in a nation exhausted by years of costly war, to return to the quiet, satisfactions and comforts—however modest they may be—of the normal life which the cessation of fighting and the coming of peace should grant even to the defeated. Calm thinking and free and open discussion of national problems are denied to them. Today's problems are complicated and the plans for tomorrow are only too often twisted or thwarted by enemies within the gate and by the Soviet Union without.

Material anxieties, multiplied a hundred-fold by the paralyzing burden of reparations press down upon them daily. Exhausted by a war they did not want or seek and tried to avoid, they slave for the

[9] Typical of the obsequious stand among non-communists was the speech delivered by Premier Mauno Pekkala at the official celebration in Helsinki on the evening of February 10. Three-fourths of the speech was devoted to abusing the Finnish people and their leaders since 1917. The signing of the peace treaty in Paris earlier in the day, he said, did not signalize a defeat. "Our day of defeat came some thirty years ago when we struck out on the path in foreign policy which led us astray. And defeat was ours on the day when we lost the peace; that is to say, when we no longer reposed our confidence in the possibilities . . . of negotiation but put our trust in the treacherous might of arms, and went to war." The communist Minister of the Interior, Y. Leino, held that the war between Finland and Russia had been caused by Finnish desire to expand at Russia's expense. The military defeat which Finland had suffered was not a defeat of the Finnish people, who had, in fact, won a victory. Defeat had been suffered only by "the wrong orientation in Finland, the wrong prophets of the nation, and the wrong social system that had prevailed in the country." These real "enemies" of the people having now been eliminated, a new and "more democratic and more progressive" society can be built on the ruins of the old. According to another communist, the reparations obligation was a mere minor detail by comparison with the destruction and impoverishment which the nation had imposed upon itself. One of the communist newspapers proclaimed that "all talk about a crushing peace means nothing more than a distortion of the magnificent picture of the future, filled with beautiful promise for the years to come." See *Helsingin Sanomat* and other Finnish newspapers, February 11, 1947.

benefit of Russia who, by her aggression, forced them into war in the first place. Unable to consider themselves penitent sinners in performing their hard labor, for they did not precipitate the war and became involved in it only after their country was invaded, they find it doubly hard to accept a lot unworthy of free men.

Nor are their anxieties limited to the economic serfdom which will be theirs for several years to come. They see the threat of a double serfdom in the political order which, under disguised Russian auspices, is gradually replacing the democratic processes of old standing. They fear continued restriction of the right to discuss and debate the problems of today and tomorrow, for they realize full well that without the right to free speech the spirit of man becomes paralyzed, his purposes pointless and he himself a being in bondage unable to stand erect among the free.

Finally, the anxieties of the Finns do not arise only from the peace treaty and what it represents. They stem also from another ominous circumstance. To them it seems that the public conscience of the civilized world has suffered appalling damage since 1939. The sense of right and wrong has become dulled to the point where it no longer functions. If aggression and conquest are open enough, if force in the subjugation of the weak is great enough, they are seemingly accepted as an inevitable part of the modern world. In the acceptance, moral judgments play little or no part, for the world has become, temporarily at least, "realistic."

Nearly fifty years ago—in 1899—the Russian imperial government by a stroke of the pen destroyed the constitution on which Finland's self-rule rested. One of the most significant features of the unequal constitutional struggle which then began between Finland and Russia was the reaction of the civilized world to it. The Russian attempt to violate the constitution of the Finns aroused the intellectual elite of the western world. Over one thousand prominent citizens of Great Britain, France, Italy, Holland, Sweden, Norway, Germany and other countries pleaded, through an address which was sent to St. Petersburg, that the sanctity of law be honored. The voice of the signatories of the address was raised in vain. Yet when a wrong had been committed, when lawless, arbitrary rule threatened a small nation's existence, over one thousand luminaries in the world of science, the arts and letters stepped forth to plead for the sanctity of the law. Florence Nightingale, Herbert Spencer, J. Westlake, Anatole France, L. Trarieux, Theodor Mommsen, Ibsen, Nansen, van der Vlugt, and Brusa, represented only a fraction of the illustrious names then found among the petitioners on behalf of justice and right.

Today the Finns face a future more ominous by far than the future which loomed on the horizon half a century ago. They face it alone. The weighty moral support abroad that sustained them in their hour of peril at the turn of the century, and added to their strength in withstanding Russia's attempt at conquest in 1939-1940, is now denied them. Looking westward beyond the confines of their land they search for men and women who are able and willing to recognize aggression, injustice and oppression and call these evils by their right names. The search has largely been in vain. In the world in which evasion has become a facile art and consciences willing and able to distinguish between right and wrong, might and right, are hard to find, the Finns have discovered but few friends whose memories go back beyond June, 1941, and whose capacities for moral judgment are equal to the challenge presented by Soviet expansion at the expense of peoples who desire only a chance to remain free and independent.

Such, then, is the situation in which Finland finds herself as the third year of her post-war ordeal draws to a close, and such appear to be the ways in which the Finns see it as they look ahead into the future. At present writing, there is no reason to believe that the situation will easily and automatically change for the better. Unless all signs fail, the grimmest kind of contest lies ahead. It is a contest for the preservation of a way of life in which western conceptions of individual liberty and freedom furnish the foundation of the body politic, social and economic. It is a contest, also, for national survival.

In the situation that is now unfolding, the years from 1939 to 1947 represent an all-important period that separates the democratic free Finland that was from the Finland that is now seemingly in the making. This book delineates a significant, not to say decisive, aspect of the events of the period. It is worth close scrutiny and serious reflection not the least because its implications obviously extend beyond Finland to the world that still retains the precious rights of independence and democracy.

JOHN H. WUORINEN

Columbia University, New York
May 1, 1947

INTRODUCTION

Finland's foreign policy and the course of events in the country during World War II involve many problems difficult to solve. These difficulties are of various kinds.

In the first place, source material is inadequate. Because of the rapid succession of events, written records of the transaction of public business were not always kept. In the exceptional circumstances created by war, the manner of handling matters often became so informal that it is not always possible, later, to ascertain how decisions actually were formulated. Especially was the division of military and political leadership loosely defined. The President having appointed a military Commander-in-Chief for the period of the war and the emergency, the executive power was divided into two parts, but the line separating them was never clearly fixed. The fact that during the war the supreme political and military leaderships were housed in different localities, added to the difficulties. Also, many of the men who knew the course of events because they participated in them have died. (For instance, Kyösti Kallio, President from 1937 to 1940; A. K. Cajander, Premier from 1937 to 1939; Rolf Witting, Foreign Minister from 1940 to 1943; R. Walden, Defense Minister from 1940 to 1944.) Furthermore, special difficulties are faced because at present no foreign source material, other than what has been released to the general public, is available. Complete familiarity with such foreign source material, however, is absolutely necessary for a full knowledge of cause and effect, since Finland's part was but a minor role in a larger picture of the war years.

Difficulties of another kind also exist. The conditions in Finland at present are such that questions concerning the war are in no sense considered—in public—with detachment or a sufficient knowledge of the facts. At present, in the unusual circumstances resulting from the Armistice, and because of the fact that the Russian (Allied) Control Commission may arbitrarily interfere with anything it pleases, freedom of speech in Finland has been curtailed to such an extent that the truth, should it prove displeasing to the Soviet Union, must be suppressed. Public consideration of the questions concerning the war, therefore, has necessarily been one-sided and sterile. In these circumstances, some groups (whose political and tactical leadership seems to come from abroad—Moscow, that is) attempt to spread the idea that Finland herself is wholly responsible for the hard fate that has befallen the country, and that Finland should gratefully perform the heavy tasks of economic slavery which the war reparations impose.

Present conditions in the world in general are such that facts favorable to Finland can hardly be expected to appear. Relations with the powerful Soviet Union are so important to all countries, whether occupied or free, that the rights of a small nation such as Finland must remain ignored. Furthermore, the former goodwill shown toward Finland is no longer felt abroad. Propaganda in recent years has managed to destroy almost all of the goodwill which Finland enjoyed in the western world during the Winter War of 1939-40. This has resulted primarily from the fact that outside of Finland it has been impossible to know all the factors which, at any given time, led Finnish policy to follow the path marked out for her by inevitable necessity.

Above all else, then, an elucidation of the circumstances under which Finland made her decisions is needed at home and abroad. Such an explanation is possible, at least as regards major matters, on the basis of material published during or immediately following the events concerned. If this material can be supplemented, at important points, by documents and the testimony given by the people involved, the picture becomes clearer still and the conclusions more binding. Information of this kind is, in fact, relatively easily available for there is nothing to hide in Finnish foreign policy. On the contrary, it is desirable that all facts throwing light on Finnish foreign policy become known, even if they can be twisted and negatively evaluated now, after the event, in the light of conditions entirely different from those that prevailed at the time. In any case, nothing is as important for Finland as the disclosure of the entire truth.

Of the questions which cannot be ignored in considering Finland's war-time policies, the following must be mentioned at the outset. The question of the nature of Finland's wars is of primary importance: in other words, how we were drawn into the war, and, above all, the question of whether we were fighting an aggressive or defensive war. In order to know who is responsible for Finnish policy during the war, it is absolutely essential to clarify the relationship of the Government's policy as a whole, and its decisions in specific instances, to the Parliament and public opinion. Closely related to this problem are the questions of Finnish war aims and Finland's attitude toward the possibilities of withdrawing from the war, which, at various times, existed or were alleged to exist. And, finally, there is the especially important question of whether the policy followed by Finland was her own, or whether it was dictated by foreign ideologies and was under the control or command of some foreign power.

These complicated questions obviously cannot be considered objectively unless one logically follows the basic rule of all historical study of past events : weigh each event in its relationship to the conditions prevailing at the time, and judge decisions made in the light of the conditions which existed and were known when the decisions were formulated. Hindsight, based on later developments and a knowledge of their consequences, is proper in party politics and propaganda, but unless carefully used, it destroys the possibility of investigation that strives for genuine impartiality.

CHAPTER 1

FINNISH FOREIGN POLICY BETWEEN THE TWO WORLD WARS

1. FINLAND'S LEGACY AS A GRAND DUCHY OF RUSSIA

The 110 years that Finland existed as an autonomous part of Imperial Russia were, with the exception of the final period of that union, a time of friendly relations between the small nation and the great Power. The Russian government honored Finland's special position and her laws, and Finland was able to continue her development along the path of western European civilization so freely that the traces of Russian influence in Finland remained infinitesimally small. The period of Nicholas II (1894-1917), however, brought a change which altered the Finns' attitude toward Russia and the Russians. When the Russian government started its Russifying policy in Finland in 1899, breaking the Finnish constitution and violating the Tsar's solemn declaration to honor the law of the land, the Russians came to be looked upon as enemies of Finland.

In the constitutional struggle which ensued, the Finns looked for help outside their borders. Some sought and found generous help in Western Europe; others established contacts with Russian revolutionary circles which have continued to the present day. The ties with the West were the stronger. The moral support from the West gave the nation courage in its fight against Russia and at the same time retarded the tempo of Russian oppressive measures. In connection with the latter, it is worth mentioning that when the Russian government, just prior to the first World War, was considering the incorporation of the Karelian Isthmus border parishes of Uusikirkko, Kuolemanjärvi and Kivennapa into Imperial Russia, the plan fell through primarily because of the unfavorable publicity the idea aroused in Western Europe. Later, Finland's war of independence in 1918 was fought on the one hand against the rebellious Finnish Left, born under Russia's influence, and against Russian garrisons who had remained in the country in spite of the fact that the newly created Soviet government had already recognized the independence of Finland. Finland thus had to purchase her independence with a

33

bitter war, and did not, as later Russian propaganda continued to
argue, receive it as a gift. The war of independence was followed
by an interim period of more than a year which closely resembled
war. The one-sided Soviet attitude dates from this period, as does
its one-sided information regarding Finland, and its deep-rooted suspicion of Finland, regardless of what Finland did or left undone.

2. Relations with Germany and Western Europe

Since Finland had received military aid from Germany in her war
of independence, it was quite natural that during the first phases of
independence German influence was quite strong. However, as early
as May, 1918, the Government of J. K. Paasikivi (the Foreign Minister was Otto Stenroth), tried to maintain Finnish neutrality in the
World War, in such a way that friendly relations with Germany
would not be broken. The German collapse in November, 1918, was
followed by the end of the pro-German orientation in Finland. From
this time on, the new groups responsible for Finnish policy rejected
the ideals of imperial Germany and sought models from France and
England, and oriented themselves politically in that direction. However, since the interest of the western Powers in Finland was not
strong enough for Finland to receive all the support she needed, Finland had to seek out countries closer to home with whom mutual
interests would guarantee common effort.

3. Orientation Toward the Baltic States, 1919-1922

The immediate alternatives in foreign policy which could be considered after 1918 concerned the relationship with the new Soviet
government and the Soviet system.

Cooperation with the White Russian forces opposing the Soviet
Union was one possibility. This question became especially pressing
when Yudenitch was approaching the gates of Petrograd in the fall
of 1919. Finland did not take part in the proposed joint operation,
however, because she considered it foolish to interfere in the internal
affairs of her big neighbor. This decision actually marked the beginning of Finland's new policy: neutrality. On October 14, 1920,
Finland signed a peace treaty with the Soviet Union at Dorpat. Her
old borders were recognized. In addition, the Petsamo region, which
had already been granted to Finland in principle in 1864 as compensation for Finnish territory on the Karelian Isthmus incorporated
at that time into Russia, was obtained. Thereafter, at least as far

as Finland was concerned, every prerequisite for normal relations with the Soviet Union existed.

A second alternative was to join the "cordon sanitaire" sponsored by France, whose object was to block Russia off from the rest of Europe. The agreements drawn up in Warsaw in 1922 had in mind a bloc of border-states for achieving this end. The Finnish Foreign Minister was present at the drawing up of these proposals, but the Finnish Parliament shelved the question of ratification and never in fact did ratify. The debate of the question in the Finnish Parliament specifically emphasized that neutrality was the only proper policy for the country in foreign affairs. This quiet burial of the Warsaw agreement was the definite end of Finland's "border states" policy.

While they lasted, Finland's relations with Russia had been anything but good. The worst stumbling block had been the Eastern Karelia question. The Soviet Union had issued a declaration in connection with the Dorpat Treaty, whereby it bound itself to grant national autonomy to the Karelians. This pledge was not kept. The result was a Karelian rebellion in which Finnish volunteers took part. When both the Karelians and the Finns made an international issue of the question, the Soviets argued that, regardless of their Dorpat declaration, the Karelian question was completely an internal Russian affair which they had the right to solve as they saw fit, without the interference of outsiders. Although Finland had no territorial ambitions in Eastern Karelia, Finnish participation in the Karelian question sufficed to rouse the ire of Russia. The Soviet Union, on the other hand, interfered continually in Finnish internal affairs through the Comintern, and aroused Finnish bitterness toward the Soviet system. It was felt that the aim of the Comintern was to carry out the conquest of Finland from within.

A third alternative was also seen at the time. It meant drawing closer to Scandinavia. Foreign Minister Rudolph Holsti visited Stockholm in 1920 for this purpose. No concrete results came of the visit, because the question of the ownership of the Aland Islands, which was then under debate, made a rapprochement difficult.

4. League of Nations Period, 1922-1935

Having become a member of the League of Nations in 1920, Finland thought that the support she needed had been found, and participated in the activities of the League. Finnish participation evidently was considered to be of some value, for Finland was represented on the League Council from 1927 to 1930. Finland tried, in fact, to have the League become an organization which would really guarantee peace and add to the security of small nations. That is why Finland in 1924 signed the Geneva Protocol, the purpose of which was to introduce peaceful arbitration of international disputes, a mutual aid pact and disarmament. With the failure of this effort, Finland in 1929 joined in the attempt to turn the Permanent Court of International Justice into a court of appeal for nationally appointed courts of arbitration. Toward the same end, Finland accepted other agreements and proposals of the League. Especially important was Finland's own proposal of financial aid to countries attacked without provocation. Finland accepted the Covenant of the League, the Kellogg Pact, the agreement defining aggression, and participated in the disarmament conference.

As a direct consequence of her membership in the League, Finland adhered more closely than ever to her line of neutrality—in other words, she avoided joining any group or bloc of major Powers.

5. Scandinavian Orientation, 1935-1938

About 1935, the international situation became particularly perturbed. In that year Germany declared she was no longer bound by the military limitations contained in the Versailles Treaty; England concluded a naval treaty with Germany; and Italy attacked Abyssinia. In the following year, Germany re-militarized the Rhineland, signed the anti-Comintern pact with Japan, and began to approach Italy. Civil war broke out in Spain and developed into an international issue.

In this storm the League of Nations proved itself completely powerless. When sanctions should have been declared against Italy, only economic penalties were applied, without effect; the Powers lacked the courage to resort to military measures. This case revealed that sanctions could lead small nations into distressing complications but would be of no benefit to them. As a result a general attempt to be rid of sanctions obligations appeared. At the same time, however, all possibilities for the League to work effectively to prevent war were destroyed.

With their hopes in the League betrayed, the small nations generally began to seek help from the great Powers or by joining one another. True to her earlier stand, Finland adhered to the line of neutrality and sought contacts with her small neighbors that embraced the same stand. Finland had already joined the so-called Oslo group in 1932. At the end of 1935 the Scandinavian neutrality bloc was formed. The President of Finland went to Stockholm in the interests of the matter, and in a speech in Parliament on December 5, Premier Kivimäki outlined the form and purposes of this northern orientation so clearly that one would have expected it to arouse interest in Moscow.

> The Finns believe that of their neighbors, Scandinavia, Sweden in particular, is least likely to become involved in war or other dangerous international complications. Scandinavia has, therefore, the best possibilities for retaining its neutrality. Since Finland's interests also demand, above all, the maintaining of neutrality, it is natural that Finland should align herself with Scandinavia, to which our country is more closely tied than elsewhere not only by bonds of history, but by economics and culture and by the consequent oneness of outlook as well. Finland sees as her responsibility the maintaining of an army for her defense (contemplated even in the Covenant of the League) in order to protect her neutrality and independence from danger no matter from what direction it may come, and in order thereby to aid the maintaining of the joint neutrality of all the Northern countries.

Spokesmen for all the various political parties supported this declaration of the Government in Parliament. An immediate consequence of this new orientation was first of all a new policy toward the League. Declining to assume responsibility involved in sanctions, the possibilities of becoming involved in conflicts between the major Powers were to be avoided. Instead, cooperation with other nations that were free from any alliance commitments was to be sought. A second consequence of this Scandinavian orientation was an attempt toward a new policy toward Russia. Its purpose was to remove the tension which had prevailed until then. The forms and extent of Scandinavian cooperation were never precisely defined.

6. Relations with the Soviet Union

In spite of Finland's policy of neutrality, it was impossible to establish good relations with the Soviet Union because of Russia's suspicions and her two-faced policies. The discussions for a non-aggression pact in 1927, begun on Russia's own initiative, were fruitless because Russia did not approve Finland's proposals for arbitration procedure in settling disputes. In Finland, on the other hand, it was repeatedly ascertained that Russia continued to interfere in Finland's internal affairs through the Comintern. When communism began to show itself in what non-communists thought were too challenging ways, the so-called Lapua Movement arose as a powerful counter movement, resulting in the dissolution of the Communist Party and the banning of communist activity in 1930. The Lapua Movement itself was later dissolved by the Supreme Court because of the lawless actions of which it had become guilty.

This period gave birth to the IKL (Isänmaallinen Kansanliike— Patriotic People's Movement) which considered its chief platform to be opposition to communism. It was born wholly on home soil; it was not an imported form of Nazism. In its beliefs and program it remained confused to the end, but in any case its opposition to communism and the strengthening of the security of the nation were its basic tenets, and were responsible for whatever success it had in elections. The votes it received were so insignificant from the very beginning that it had in fact no important influence in parliamentary life, and its support among the voters progressively declined. At its peak, early in the 1930's, it had fourteen out of the 200 representatives in the Parliament but at the outbreak of World War II its number of seats had dropped to eight. In foreign policy, it had no importance whatever. In Soviet Russia, however, the outlawing of communism in Finland was taken seriously: Albrechts, serving at that time in a highly responsible position in the Soviet, wrote that when the Lapua Movement carried out its big demonstrations in Helsinki in the summer of 1930, the Soviet Union prepared for war against Finland, but fortunately nothing came of it.

A second issue which had continued to irritate the Soviets was the Eastern Karelia question. This question was born of the fact, on the one hand, that the East Karelians were Finns, and on the other, from the Russian failure to carry out the promise to grant self-government to the East Karelians. These factors furnished enough material, in Finland, for nationalist-romanticist aspirations whose spokesmen became the Academic Karelia Society composed of university students. Later this Society made the Finnization of the Helsinki University the main point of its program, and brought upon its head the wrath of the Swedish-speaking intelligentsia. The Society had no influence in Finnish foreign affairs. But by its declarations about a "Greater Finland" the Society gave fuel to propaganda harmful to Finland. In any case, Finland's official foreign policy was completely free of plans to enlarge Finland's territory. A large majority in Parliament was always a guaranty that Finnish foreign policy would continue to center on complete neutrality, and all of Finland's Foreign Ministers before and during the war of 1939 were free of the nationalist-romanticist taint of the Academic Karelia Society. The Soviet Union must have known this quite well enough.

If Russia had previously been suspicious of all foreigners, from the beginning of the 1930's it may be said to have hermetically sealed itself. A deliberate and large-scale preparation for the coming war was then begun. The many-sided contacts and ties which other European states had at the time among themselves generally, were out of the question with Russia. For example, economic relations between the Soviet Union and Finland remained absolutely insignificant, although natural prerequisites for trade were abundant, and Finland made several attempts to extend commerce with Russia.

Finland did all she could to establish good relations with the only neighbor capable of threatening her security. In 1932 Finland signed the non-aggression pact proposed by Russia, and renewed it in 1934 for ten years. When Russia was admitted into the League of Nations in 1934, her admission took place without any investigation or reservations, in spite of the fact that Finland at least would have had more than sufficient reason for making them. At this time Russia already felt herself strong enough to use procedures in her foreign relations that would have been out of the question in the 1920's. Her foreign policy began to develop a clearly imperialistic aspect. In this connection, a statement by Commissar for Foreign Affairs Litvinov early in 1933 is especially revealing. He declared that it was of advantage to Russia to maintain the complete independence and neutrality of the Baltic countries and Finland, but that Russia also was concerned with the development of those internal policies which might prove to be a threat to the independence of these countries. In this connection Litvinov mentioned for the first time those guaranties of the Baltic States' independence and security which later proved so fateful. The Commissar of Leningrad, A. A. Zhdanov, spoke a still clearer language in a speech on November 2, 1936:

> We people of Leningrad sit at our windows, looking out at the world. Right around us lie small countries who dream of great adventures or permit great adventurers to scheme within their borders. We are not afraid of these small nations. But if they are not satisfied to mind only their own business, we may feel forced to open our windows a bit wider, and they will find it disagreeable if we have to call upon our Red Army to defend our country.

After 1939 it was easy to understand just what was contained in that statement.

It is evident that Finland did not realize how great a significance for foreign policy lay in the defeat of Trotsky and in the rise of Stalin to the dictatorship of Russia. When the Russians temporarily gave up striving for a world revolution and contented themselves with the development of socialism in their own country, they soon embraced the same imperialistic ᐟaspirations of territorial growth which nineteenth century Slavophilism and Pan-slavism had defined. Basically, Soviet foreign policy was no longer communistic, but imperialistic and militaristic. The position of Russia's small neighbors had now fundamentally changed. The significance of this change was not sufficiently understood in Finland, but most other countries also made the same mistake.

In order that nothing would be left undone in establishing good relations with Soviet Russia—a basic prerequisite of the Scandinavian orientation of the nation—Finland's Foreign Minister Holsti went to Moscow in February, 1937. The purpose of the visit was to remove the irritations which had existed between the two countries. But it became evident that a peculiarly deep-rooted distrust toward Finland existed in Soviet government circles. Above all, they suspected that Finland was in cooperation with Germany, and that Germany's object was to attack Russia through Finland. It was claimed, for instance, that the Germans had established poison gas factories in Finland and were building airports in Finland for military purposes. It was naturally impossible to ascertain whether these claims were due to the stupidity of Russian spies, or whether they were arguments invented for the occasion. Finland for her part gave every assurance of being loyal to the Scandinavian neutrality bloc and the League of Nations, and declared that Finland would consider every encroachment on her territory as a hostile act, especially if it were to lead to Finland's becoming the battleground in a war between great Powers. During Holsti's visit detailed questions were not discussed, and regarding the major issue, it is difficult to say if the Soviet leaders comprehended Finland's desire for neutrality. The one positive result of the visit was the proof given to the other Scandinavian countries of Finland's desire to maintain good relations with her neighbor and in giving the lie to rumors which had circulated throughout Europe that Finland was a party to some secret military alliance directed against the Soviet Union.

CHAPTER 2

FINLAND'S FOREIGN POLICY, 1938-1939

1. The Threat of a World War

In 1938 the Germans maneuvred continually to change the political map of Europe and threatened general peace. Early in that year Austria was annexed by Germany, and toward the end of the year the Sudetenland was taken from Czechoslovakia. The pact signed between England and France then came as a counter stroke. And some quarters believed at first that the Munich Pact removed the threat of war, but it soon became evident that it, too, was only a pause and that new surprises were in the offing. In this situation, the small states naturally felt a greater need than before of remaining outside of great Power conflicts.

2. The Finnish Policy of Neutrality and Peace

Finland declared officially that the prime objective of her foreign policy was the maintaining of permanent neutrality. On May 27, 1938, the Scandinavian states made a statement explaining their neutrality, and the heads of their respective states made a plea to the great Powers to refrain from the use of force in the settlement of their differences and to resort to arbitration instead.

The Aland Islands, demilitarized in accordance with the international treaty of 1921, were considered the weak point in Scandinavian neutrality policy because of the fear that with the outbreak of war a major Power would rush to occupy them. The Foreign Ministers of Sweden and Finland therefore agreed early in 1939 that Finland would receive Swedish permission for a partial re-militarization, with Sweden's aid, of the islands. When this was proposed to the signers of the 1921 agreement and to the League of Nations, the answer was favorable. Russia, however, to whom this proposal was also presented, although she had not signed the 1921 agreement, delayed her answer and let it be known by a roundabout way that she would not grant her permission, or would do so only on condition that Russia receive the same status as Sweden in defending the neutrality of the islands. A Soviet spokesman explained that the U.S.S.R. would not

permit the erection of either strong or weak fortifications, since some
foreign power, Germany for example, might seize them. With this
opposition, the first concrete move for action of the Scandinavian
neutrality policy fell through.

In spite of all signs of impending war, Finland continued her peace
policy. This is clearly proven, for instance, by the reduction of the
Finnish foreign debt despite the threat of war. The total foreign debt
amounted to 10,160 million marks in 1931; by 1938, it had been reduced to 440 million. At the time when the great powers began
hurried preparations for war, Finland was preparing for the Olympic
Games of 1940, which were to be held in Finland. In November,
1938, the Parliament granted 200 million marks for this purpose,
and the money was almost completely spent. In addition, the city
of Helsinki alone expended 138 million marks in preparation for the
event. The people of Finland literally competed for tickets to the
games and were almost more disappointed by the cancellation of
the Olympics than by the coming of war.

Finland did not, however, neglect her military defense, at least
not in comparison with the other Scandinavian nations. In the
1920's, Finland had used English military experts in setting up her
army system, and in the early 1930's the army was revised according
to a regional scheme of organization which was considered best for
those defensive purposes which the Finnish military organization
would have to meet. With the approach of danger of war, modest
additional funds were granted for basic purchases, but even they were
spent with extreme frugality. Shortly before the beginning of the
second World War, the then Premier Cajander in a speech to the
Officer Corps explained that the policy of saving stemmed primarily
from the fact that it was not considered wise to procure materiel
which would be rapidly outmoded technically and therefore would
soon have to be scrapped. That is why, when Finland was drawn
into war, she lacked important and necessary weapons for defense.

3. Relations with the Western Powers

In general, Finland's relations with all western European countries except Germany were good. The relations with Germany were
frankly cool. As in the other Scandinavian countries, the Nazi system of Germany had been sharply criticised in Finland. Partly as a
result of that criticism, the position of the German language in Finnish culture came to be considered too prominent. Shortly before the

war, Premier Cajander declared in several speeches that too much time was devoted to the study of German in the schools and that in general the German language had too important a position in Finnish cultural life. These speeches attracted annoying publicity in Germany.

Politically also, Finland indicated she was travelling along other paths than those of Germany. Finland's rejection in 1939 of a mutual non-aggression pact with Germany was received in the latter country with considerable chagrin; on the other hand, England was satisfied with the Finnish decision. In this connection the conclusions of the United States Ambassador to Russia, Joseph E. Davies, formulated during a visit to Finland in July-August, 1937, are completely accurate. In his report, dated Helsinki, August 2, 1937, he indicated that in European policy Finland followed England's signals, since England was Finland's best customer. He saw Finland's adherence to the Scandinavian bloc as another step bringing Finland and England closer together, since that bloc was in close cooperation with the British Foreign Office. Nevertheless, he declared, there was in Finland a latent friendship toward Germany, a friendship going back specifically to the period of Finland's struggle for independence. This, however, he did not consider to be of any great significance, because he had been able to ascertain that the Finns were a democratic, freedom-loving and independent people, and that the Finnish government despised Hitler's ideology and methods of government. Finland was, therefore, instinctively anti-German. Situated between two great Powers, Finland was realistically neutral, careful not to injure anyone, and she took care not to become the battlefield of any Powers.

Undoubtedly there were Nazi-sympathizers in Finland, but surely no more than there were in England, for example. It is revealing that among the Jägers (Finns who had fought in 1918 for Finland's independence, aided by the Germans, and had received their military training in Germany) a pro-German attitude was very rare, and acceptance of national socialism unknown, with but few exceptions. As an organization the IKL was sufficiently indefinite and confused in its program that as a whole it could not be considered Nazi. The national socialistic organizations, on the other hand, which were founded in Finland after German patterns, as for example the Ruutu, Kalsta and Snellman organizations, were completely insignificant. Only a handful of youth belonged to them, hardly knowing themselves what they wanted; for a time they printed starving journals which died a natural death. To the extent that these organizations had not been removed from the rosters of functioning organizations earlier, their ending by decree in 1944, at the demand of the Armistice Commission, was simply an act of bookkeeping.

4. Relations with the Soviet Union

It is easy to realize now, after the event, that many of Russia's actions and pronouncements in 1938-1939 were a clear preparation for war and aggression: for example, the closing of the Finnish Consulate in Leningrad, and the ending of Finnish traffic rights on the Neva River, which had been guaranteed by the Dorpat Treaty in 1920. The Finns were literally in a quandary over the question of what should be done in order to establish good relations with Russia which represented the only problem in their foreign policy.

The real objectives of the Russians began to emerge only at the time of the secret discussions which a special Soviet emissary, Yartsev, initiated (without the knowledge of the Russian Minister in Helsinki) in the spring of 1938 with the Finnish Premier, his secretary, the Foreign Minister and Väinö Tanner. The reason for the discussion, according to Yartsev, was the possibility that Germany would begin a war against Russia, and that the left wing of the German front would land in Finland. If such a landing were allowed to take place without Finnish resistance, the Soviet Union would not wait for the enemy to reach the Russian border but would fight in Finland. With this possibility in mind, Russia now demanded the right to aid Finland. The Finns explained that their country would in any event defend its own neutrality and would not permit the use of Finnish territory as a base for attack against Russia. Yartsev insisted, in spite of this assurance, that the Finns accept Russian aid, and promised Finland permission to fortify the Aland Islands if the Russians could share in the work and send their own observer. Further, he demanded the right for the Soviet Union to fortify the Finnish Suursaari island (Hogland), in the Gulf of Finland. In return for these concessions, Russia was prepared to guarantee Finland's inviolability, to help her militarily, and to grant her a favorable trade agreement. At one stage during the discussions Yartsev threatened Finland with aggressive measures, but later he withdrew the threat. When the Finns expressed surprise that their assurances of neutrality did not satisfy Russia, Yartsev declared the Russians started from the premise that the Finns alone could with-

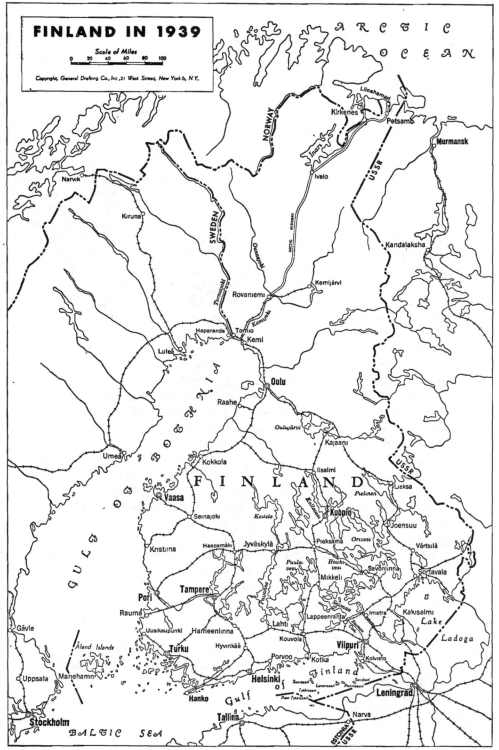

FINLAND IN 1939

Scale of Miles

0   20   40   60   80   100

Copyright, General Drafting Co., Inc., 21 West Street, New York 6, N.Y.

(Courtesy of Mr. Otto G. Lindberg, President, General Drafting Co., Inc.)

45

stand a German attack for only a short time. The Finnish contention that the German road to territorial expansion eastward could hardly go through Finland was without effect.

When the conversations with Yartsev ended without the results desired by Russia, since the Finnish representatives felt—doubtless quite correctly—that a promise of aid would mean the loss of neutrality and, possibly, even of independence, the Soviet Union gave up its demand and took up a new line. It demanded the use or outright cession of Finnish islands in the Gulf of Finland. This phase of discussion began in Moscow on December 7, 1938, at the opening of the new Finnish Legation, when Foreign Trade Commissar Mikoyan explained to the representatives of the Finnish Foreign Office that fostering of trade involved political conditions. According to his declaration, Moscow had noted with satisfaction the Scandinavian orientation of Finland, but the Soviet government did not consider that to be enough since Finland would hardly be strong enough to ward off violations of her neutrality if some third nation sought to expand eastward and were to threaten that neutrality. When the Finns emphasized that there was no spot as weak in Finnish defenses as the Aland Islands and that it was hoped, therefore, that Russia would agree to the Finns' building fortifications on the islands, Mikoyan changed the subject and asked if Finland could not cede Suursaari (Hogland) to Russia. The Finns declared that Suursaari remained unfortified, in accordance with the provisions of the Dorpat Treaty of 1920, but if the conditions of the treaty were to be changed, Finland could erect the fortifications herself. This conversation, too, failed to give Russia what she wanted.

The Finns now began to explore more energetically the question of the fortification of the Aland Islands. In this connection, the Commissar for Foreign Affairs, Litvinov, took up in March, 1939, his government's earlier demands with the Finnish Minister to Moscow; Litvinov now proposed that the Finns should lease Suursaari, Lavansaari, Tytärsaari and Seiskari to the Soviet Union for thirty years to guard the channels to Leningrad; Russia would not fortify the islands. If this were agreed upon, Russia would in turn guarantee that trade agreements and the Aland Islands question would be decided promptly and favorably.

The Finns replied that no prospect of leasing the Gulf of Finland islands existed because they were integral parts of Finland, and that to lease them would be a violation of Finnish neutrality. Litvinov thereupon proposed that the islands be exchanged for land in Eastern

Karelia. This suggestion also was rejected. Litvinov did not drop the matter but requested Ambassador Boris Stein, who was sent on a special mission to Finland, to pursue the conversations in Helsinki with the Finnish Minister for Foreign Affairs.

In the ensuing negotiations with Foreign Minister Erkko, the cession of the Gulf of Finland islands was again proposed, either by means of a lease or exchange of territory. The answer remained as firmly negative as before: Finland could not negotiate regarding her territory which, according to the Constitution, is indivisible, and could give her islands neither to Russia nor to Germany, since doing so would infringe upon Finnish neutrality. Stein was not satisfied with the answer and requested the Government to reconsider the proposal. The reply was again negative, but the Minister for Foreign Affairs qualified it with the announcement that Finland was desirious of continuing discussions concerning guaranties of the security of the Soviet Union. That is, Finland refused to cede any of her territory but was willing to make some kind of a political agreement. When the answer was delivered to Litvinov, he replied he had expected concrete proposals. The Finnish Foreign Minister assured him that Finland would defend her neutrality under all circumstances against any and every aggressor. Stein explained that the Soviet government placed no value on promises unless additional measures were also undertaken, and on leaving Helsinki on April 6, 1939, he frankly declared the matter was not at an end: the Soviet government. could not accept Finland's negative answer, and it did not give up its demand for the Gulf of Finland islands because they are of great strategic significance for the security of Russia.

Today, when we have seen what large territories and other wealth Finland lost in the war, it is easy to criticise the pre-war foreign policy of Finland for its stubbornness in not agreeing to Russia's "moderate" demands.

The justice of such criticism is not indisputable or clear. A mutual aid agreement would actually have meant giving up strict neutrality and would have led to a military alliance with Russia. In this case Finland would in all probability have become a battlefield of the great Powers, would have been occupied by Russia with the consequences which Russian occupation has brought with it elsewhere, and would possibly have lost her independence as well. Whether the cession of the Finnish islands would have safeguarded Finland from additional misfortunes is very debatable. First of all, it is more than unlikely that the Parliament would have agreed to lease or exchange them, since that too would have meant a questionable departure from the policy of neutrality, and above all, it would have significantly weakened Finland's own defenses. It must be kept in mind that at the time a total war had not yet lowered international political morals to the present level where great powers but not the small ones have the right to look to their security.

While these negotiations were under way, no information regarding them was given to the people of Finland, and they were first publicly mentioned in connection with the criticism that Soviet agents made, after the war, of Finland's earlier policy. The negotiations had been kept secret at the request of the Soviet government. Finland's correctness in this respect was perhaps carried too far. At least at the end of the discussions Parliament should have been given an account of their contents and progress. If the right of Parliament to decide on war and peace is conceived to be as broad as it has been argued at times it is, the final decision should have rested with Parliament, since these negotiations pointed out the road which led Finland, against her wishes, into war. Actually the final result of the negotiations would not have been changed by Parliament, but to have made Russia's demands more widely known would have been of inestimable help in that Finland might have been better prepared when her ordeal began in earnest in the fall of 1939.

CHAPTER 3

FINNISH FOREIGN POLICY ON THE EVE
OF THE WAR, 1939

1. The Western Powers' Negotiations at Moscow

At the time of the Munich Pact, Russia had been completely ignored. But when the great Powers began to jockey for position after the Munich agreement, neither of the potential opponents could avoid trying to obtain the support of mighty Russia. In this situation, Russia was like an auctioneer, accepting bids and banging the gavel only when the highest bid had been made. The Russians had for some time felt themselves strong enough to demand the rank and respect due a first-rate Power, if not indeed the deciding voice in Europe and Asia. She recalled to mind nothing as much as the Russia of the Tsars, and her most immediate territorial objective was the extension of Soviet Russia's boundaries to correspond to those of her Tsarist predecessor. The situation now seemed favorable, in all respects, for achieving this aim.

One can only guess at Russia's conception of the general situation and her own ambitions in the summer of 1939. At any rate it seems certain that the U.S.S.R. considered advantageous to herself the provocation of a European war in which Russia would not take part until the U.S.S.R. herself thought it advantageous to do so. When France and England began their negotiations in Moscow in March, 1939, for joint action against Germany, the Soviet Union demanded an agreement which would provide that certain specified European countries, Finland included, were to be given the Allies' guaranties of aid against an attack. "Attack" was defined so as to include "indirect attack," by which was meant, for example, possible inclination of some small country toward an attitude friendly to Germany. No authoritative explanation is available of all that might have been involved in the proposed "guaranty," but it certainly must have included an opportunity to interfere in the internal affairs of the nations guaranteed if they could be considered to be developing along a line leading to a pro-German trend. And it probably also included provisions for the granting of military aid to the small nations even

if they did not request it—that is, to occupy them or to take over strategic areas within their borders. Understanding this, all the small
countries asked France and England not to enter into an agreement
of this kind. This view was so unanimously held in Finland that no
demand for the acceptance of these guaranties was presented by anybody. Finnish diplomacy did all it could for the rejection of these
proposals, receiving support in the undertaking from Sweden. Specifically, it is known that leaders of English foreign policy had declared they understood that such guaranties were not desired. That
was, in all likelihood, the reason why no agreement was reached in
Moscow. There were possibly other reasons as well, but since the
negotiations have been kept very secret, they are as yet unknown.

2. THE MOLOTOV-RIBBENTROP PACT

While these negotiations with the western Powers were under
way, Moscow was obviously negotiating with Germany. The Soviet
Union also seemed to be awaiting the moment when fear that the
opponent would succeed in reaching an agreement would force the
other to accept Moscow's demands. A proposal acceptable to Russia
was made by Germany, and at Moscow on August 23, 1939, the
German-Russian non-aggression and arbitration pact was signed.
The boundary agreements and friendship pact of September 28, 1939,
after the defeat of Poland, completed the arrangements. The information given to the public disclosed nothing and did not even give a
hint of what really had happened.

In Finland the pact caused no anxiety. It was rather felt that now
that the two great Powers nearest Finland had come together, the
possibilities of continued peace in that part of Europe had become
greater. This conception seemed to be strengthened by reports from
Germany. The German ambassador to Moscow, Count von der
Schulenberg, declared emphatically on August 30, 1939, that in the
negotiations for the Russo-German pact there had been no discussion
of any spheres of influence to which Finland might belong. The later
course of events showed that this declaration was wholly untrue.
,The details of the agreement are still unknown, for even after the
changes that have occurred since 1941, neither Germany nor Russia
would derive pleasure or honor from the publication of its content.
During Finland's Winter War some details were discovered, but
they could not be definitely verified. Premier Daladier of France
had permitted the Swedish Consul in Paris to read a document
alleged to be a copy of the Molotov-Ribbentrop pact. According to

that document, Germany had granted Russia the right to act in the Baltic countries as she later in fact did act. As for Finland, Germany had given Russia a free hand to push the Russian borders to Viipuri and the right to take parts of Petsamo. If Russia could not get these areas by peaceful negotiation, she was given the right to seize them by force. Should Russia take more extensive territories in Finland, Germany was to have the right to take control over some portions of western Finland (the Aland Islands?) in order to maintain the balance of power in the Baltic.

Certain facts suggest that at least parts of this document were authentic, for example, the evacuation of Baltic Germans in the fall of 1939, and Molotov's announcement in 1940 that he had not taken up the Aland Island question in the Russo-Finnish settlement "so that new difficulties would not arise." Ribbentrop himself later admitted that by the agreements of August 23 and September 28, 1939, Germany assigned Finland to the Russian sphere of influence. In his note to the Soviet government on June 21, 1941, he declared that by the Russo-German agreements, the two Powers had bound themselves to maintain friendly relations, and had defined the respective spheres of influence in such a fashion that the German Reich gave up all claims to influence in Finland, Latvia, Estonia, Lithuania and Bessarabia, and that Polish territory east of the Narev-Bug-San line was to be incorporated into Russia at the latter's request.

When the Soviet Union, in carrying out these agreements, had overrun almost all of the province of Viipuri, it obviously deemed itself acting within the terms of the Molotov-Ribbentrop pact, and felt that Germany was not justified in seeking any compensation. The Russian disapproval of possible seizure of the Aland Islands by Germany, communicated to Germany in the spring of 1940, must have resulted from this Russian view.

It is possible today to argue, with the aid of hindsight, that a more far-sighted policy on Finland's part would have prevented Finland from becoming the subject of the Molotov-Ribbentrop agreements. This seems, however, very unlikely. If either Power had considered it to be in her own interests to protect Finland in these negotiations, Finland would already have had to be—by August, 1939—the vassal of the Power "protecting" her. That is to say, she would already have had to be in the position to which the negotiations sought to assign her. The Soviet Union obviously had a clear-cut program which it was carrying out without bothering about the small obstacles in its path. The Germans later argued that if Finland had not rejected the non-aggression pact proposed by Germany in May, 1939, she would not have fallen into the Russian sphere of influence. At the time, however, nothing was said of what Finland's position would then have become, or of how the non-aggression pact would have strengthened Finland's position. Later, when it was seen how little a non-aggression pact safeguarded Denmark against the attack by Germany, such arguments were no longer presented, even to the Finns.

This Molotov-Ribbentrop pact was the actual go-signal for the start of the new World War. Immediately following the German invasion of Poland, Finland individually, and jointly with the other Scandinavian countries, issued a declaration of complete neutrality. Even Russia was at first neutral. It is known, for example, that as late as the middle of September, Losovski, press chief of the Commissariat for Foreign Affairs, declared that the Red Army would not be led by any excuse—for instance, a revolution in Poland—into crossing the Russo-Polish border of its own accord. The attack nevertheless took place on the 17th of the same month. When this attack was begun on Poland whose military machine had already been smashed by the Germans, the Soviet government issued a neutrality proclamation to all possible countries, including the Baltic nations and Finland. What purpose this peculiar and anything but bona fide "guaranty" served, remains a mystery. It is possible that Russia feared that some countries had agreements for joint action in case of just such an attack.

3. The Soviet Union's Demand for Security

Novel and surprising examples of the spirit characteristic of the second World War and of Russia's way of illustrating it came after the Russians had taken their portion of Poland and began to exploit the possibilities offered by the Molotov-Ribbentrop pact. It is well known how each of the Baltic states, Estonia, Latvia and Lithuania, individually received the suggestion, tantamount to a command, that their Foreign Ministers be sent to Moscow to negotiate, and how these negotiations led to the Baltic states being forced to accept Russian demands granting the Soviet Union bases and mutual aid pacts. Thereafter nothing was left of the independence of these countries except the name, and even that only temporarily.

After the Baltic countries, Finland's turn came on October 5, when Helsinki received the suggestion that Foreign Minister Erkko or his representative be sent to Moscow as soon as possible, since "with the change of the international situation caused by the war, the Soviet government now desires an exchange of ideas with the Finnish government regarding certain concrete political questions." When results of this invitation were not immediately forthcoming, Molotov urged speed on October 7. From the conversation which the Russian Minister in Helsinki had with Foreign Minister Erkko on the 8th, it became clear that Russia, in order to arrange such conditions in the Baltic as would prevent Russia and her neighbors from being drawn into the war, wanted to carry on the same kind of negotiations with Finland that she had conducted with the Baltic countries. On the following day the Soviet government was informed that Finland was sending a representative to Moscow. To prevent any surprises, several classes of reserves were called up on the 10th for "supplementary maneuvres," which was tantamount to partial mobilization.

Minister Paasikivi was the Finnish delegate sent. According to his instructions, he was to stress that Russo-Finnish relations had been regularized by the peace treaty of 1920, and that their political relations were based on that treaty and the non-aggression pact which the two countries had signed. Further, he was to prove that Finland's Scandinavian orientation gave assurance of Finland's desire for peace and of her unqualified determination to remain outside all conflicts. In any case, Finland would fight to defend her neutrality, and would not permit herself to be used as a base for attack against anybody. If the Soviet Union were to make proposals involving territorial demands or demands violating Finnish independence, Russia was to be informed that no commitments could be made, since, in accordance with the parliamentary system that prevails in Finland, the approval of the legislature is necessary. Questions of granting military bases on Finnish territory, as well as changing the border on the Karelian Isthmus, were not to be discussed. On the other hand, the exchange of certain Gulf of Finland islands for other territorial compensation was possible. Finland was not prepared to conclude a mutual aid pact with Russia, because such a pact would be in conflict with her neutrality policy, and because Finland had declared her decision not to conclude alliances with anybody.

Finnish public opinion unanimously and strongly opposed large concessions to Russia, at least until it was known what the demands would be. The reaction to Russia's demands was as uncompromising as if the earlier constitutional struggle under Nicholas II had once more been involved, and the possibly different consequences now were not seen.[1] A firm stand was strengthened by the knowledge that Finland had the goodwill of the whole civilized world behind her. In general it was felt that the relations between Finland and Russia contained no unsolved problems and that neither had anything to demand of the other. Since the Russians had trumpeted, beside their slogan "Proletariat of the world, unite" the much quoted words of Stalin, "We neither desire to gain even a single foot of foreign soil nor are we willing to lose even an inch of our own," it was considered obvious in Finland that territorial cessions were out of the question. At the time, and later, no one could comprehend a "peace" policy the first point of which was territorial demands on a weaker neighbor. Not only were Russian territorial demands considered wholly un-justified, but it was predicted that to grant them would be simply a prologue to other demands later, as past experience of how the Russians kept their word had shown. Demands to cede certain Finnish border parishes to Imperial Russia had been successfully withstood in the time of the Tsars, and there could be no question of cession now, because the area in question was ancient Finnish territory which had been wrested from the wilderness by Finnish toil. Talk of Russia's and Leningrad's security requirements were considered nothing more than excuses since the Finns knew their own desire for peace and considered it obvious that as long as the Soviet Union left Finland in peace, the northern flank of Leningrad was at least as safe as the southern. Furthermore, it was considered obvious that be-cause of Finland's isolated position, no great Power could use Finland as a base for attack against Russia, until so much had happened and such a long time had elapsed that there would be ample opportunities for repelling such an attack whether Russia had bases in Finland or not. In fact, this view was later confirmed as correct. It was felt, therefore, that the real reason for Russia's demands was something other than the desire to increase her security which, as far as Finland was concerned, had already been guaranteed by the terms of the Dorpat Treaty and by the special boundary agreement in 1922 which imposed restrictions on Finnish military establishments in the islands and border regions from which the Soviet Union could be directly threatened.

---

[1] The reference is especially to the years after 1899, when Russification began to bear down heavily upon the Finns. During the years in question the nation showed singular unanimity in her opposition to the illegal and unconstitutional procedures of Russia (Ed.).

Today one may claim that Finland should have submitted to Russia's demands in the fall of 1939. In the light of the Moscow peace of 1940 and the terms of Russia which had to be accepted in September, 1944, that argument perhaps does seem justified. In the fall of 1939, however, the situation was different, and no Finnish government could have granted the concessions demanded without being overthrown. For such submission to Russia's demands to be possible, Finland would have had to be less democratic than she was. The unanimous opinion of the nation, expressed in all the ways in which public opinion usually makes itself felt, opposed the concessions proposed. It was understood then, rightly or wrongly, that the question involved the foundations of Finnish national existence. It has been argued that this conception was the result of wrong education and misinformation; that argument, however, first appeared with the later emergence of opportunistic politics. In the fall of 1939 the people of Finland felt that an attempt was being made unjustly to violate their rights, and that to accept Russia's proposals would have meant going along the road leading to extinction. It is impossible to say in what situation Finland would now be if she had granted bases and agreed to a mutual aid pact as the Baltic countries had done. The Soviet government would perhaps have employed in regard to Finland the procedures used elsewhere. The later experimentation with the Kuusinen puppet government lends support to this supposition.

In the first meeting at Moscow a mutual aid pact and territorial concessions were proposed to Finland. On October 14, Russia's demands were presented in detailed form. Giving up the demand for a mutual aid pact, the U.S.S.R. wanted first of all to strengthen the security of Leningrad and secondly to receive guaranties that Finland would continue good relations with Russia. Therefore, in order to close the Gulf of Finland, Russia demanded a thirty-year lease of the harbor of Hanko, the Bay of Lappohja as anchorage for the Russian Navy, and the Finnish islands in the Gulf of Finland, and offered territorial concessions in exchange. Further, on the Karelian Isthmus, the Soviet boundary was to be moved northward and northwestward. In Petsamo, Finland was to give up the Shredni peninsula since the boundary there, it was claimed, had been drawn "artificially and clumsily." The non-aggression pact was further to be strengthened by both parties guaranteeing to refrain from joining nations or alliances inimical to the other. The fortifications on the Karelian Isthmus were to be destroyed, but Finland could fortify the Aland

Islands on the condition that no other nation (including Sweden) participate. The Finns presented a report from their military experts which proved that no great power could invade Russia by way of Finland, but the Russians did not care to discuss the report.

When Paasikivi returned to Helsinki to receive new instructions, the negotiations were interrupted for a relatively long period, because President Kallio and Foreign Minister Erkko were in Stockholm at the conference of the chiefs of the Scandinavian states on October 19. The support that Finland would have needed then, however, was not forthcoming from Scandinavia. President Kallio did not bring up the matter for discussion at all, because he feared a refusal in any case. Foreign Minister Erkko was given to understand that in the event of a conflict no aid from Scandinavia was to be counted upon. It has been claimed in Sweden that at one stage Germany had declared she would consider official Swedish aid to Finland a cause for war. The French Minister in Stockholm was informed to this effect, and Finland's Minister was also told of it. German sources later firmly denied it and explained that Germany would have interfered only if the western Powers had landed their forces in Scandinavia.

The next Moscow meeting, at which the chief of the Social Democrat party, Väinö Tanner, was present at Paasikivi's demand, did not take place until October 23. In order to maintain peace and good relations, Finland now made concessions which the Government considered far-reaching. Specifically, it was proposed to give up the Gulf of Finland islands (with the exception of the thickly-settled Suursaari), as well as the so-called Kuokkala area on the Karelian Isthmus, in exchange for Russian territory. The other Russian proposals were rejected as prejudicial to Finnish neutrality, but it was announced that Finland was prepared to amplify the non-aggression pact by having both parties bind themselves not to aid any country which had undertaken an attack. Having received Finland's reply, Stalin insisted that Finland offered too little, and that the Russian demands were so minimal that it was not worth bargaining about them "since someone might attack Leningrad." When the question was raised as to who might make this attack, France and England were mentioned several times, but Germany was also listed. The Finnish offer to eliminate the Kuokkala area on the Isthmus by ceding the area to Russia, was scornfully rejected. All the Russian proposals called for territory as far as Koivisto. When the Finns called attention to the Dorpat Treaty and the non-aggression pact, both still in effect, the answer was that they had been concluded under

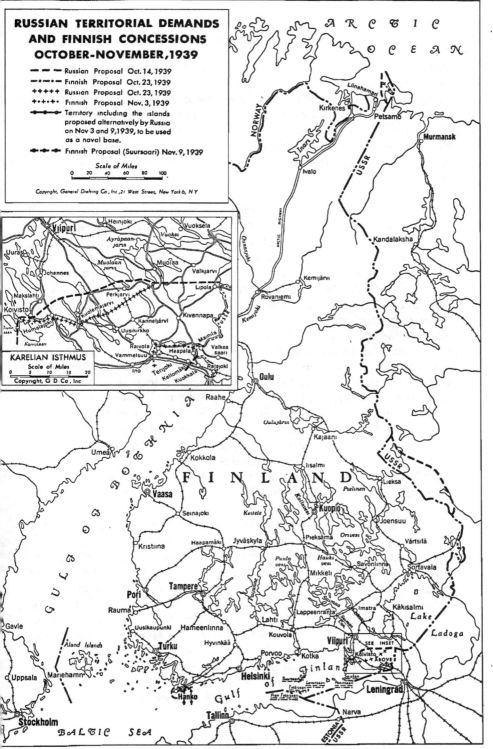

RUSSIAN TERRITORIAL DEMANDS
AND FINNISH CONCESSIONS
OCTOBER-NOVEMBER, 1939

- – – – Russian Proposal Oct. 14, 1939
- –•–•– Finnish Proposal Oct. 23, 1939
- +++++ Russian Proposal Oct. 23, 1939
- +•+•+• Finnish Proposal Nov. 3, 1939
- •––•––• Territory including the islands proposed alternatively by Russia on Nov 3 and 9, 1939, to be used as a naval base.
- •–•–•– Finnish Proposal (Suursaari) Nov. 9, 1939

Scale of Miles
0   20   40   60   80   100

Copyright, General Drafting Co., Inc., 21 West Street, New York 6, N.Y.

KARELIAN ISTHMUS
Scale of Miles
0   5   10   15   20
Copyright, G D Co., Inc.

(Courtesy of Mr. Otto G. Lindberg, President, General Drafting Co., Inc.)

57

different circumstances. In the memorandum which was presented late that same evening, the Soviet government stuck to its former demands, except for a few altogether minor concessions.

The Finnish delegates again had to return to Helsinki for additional instructions. These were completed after many changes, and the parliament groups which discussed them approved them unanimously. Although this democratic procedure involved informing a comparatively large group of the course of the negotiations, no information leaked out to the public.

In Russia the situation was quite the reverse. While the Finnish representatives were again en route to Moscow, the Russian radio announced that on October 31 the Commissar for Foreign Affairs, Molotov, had delivered an address in the Supreme Soviet in which he discussed the negotiations with Finland and announced the details of Russia's demands which he alleged had come about because "Russia not only had the right, but the responsibility to take serious steps to increase her security." He mentioned, as one of the reasons for altering the border on the Karelian Isthmus, the fact that Leningrad's population was about as large as that of entire Finland. In the official version of the speech, which appeared a few days later in an edition of ten million copies, the following note was added by the publisher: "laughter in the hall," indicating that Soviet imperialism was not only a policy approved by the Soviet inner circle but was a feature of the whole Soviet system. Molotov also pointed out that Finland was under influences emanating from some third state or states, and criticized in this connection the recent statement of President Franklin D. Roosevelt, which expressed the hope that good and peaceful relations between the Soviet Union and Finland would be preserved.

The Russian publication of their demands was rightly considered to mean a very serious change in the nature of the negotiations. It was felt that the demands having been made public, the "prestige" of Russia as a great Power would permit no retreat from the position taken by the Soviet. Molotov's speech was therefore considered improper in Finland. As soon as it became known, the Minister for Foreign Affairs, Erkko, decided to call back the delegates, reconsidered, and finally left it up to them either to return or to carry out their assignment to the end. The party continued to Moscow. In a release to the press, published on November 1, Foreign Minister Erkko announced that Russia's publication of her stand had changed the nature of the negotiations and made it more difficult to continue them in a spirit of confidence. Finland for her part had tried, independently and without the influence of any foreign nation, to find a solution to the questions presented to her, although it had been difficult to do so because of Finland's neutrality policy. With reference to Molotov's open threat of "serious measures," Mr. Erkko pointed to the non-aggression pact which was still in force.

After this information had been given to the press, the Finnish government convened. A cautious atmosphere prevailed, and it was even proposed to make more far-reaching concessions to Russia, but the firm opposition of the Premier and the Minister for Foreign Affairs prevented further consideration of this proposal.

In the memorandum which the Finnish delegates presented in Moscow on November 3, it was stated that Finland still adhered to and insisted on her inviolability and neutrality and could not, therefore, lease Hanko or Lappohja Bay. The small Gulf of Finland islands would be ceded, however, for exchange of territory. Finland was also prepared to discuss measures regarding Suursaari (Hogland) in a way which would guarantee the security of both countries. On the Karelian Isthmus, on the other hand, Finland considered Russia's security sufficiently protected by the cession of the territory south of the Vammeljoki-Lintulanjoki-Kaukjarvi line. Finland was further prepared to discuss giving up the Kalastaja Islands (Shredni Peninsula) off Petsamo. However, Finland did not feel she could agree to the demolition of the fortifications on the Karelian Isthmus, since the measures undertaken by the Finnish government along the border were purely for defense and security, and since Finland's absolute neutrality demanded the securing of her boundaries. Molotov declared that Finland's answer was unsatisfactory in every respect, and stated, dissatisfied, that "We civilians seem unable to accomplish anything more. Now it is up to the military to have their say."

The next day (November 4), Stalin himself took part in the negotiations. He said that no other Russian government except the Soviet would tolerate Finnish independence, but in return it demanded that its own security be guaranteed. Russia, therefore, absolutely had to have the use of Hanko, and Finland could clothe her concession in any legal form she chose. When the Finns announced that ceding Hanko was out of the question, Stalin proposed the cession of some islands around Hanko, but lacking instructions, the Finns were unable to continue the discussion of this proposal. Upon receipt of further instructions, the Finns stated, on the 9th, that the islands surrounding Hanko could not be ceded for the reasons that applied to Hanko itself, whereupon Stalin asked if at least the island of Russarö could be had. Since the discussion did not continue on that point, it did not become clear if Stalin's question contained a hint of willingness to reduce the original Russian demands. When the Finns stated that the ceding of the southern half of Suursaari was possible, Russia to fortify her part of the island, Stalin immediately rejected the idea as "meaning two masters—that will not work." The Finns were prepared to cede territory on the Karelian Isthmus as far as Ino and possibly more if the Russians would give up their demands on Hanko and Koivisto, but since the Russians did not abandon these demands, the change of the boundary on the Isthmus was not discussed further.

The negotiations seemed to have come to a standstill, and no reason appeared to exist for their continuation. That same night, however, Molotov added to them a peculiar written postscript. He argued that the Finnish refusal to grant a foreign power military bases within Finland's own territory was unrealistic and meant a falsification of Russia's real attitude, and he proposed that Finland sell or exchange the Hanko area or at least the Hanko islands, in which case they no longer would be Finnish territory or inside the Finnish borders. In its written reply the next day, the Finnish delegation declared that the Finnish government would not agree to grant bases on the Finnish coast, and that the Hanko islands, regarding which the proposal now presented was more extensive than that previously advanced, would still remain inside Finnish territorial waters. The Finnish government, honestly desirous of strengthening its relations with the Soviet Union, would be prepared to make even extensive concessions to satisfy the wishes of Russia, but it could not go so far as to surrender the country's life lines, which the granting of military bases to a foreign Power at the mouth of the Gulf of Finland would mean.

That was the last exchange of views in the negotiations. When the Finns left word on the 13th of November that they intended to go home, and expressed the hope that future negotiations would lead to results satisfactory to both parties, they received no reply. Nor did the Soviet government take advantage of the hint in the statement that Finland was still ready to seek means to satisfy her great neighbor. On the contrary, the Soviet press and radio began a violent propaganda campaign against Finland; the central theme was the charge that Finland's "ruling circles" had now shown their extreme hatred of the Soviet Union (that is, by refusing to give up important parts of their territory!).

In Finland the impression was still general that Russia would not resort to force. The Finns remembered Russia's assurances of peace repeatedly reiterated for two decades. Russia's proposals for disarmament were recalled. Russia was known to be so vast in size that she needed no additional territories, and it was impossible to conceive that any danger threatened Russia from Finland. Since it was not believed that Russia would attack, Finland's defense preparations were slowed down. Evacuees from the cities and border regions returned to their homes, the schools were opened and reservists who had been called up began to be sent home on furlough.

4. Relations with the Western Countries at the Beginning of the Crisis

France and Britain were naturally not altogether satisfied by the fact that the guaranties which had been considered during their negotiations with Moscow in the summer of 1939 had not been accepted by Finland, but they understood the reasons for the small countries' attitude and had not wanted to use pressure on them. When Russia signed the pact with Ribbentrop, and it was not clear how far Russo-German joint action would develop, Britain and France were prepared, albeit cautiously, to give their moral support to Finland. For example, it is known that during the meeting of the heads of the Scandinavian states at Stockholm, Britain expressed to Russia the hope that her demands on Finland would be reasonable and not lead to complications between the two countries. The belief prevailed in Britain also that, in spite of her threats, Russia would not go to war.

The United States was considerably more active. Though she had perhaps previously seen a potential ally in Russia during the period of the French and English negotiations in Moscow, and had rather hoped that Finland would submit, after the Molotov-Ribbentrop pact she saw Russia as the same kind of a dictatorship as Nazi Germany and offered moral support and diplomatic aid to Finland, who had a good reputation for payments of her debts, her athletic prowess, and as a democratic state. In his letter of October 11 to Soviet President Kalinin, Roosevelt expressed his concern for Finland and the hope that "the Soviet Union will make no demands on Finland which would be inconsistent with the maintenance and development of amicable and peaceful relations between the two countries, and the independence of each." Kalinin replied that the Russo-Finnish negotiations had taken place on the basis of their former relationship, and that the aim of the negotiations was to further the relationship and strengthen friendly cooperation for the purpose of consolidating their mutual security. Molotov, in explaining this exchange of notes on October 31, ironically suggested that after all Finland was in a better position than the Philippines and Cuba, who had vainly petitioned the United States for freedom and independence. In order to give Finland still stronger moral support, Roosevelt sent a telegram to the King of Sweden on October 18, on the occasion of the meeting of the Scandinavian states in Stockholm, announcing his support of neutrality and those fundamentals of law and justice which the states represented in Stockholm also had ever upheld. Later the United States Secretary of State thanked Finland for her firm stand in the Moscow negotiations.

The representatives of the Scandinavian states had all separately submitted identical notes to the Soviet government on October 10, each expressing the expectation that Russia would demand nothing of Finland that would prevent her maintaining her independent position of neutrality. These statements were allegedly not accepted by Russia, presumably on the grounds that "third parties" had no business to interfere in matters which did not concern them.

It is thus easy to see that the "influence of third parties" on Finland's behalf, which Molotov mentioned in his famous speech, was of purely moral nature.

5. The Outbreak of War

In his speech of October 31, Molotov had already indicated that the rejection of the agreement which Russia demanded "naturally would cause Finland grave damage," and on November 3 he had casually mentioned to the Finnish representatives that the military's turn to speak had now arrived. On the latter date *Pravda* used still stronger language:

> We are embarking on a road of our own, let it lead where it will. We will guarantee Russia's security, without caring for anything, breaking through all obstacles, of no matter what sort, to gain our goal.

How seriously these threats full of imperialistic spirit should have been taken was understood only when the famous shelling at Mainila on November 26 had become the basis of new demands and the opening round of a huge propaganda campaign for war.[2] At the time, Finland could ascertain only that seven salvoes were heard from the Russian side of the border. (The Finnish artillery had been placed so far to the rear that its range fell short of the Russian boundary.) It was believed the Mainila incident would never be explained, but some prisoners of war captured in the summer of 1941 volunteered the information that the Mainila shelling had been a clumsily arranged provocation. In any event, because of it, Molotov demanded that Finnish forces be withdrawn to 20-25 kilometers from the border, and bluntly rejected the Finnish government's proposal that both armies should be withdrawn and that the Mainila shelling be investigated in accordance with the existing boundary agreements.

On November 28, the Soviet Union unilaterally renounced the non-aggression pact of 1934 in contradiction to its specific terms. Before the Finnish Minister could deliver an answer to the note, the Soviet government broke off diplomatic relations with Finland on November 29. Nevertheless, Finland's answer was ultimately delivered. It proposed that peaceful arbitration provided by the non-aggression pact or some neutral go-between be used, and as further evidence of Finland's honest desire for peace, it was announced that the Finns were prepared to withdraw their forces on the Karelian Isthmus so far back that they could not in any way be considered a threat to the security of Leningrad.

No answer to this note was received. The Soviet government had obviously long since decided to let arms speak. On November 29 a Russian force had pushed across the border at Petsamo and had taken a few Finnish boundary guards as prisoners. On the 30th, the Red Army began a full-scale attack with air raids on several cities and industrial centers, especially Helsinki. The Soviet radio claimed that the Finnish reports of these raids were lies, and that the Russian airforce had merely dropped bread to the poor people of Helsinki. The unerring humor of the Finns thereupon dubbed the incendiaries as "Molotov's bread-baskets." War had begun. It was as if we had slipped into it without understanding that war really could be so near.

[2] The Russians claimed that Mainila, which was a few miles inside the Russian border on the Isthmus, had been shelled by the Finns. Seven shells had been fired, it was alleged, and thirteen Russians killed or wounded. The Finns denied that any shelling had occurred, and proposed that the incident be investigated by impartial investigators, or, if Russia preferred it, in accordance with the provisions for settling disputes which were defined in existing Russo-Finnish boundaries convention. Russia resolutely rejected the proposal (Ed.).

The attack of the Red Armies was carried out in surprising force on a wide front on the Karelian Isthmus and along the border from Lake Ladoga to the Arctic. Only then did it become clear that Russia had prepared for the invasion of Finland a long time in advance, having among other things built military roads passable in winter across uninhabited wastes to the Finnish border, which would have been useless if not dangerous to the defense of Russia, and which could have had no other purpose than to aid in the attack that had been planned.

CHAPTER 4

THE WINTER WAR AND THE PEACE OF MARCH 12, 1940

1. Attempts to Have Russia Halt Her Attack

As soon as the Soviet attack became known, the United States offered her good offices to settle the conflict by peaceful means. Finland naturally declared that she would gratefully accept the offer, but it was haughtily rejected by Russia.

Since Soviet propaganda had violently attacked the Finnish government and its individual members—for example, Premier Cajander had been called a "scarecrow," a "fool," and a "marionette" by *Pravda* on November 26—the Finnish government resigned, in spite of a unanimous vote of confidence in Parliament, in order to give a new Government a freer hand in seeking peace. The Director of the Bank of Finland, Risto Ryti, became Premier; though he had hardly taken part in politics, he was known for his friendly orientation toward England. The leader of the Social Democratic party, Väinö Tanner, became Minister for Foreign Affairs. The new Government, which was appointed on December 1, 1939, defined the reestablishment of peace as its main objective, but was determined to wage war as successfully as possible until peace could be concluded. With this in mind, the Government proposed to Russia on December 4, through the Swedish Minister in Moscow, that negotiations be resumed. At the same time Finland declared she was prepared to make new, concrete proposals for the satisfactory solution of the questions between Russia and Finland. This proposal was rejected by the Soviet government, with the explanation that it was willing to negotiate only with "the only legal government of Finland" which, it stated, was the so-called "Finnish Democratic government" which Russia had set up on December 1.

This puppet government of Russian hirelings set up at Terijoki, which was headed by O. W. Kuusinen, an officer of the Comintern, had nothing to do with the Finnish people, any more than did its so-called "People's Army" formed from Finnish-speaking Russian citizens as well as pure Russians. This government, it was claimed, had turned to Russia requesting her to "stop by force" the war which had been brought about by Finland's former "rulers." The Soviet government had concluded, on December 2, a mutual aid pact with this agent of its own creation. The Kuusinen government naturally had no practical significance, but it enriched political science with a new concept which was completely identical with the later "Quisling" concept. The document which "established" this puppet government contains a statement that deserves attention. According to it, both Finland and Soviet Karelia would now become subject to the Kuusinen government.

> Since the Finnish people have formed their own democratic republic, which is totally dependent on the people's support, the time has come to establish good relations between our countries [Russia and Finland] and to guarantee together the security of our states; the time has come to bring about the centuries-old desire of the Finnish people to have the people of Karelia rejoin their compatriots, the Finnish people, in a united Finnish nation . . .

The Soviet Union, expecting soon to overrun all Finland, thus publicly admitted that the people of Eastern Karelia and of Finland were one. In any case, the Kuusinen experiment showed that Russia's objective was the conquest of all Finland. A valuable chronological item in the making of the final decision to take over all of Finland is the fact that on November 13, Arvo Tuominen, a former Comintern official then residing in Stockholm, was offered the post of leader in this shadow government. On the same day the Finnish delegation had announced its departure from Moscow, and negotiations came to an end. Presumably, shortly before this time, then, the leaders of the Soviet Union had decided to resort to military measures in order completely to conquer stubborn Finland.

2. WESTERN OPINION AND THE LEAGUE OF NATIONS

The Russian invasion of Finland created a situation in which the world's largest country was fighting a small country which was isolated and alone. This in itself was enough to arouse universal sympathy for Finland in her solitary and unequal battle. Old memories of David against Goliath, the Greeks against the Persians, came to mind everywhere and aroused sympathies, friendly concern and admiration for the Finns. But other factors also favored Finland. The antipathy of western nations toward Nazism was extended to embrace Soviet Russia because the U.S.S.R. was in close cooperation with Germany. When the Finnish Parliament appealed to the civilized world on December 10 not to desert Finland, fighting her mighty enemy alone, and stated that Finland expected active help from the civilized western world, the appeal fell on favorable soil. The opinion that Finland should be given aid was practically universal. As a typical example of this sympathy, it is worth recalling a part of a radio address by Winston Churchill on January 20, 1940, in which he said:

> Finland alone—in danger of death, superb, sublime Finland—shows what free men can do. The service that Finland has rendered to humanity is magnificent . . . We cannot say what Finland's fate will be, but nothing could be sadder to the rest of the civilized world than that this splendid northern race should at the end be destroyed and in the face of incredible odds should fall into a slavery worse than death. If the light of freedom which still burns so brightly in the frozen North should finally be quenched, it might well herald a return to the Dark Ages, when every vestige of human progress during two thousand years would be engulfed.

The theoretical goodwill of the western nations toward Finland was best shown in the League of Nations. On December 3, Finland requested that the League Council take action to stop the attack, referring to articles 10 and 15 of the League Covenant. When the Council and the Assembly of the League convened in response to this appeal, the Soviet government in its reply of December 5 started from the fiction that the Kuusinen "government" represented Finland, and consequently argued that Russia was not at war with Finland. She therefore declined the invitation to attend the meeting. On the 9th the Council decided to refer the matter to the Assembly. To the proposals of the Assembly's committee, formed to handle the matter, Russia replied on the 12th that she could take no part in discussions of the Finnish question for reasons previously stated. On the 14th the Assembly approved a resolution which stated that since Russian activities were contrary to general treaties, as well as specific treaties with Finland which Russia herself had signed, League members should give all possible aid to Finland, and it was further declared that Russia had acted in violation of the League Covenant and consequently was no longer a member of the League. Immediately thereafter, the League Council formally announced Russia's expulsion from the League. This was an unusual action, and turned out to be the last achievement of the League. It could hardly have chosen a worthier way of ending its labors.

Even after this, however, an attempt was made by the Finns to establish contact with the Soviet government. In a radio speech of December 15, Tanner addressed Molotov and proposed a continuation of the negotiations, but the only answer was a news item of the Tass agency to the effect that the appeal would hardly get an answer.

3. Foreign Assistance

The goodwill shown Finland probably assumed, in many instances, only a diplomatic form. Its extent and influence, therefore, are still but partly known. However, it can definitely be taken for granted that it was not without effect on the Soviet Union. The League of Nations' appeal for material and humanitarian help to Finland had few results at the Finnish front, but it nevertheless sustained the front and the whole nation's ability to resist. This aid was all the more valuable in that in most instances it was completely voluntary.

Finland was not prepared to wage war, and arms and men were therefore most sorely needed. But because all nations were now rearming it was very difficult to obtain arms or men. The material help from Sweden was most substantial and actually became of really decisive importance both because of its quantity and the ease with which it could be transported to Finland. From Sweden it was possible to buy, without loss of time, arms and ammunition absolutely vital at the front. Volunteers also came from Sweden, though only two reinforced battalions reached the front in time. Volunteers from other countries near and far also came to fight for Finland's freedom. Like Sweden, England permitted the public recruiting of volunteers. Their transportation to Finland, however, had to be carried out in purely civilian ways, since Sweden denied transit to all uniformed units. None of the foreign volunteer units from countries other than Sweden reached the front before the war had ended, except for a company formed of Finnish Americans which reached the Karelian Isthmus a few days before the peace. The significance of volunteers in modern warfare is, however, chiefly moral. No effective help can be organized in this fashion; only organized groups, trained together, are fully usable in service at the front.

Very important was the help which the 30 million dollar loan from the United States signified. Its use, however, was limited to civilian purchases. Because of America's neutrality policy at the time, no old weapons were sold or allotted to Finland, though the same neutrality policy did not prevent their being given to England two months later. Still, certain supplies, and especially airplanes, were bought in the United States, but they did not reach Finland until after the war.

Germany, on the other hand, assumed not only a cool but a definitely inimical attitude toward Finland's struggle. Her coordinated press and radio showed not the slightest sympathy toward Finland. On the contrary, it tried to minimize the whole Finnish question. Germany prevented arms bought in Italy and Western Europe, and volunteers from Hungary from passing through, thus showing that German neutrality was friendly toward Russia but not toward Finland. On at least three separate occasions Germany "advised" Sweden not to take part in the war on Finland's behalf; these demarches are known to have been made on December 12, 1939, and on February 28 and March 4, 1940. Germany is known to have seriously considered, in December, 1939, recognizing the Kuusinen government. It is clear that the reaction to Germany in Finland was determined by these facts. The attitudes caused by them changed only under the compulsion of new and later difficulties.

4. THE WESTERN POWERS' OFFER OF ARMED ASSISTANCE

At the beginning of Russia's attack, the western world probably felt only pity for Finland. The granting of military assistance undoubtedly seemed useless. It was very generally expected that, in view of the odds, Finnish resistance would soon crumble and that it would be useless to send weapons which would only fall into the hands of the Red Army. This fear proved unfounded. The Russians had believed—trusting their agents' distortions or reports colored by wishful thinking—that the Finns would scatter at the first blow, and that the Red Army divisions in their concentric attack would occupy in three or four weeks the most important centers of the country and cut it off from the rest of the world. These hopes were dashed. The Red Army met in Finland a single-minded people's army, which in retreat left its own earth scorched, and offered such well-directed and firm resistance that the attack on the Karelian Isthmus was halted for two months on the Finnish main line of defense, thus changing the enemy's offensive into a costly warfare of position, and that north of Lake Ladoga several divisions were surrounded and destroyed. A miracle had occurred, contrary to all common-sense calculation which arrives at conclusions only on the basis of quantitative comparisons.

At the beginning of February, however, the war took a new turn. The Red Army had concentrated new forces on the Karelian Isthmus so heavily that finally at least thirty infantry divisions were in the line, reinforced by strong artillery and armored forces. The big offensive of the Red Army begun on February 1 was at first checked, but on February 11-13 the Russians succeeded in a break-through on the Summa front which the tired Finns, almost completely without reserves, could not hurl back. A withdrawal along the whole western part of the Isthmus had to be undertaken which reached Viipuri at the beginning of March. At the same time Red Army units succeeded in crossing the ice to the western shore of Viipuri Bay. Resistance still continued in force, however, and there was no cracking up or rout. The spring thaw would soon begin. It would undoubtedly mean immense difficulties for the Red Army supply service.

At the beginning of this new phase, France and England decided to give Finland direct military support. They had already informed Sweden on December 27-28, 1939, that, in accordance with the League of Nations decision, they were prepared to give indirect aid to Finland (technicians and certain supplies) and requested Sweden to expedite their effort. On January 3-4, 1940, the Swedish government declared that it was willing to assist, but preferably on condition that the supplies to be shipped to Finland appear at least nominally as Finnish purchases from abroad. In addition, the permission granted in January to recruit volunteers in Britain, and the British request of January 13 to the Swedish government that their transit be facilitated, testified to Britain's desire to give Finland concrete help. The western Powers had originally planned a naval expedition and landing in Murmansk but abandoned the plan because of technical and military reasons. The definite decision to give direct military assistance was not reached by the Allied Supreme Council until February 5.

It is obvious that the motives of the western Powers in offering help to Finland were not merely idealistic and that they saw in the support of Finland a way to advance their own interests. French High Command documents seized by the Germans and published by them, reveal that early in 1940 the Finnish front was considered to have the same significance for the western Powers as the Macedonian front in the first World War. The objective of the western Powers was now to blockade Germany from all sides and limit its sources of necessary raw materials. By helping Finland, it was assumed, Norway and Sweden might perhaps also be brought to join the anti-German front, and, in any case, Germany's supply of iron ore from Sweden would be cut off. Simultaneously, it was the intention, on the southern front, to bomb the Caucasian oil fields in order to decrease Russia's oil exports to Germany. In general, the western Powers considered the continuation of the Finnish war an advantage to themselves, since it expanded the war, disturbed Soviet economy and prevented Russian aid to Germany. Daladier was especially active in developing these plans for extending the war. France was prepared to go so far as to break off diplomatic relations with Russia, but England was more cautious, presumably desiring to leave open the prospect of again seeking cooperation with Russia if a change in the situation should occur. However, the British Ambassador did quit Moscow on January 3, 1940.

These considerations and calculations were naturally not known in Finland during the war, but it was realized, of course, that the western Powers were not offering military assistance without benefit to themselves.

From the Finnish point of view, two factors in the British-French proposals were of decisive significance. In the initial plans, the actual size of the expeditionary force was estimated at from only 6,000 to 12,000 men. They were to be sent via Norway and Sweden to the Finnish northern front. In addition, other units would have been left to protect supply lines, and presumably also to occupy the mines of northern Sweden to prevent their exploitation for the benefit of German war industries. The transportation of this force, however, would of necessity have taken so long that it was doubtful if it would arrive in time to be of help. Slowly the proposed size of the force was enlarged, and enlarged again: on February 24 the British Minister to Finland announced that the plans called for 20,000 to 22,000 men. The same source gave the assurance on February 28 that by the end of April 12,000 or 13,000 men would be concentrated in Finland, with additional thousands in Sweden to support the expedition.

On March 1 the Government of Finland inquired if the western Powers could immediately send at least 50,000 men, who were to arrive at their destination in March, and later more, and whether they would be available for use on all fronts as need arose. At the same time, a request was made for a force of at least one hundred bombers with crews. On the same day, the western Powers did agree to send 50,000 men who, it was promised, would arrive by the end of March. The last specific offer was considered by Finland on March 7. It was the assurance of Daladier and Ironsides, given on March 4, to send an expeditionary combat force of 57,000 men of whom the first 15,000 would embark on March 15. The amount of military aid was thus increased by Britain and France, but the problems of transportation and time became more difficult to solve. The air support which had been promised, on the other hand, was of relatively significant proportions and the transportation of the airplanes and their ground crews could have been carried out more speedily.

The second decisive factor in the problem was that this help could arrive only by way of Norway and Sweden and depended on their consent. On March 2 they refused to grant this consent because it would have violated their neutrality, Sweden firmly and Norway less so. The western Powers therefore proposed to send the expeditionary force on the condition that Finland present an official request for aid by March 5.

Finland now momentarily held an exceptional position in world affairs. If she had requested the help which had been offered, closer cooperation between the Soviet Union and Germany would undoubtedly have resulted, and it might have led to a Russian-German military alliance. Thus a complete change in the later progress of the war might have come about. To force transit through Norway and Sweden, however, would have drawn these Scandinavian sister nations of Finland into the war, and would have made of them and Finland, the battleground of the big Powers. The help offered was too small to have affected the outcome on the Finnish front, and it was not certain that it would reach Finland in time. The only certainty was that the acceptance of this military aid would not have helped Finland in her efforts to attain peace; on the contrary, it would have bound Finland to the war of the major Powers, nobody knew for how long. Considering Finland's own advantage, this aid could be accepted only if no other means of solving the problem could be found. It might be argued, with the aid of hindsight, that the rejection of the assistance offered by the western Powers was the greatest of all errors, for Finland thereby discarded the chance to get on the side of the victorious West. But would the West have been victorious if it had had to fight against the Soviet Union? Should not the present victors be thankful now that in 1940 Finland was so cautious and hesitant?

From Finland's point of view, however, these questions are purely theoretical. The deciding factor was that the help promised would have been "too little and too late." It was presumably this expeditionary force, originally intended for Finland, that made the unsuccessful landing in Norway in the spring of 1940. It is not probable that the result on the Finnish front would have been any better.

There were other possibilities than continuing the battle to the end. The Soviet government had meanwhile realized that the Kuusinen "government" was an unprofitable venture. For many different reasons Russia had at least temporarily abandoned her plan to conquer all of Finland and was ready to make peace with Finland's legal government, if only peace were made on Russia's terms. Since the Finnish government had continued to seek for peace throughout the war, it was clear that negotiations could soon begin.

5. Peace Negotiations and the Dictated Peace of Moscow

After the Russian attack, efforts to make direct contact with Moscow having been unsuccessful, the Finnish government considered the use of an intermediary. It was assumed that the best chances would be offered by Germany, because Germany was in a way Russia's ally. If Germany refused, or if the attempt were unsuccessful, a collective effort under United States' leadership was visualized. During January, 1940, it became clear that none of these procedures would bring results. Germany, after having sounded out Moscow, replied on January 19 that in her opinion no prospects of success existed at the moment. Since a collective effort did not seem to hold out any greater promise, attempts were made to establish contact with the Soviet Union through private channels. Foreign Minister Tanner requested Madame Hella Vuolijoki, who knew Madame Kollontay, the Russian Minister to Stockholm, to use this contact to find out the war aims of the Soviet Union, and what the possibilities were for getting peace. Only when the attempt led nowhere and the Swedish Foreign Minister, Günther, offered Sweden's mediation on January 25 did it become clear that the Soviet Union was prepared to begin negotiations with the Government of Finland whose legality it had earlier denied. One can only guess at the reasons which had changed the attitude of the Soviet. It is possible that it had been primarily influenced by the knowledge of the intention of the western Powers to send military help to Finland.

At the beginning of February Finland thus stood at the crossroads, faced by three possibilities. In the order of their importance, the Government classified them, at a discussion held at Army Headquarters on February 10, as follows:

1. Peace with the Soviet Union.
2. Military aid from the Scandinavian nations, in which case the war would remain localized.

3. Military aid from the West, in which case Finland would be involved in the World War.

In order to utilize all means for saving the country, these three alternatives were simultaneously explored. This fact was not hidden from anybody concerned in the negotiations, nor did Finland at any point violate the rules of honest play.

On January 29, Sweden's Foreign Minister received word from Molotov, for transmittal to Finland, that Russia did not consider it impossible to reach an agreement with the government of Ryti and Tanner. To begin negotiations, Finland should make proposals of territorial cessions which had to be larger than those discussed in the negotiations in Moscow during October-November in 1939. Since blood had been shed, allegedly against the Soviet Union's wishes and without Russia's being to blame, she demanded additional guaranties for the security of her boundaries. The promises made to the Kuusinen "government" would not apply to the Ryti and Tanner government. The negotiations were to be kept absolutely secret.

In its answer on February 2, which Premier Ryti himself delivered in Stockholm, the Finnish government announced it was prepared to negotiate. Since, according to Finland's conception of the matter, a common basis for discussion could be reached only through compromise, it was proposed that the negotiations take as their starting point the result which had been reached in the Moscow negotiations in the fall. The Finnish government stated, however, that it was prepared to make additional concessions, particularly on the Karelian Isthmus, but territorial cessions could be made only in return for territorial compensations. The neutralization of the Gulf of Finland by international agreement could also be considered. On February 6 the Soviet government announced it could not accept Finland's answer as a basis for negotiations.

Foreign Minister Tanner was in Stockholm at the time and in contact with the Russian Minister there (who was not empowered to negotiate) and he requested information regarding Russia's demands and expressed his own personal opinion that Finland might cede, in the place of Hanko, some island at the mouth of the Gulf of Finland, in exchange for Repola and Porajärvi. During the next two weeks little happened. Russia presumably expected military developments on the Karelian Isthmus gradually to soften Finland, and to bring her to the acceptance of the new demands in which it was known Hanko would definitely be included. Finland was not yet ready for this, as a conference on February 10 at military head-quarters indicated. Immediately afterward, Finland heard via Stockholm that Russia would demand Hanko, all of the Karelian Isthmus, and territory north of Lake Ladoga. This proposal was not delivered officially to the Finnish government, and no negotiations were begun, since the gap between Russian demands and Finnish offers was too wide.

An important development in the search for peace was Tanner's second visit to Stockholm on February 13 when he renewed Premier Ryti's proposal of February 2 to Sweden, left open at that time, that Sweden send Finland volunteers in complete units, as Germany had done during the Spanish Civil War. If Finland could not secure this help, she would have to accept the western Powers' offer of aid, but that in turn would involve the northern countries in the World War.

The answer of Sweden's Prime Minister was negative. The discussion and the negative result were disclosed on the 16th in the Stockholm newspaper *Folkets Dagblad Politiken,* and the Swedish Prime Minister immediately hastened to issue a communique on behalf of his government, in which the content of the news item was confirmed in language unfortunate from Finland's point of view. On the 19th, the King of Sweden issued a statement which somewhat softened the Prime Minister's communique, but in fact it underscored the communique: Swedish military assistance to Finland was impossible in any official form. After this, Finland's hopes for armed aid from Sweden had to be considered lost. In Finland it was felt that involvement in the situation by the western Powers could no longer change the outcome: their offers were in general wavering and indefinite.

The Soviet Union could now consider Finland ripe for the acceptance of even harsh terms. On February 20 and 22, Molotov informed the Swedish Minister in Moscow that Russia's minimum demands, which its military leaders considered absolutely necessary for Leningrad's security, included all of the Hanko peninsula, all of the Karelian Isthmus, including Viipuri, land on the northern shore of Lake Ladoga, including Sortavala—or roughly the boundaries of Peter the Great, laid down at Nystad in 1721. In addition, Russia demanded that Finland join Russia and Estonia in a pact for the defense of the Gulf of Finland. These terms included the threat that if they were not accepted, additional demands would be presented in the future.

On receipt of these harsh terms, the Finnish government asked Sweden once more, on February 23, if she could grant permission for the transit of men and materiel in accordance with the League of Nations pact, Article 16. On the next day Sweden replied, as before, that she was unable to increase her aid, or to permit any aid which would involve Sweden in the war, and therefore could not allow military units of nations at war to go through Sweden. In order to have some kind of support before making the final decision, the Finnish Foreign Minister asked the Prime Minister of Sweden on the 27th if Finland, having accepted Russia's terms, could count on economic support from Sweden, and if a defense alliance could be considered, since otherwise there would be no guaranties that Russia would not make new demands and begin a new war. The granting of economic aid, Sweden declared, was possible, but as regards the question of defensive alliance, the only answer was that it could be taken under consideration.

In the meantime, Russia tried to use Britain as an intermediary, asking her on the 26th to transmit to Finland the terms outlined above. Lord Halifax, the Foreign Secretary, declared that he considered the terms altogether unreasonable and refused to transmit them. Ambassador Maiski then threatened that this attitude of the British government might lead to unexpected developments in the relations between Britain and Russia, but received the retort that it was hard to prevent conflicts from arising if Russia stubbornly continued the war against Finland and presented demands which were difficult to accept. The nature of the Russian calculation which led to the attempt to use England's mediation is still a matter of conjecture. Presumably it was only a trial balloon by the aid of which Russia attempted to discover how serious the western Powers' plans for intervention were.

On February 28, Russia informed the Foreign Minister of Sweden that Finland must give her answer to Russia's demands within forty-eight hours. Finland's reply, delivered via Stockholm to Moscow on March 1, requested more specific definition of the new boundaries and asked what Finland would receive in return for the cessions. At the same time, the western Powers increased and made more definite the scope of the military assistance they had offered, and requested that Finland's reply to the offer be given by the 5th. On that date Moscow replied, via Stockholm, to the Finnish inquiry of March 1. The Soviet Union stated that it would not abandon its demand for

Viipuri and Sortavala, and that it would wait a few more days for the final acceptance of the terms that had been submitted. The note contained the threat that if the demands were not now accepted, the Red Army would march deeper into Finland, the terms would become harsher, and the Soviet Union would make a final definitive agreement with the Kuusinen "government."

In considering the alternatives before it, the Finnish government still put peace in first place. Since the military situation was growing increasingly more alarming, and the possibilities of getting help from the outside promised little at best and seemed to recede into the distance, the harsh peace terms offered were perforce considered preferable to the catastrophe that threatened. The Finnish government therefore announced on March 5, via Stockholm, that it would accept the Russian terms in principle, as a basis for peace negotiations, that it awaited a proposal of where and when the negotiations were to take place, and suggested an armistice on the basis of the status quo. In delivering this note, the Swedish government added a suggestion of its own to the effect that hostilities between Russia and Finland cease on the 6th. On the 6th, Molotov declared that Russia was prepared to begin negotiations in Moscow for peace and the ending of hostilities, but would not agree to an armistice. On the same day the Finnish government decided to send a peace commission to Moscow, to which Ryti, Paasikivi, Walden and Voionmaa were appointed.

When the negotiations began in Moscow on the 8th, Sweden gave Finland diplomatic support by stating that if the Russians went so far in their demands that the Finnish government could not accept them, a dangerous reaction in public opinion in Sweden and in the stand of the western nations might result. This demarche carried no weight, however, for on March 9 it was disclosed that in addition to the terms previously known, several new conditions would be presented to the Finns. The Soviet Union now also demanded the large border area of Salla and Kuusamo, and the building of a railroad from Salla to Kemijärvi.

The Finnish government was now faced with an exceptionally difficult decision. The premises on the basis of which the negotiations had begun, had been unexpectedly changed by the additional demands of the Russians. This forced a reconsideration of the offer of help from the western Powers. On the 8th the following communication was received from the French Prime Minister Daladier:

We have waited for several days for Finland to make her appeal, so that we can come to your aid with all the means at our disposal. It is difficult to understand why this request is still postponed. We know the pressure Sweden is exerting on you to make a peace which would leave you at Russia's mercy. We know Russia fears you will appeal to the Allies, because she fears that an Allied intervention will lead to a Russian catastrophe. To avoid the catastrophe, Russia is now ready to negotiate in order to be able to destroy you later. I assure you once more, we are ready to give our help immediately. The airplanes are ready to take off. The operational force is ready. If Finland does not now make her appeal to the western Powers, it is obvious that at the end of the war the western Powers cannot assume the slightest responsibility for the final settlement regarding Finnish territory. I request the Government to make its decision soon.

Daladier had agreed orally that the request could be presented by March 12 at the latest, but preferably earlier. He had declared he understood the difficulty of Finland's position, but requested that his position be appreciated as well, since he had energetically crusaded against Stalin. It was known that England had promised to send fifty bombers with crews.

On the other hand, many reasons pointed to Finland's submitting to the stiffer demands of Russia. Sweden in particular did everything she could to steer Finland to this point of view. The decisive factor, however, was Commander-in-Chief Mannerheim's statement on March 9 that the situation on the Karelian Isthmus was untenable, that foreign help, even under the best conditions, would take five weeks to arrive, and that even then it would be of insufficient strength. On the evening of the 9th, therefore, the Government decided to give the delegation in Moscow full powers to make peace, and on the 11th it informed the delegation that the military situation compelled acceptance of the Russian demands. At the same time, however, it was decided to inquire officially once more of the possibilities of aid from the governments of Norway and Sweden, and their final decision in regard to the transit of the expeditionary force of the western Powers through Norway and Sweden. Sweden was asked whether she stood ready to consider a defensive alliance with Finland after the war had been brought to a close.

In order that the decision would be formulated on as broad a basis as possible, the peace question was submitted to Parliament's Committee for Foreign Affairs. On the 11th it voted thirteen to four in favor of making peace. On the same day, news of this vote leaked out to the Swedish press. This of course decisively influenced the negotiations in Moscow and the attitude of Norway and Sweden. Thereafter neither moderation in Russia's terms nor a more affirmative answer from the Scandinavians than had already been received, could be expected. On the other hand, the declaration over the radio of Chamberlain and Daladier, in which the western Powers promised to come to Finland's help, if requested to do so, gave Finland support. The Government's decision had already been made, however: on the 12th it telegraphed its delegation in Moscow full powers to sign the peace. Two members of the Government (Hannula and Niukkanen), who had favored approval of the offer of aid from the West thereupon resigned from the Cabinet. The last query of England and France on the 12th, for transit permission from Norway and Sweden, no longer influenced the course of events. No answer was needed, for on the evening of the 12th of March, 1940, Finland signed the terms of the Moscow peace.

The Moscow peace terms could not and cannot be considered as anything but altogether unreasonable. Finland had to cede, in the southeast, an area vital to her economy, the conquest of which the Soviet Union had not even tried to defend in the name of its "security." On the contrary, on October 31, 1939, Molotov had branded as groundless lies, arguments that Russia wanted to take Viipuri and the north shore of Lake Ladoga. The whole Finnish industrial area was senselessly cut up. For example, the extensive lake system was cut off from the sea because the mouth of the Saimaa Canal was now in Russian hands. Ten per cent of the Finnish population had lost their homes. Finnish defense possibilities had been catastrophically worsened. Russia herself seems to have been ashamed enough of her appetite, for an attempt was made to explain the seizures with the aid of arguments made out of whole cloth. *Pravda,* for example, justified on March 25 the occupation of land north and northeast of Lake Ladoga by presenting the remarkable claim that in order to destroy the Volga Aluminum Combine established in 1931, Finland, at England's command, had immediately built a military airport at Sortavala as a base for air raids to destroy the aluminum plant. Molotov himself felt it essential to try to prove, on one occasion, that Finland could exist even with what the Moscow peace had left her.

Opinion in Parliament differed as to whether the Moscow terms should be accepted or whether the aid offered from the West should still be welcomed. The question can be argued endlessly, even now.

It cannot be answered objectively. At any rate, Finland had had time to show that she was willing to fight for her independence. In the western world, too, the compulsion under which Finland had submitted to Moscow's dictated peace was understood, and in his message to the Finnish people, Lord Halifax declared that he honored Finland for the bravery she had shown, and expressed his hope and belief that that bravery would in the future bring its full reward. Furthermore, he gave assurance that when the Allies achieved victory, Finland would surely participate in those advantages which a a true and just peace would bring. That reward and the advantages, however, were received in 1944 in a way that no one could foresee in 1940.

CHAPTER 5

FINLAND UNDER THE MOSCOW PEACE

1. Relations with the Soviet Union

The entire Finnish people considered the Moscow peace a gross injustice but submitted to it and proceeded honestly to fulfill its terms. They did not want to build the future on chance developments, and no thoughts of revenge were entertained. The proof that the Moscow peace was considered final is conclusive. For example, refugees who had lost their lands were given compensation. A heavy national property tax was levied, and an emergency housing and settlement law was enacted and put into effect with full speed. Such gigantic reforms would not have been carried out if there had been thoughts of correcting the injustice that had been suffered, and cancelling the hardships, through revenge. It is no doubt true, to be sure, that practically everybody in Finland would have found it easy to witness the Soviet getting what it deserved because of its lack of international morality and because of what it had done to Finland by the unprovoked attack.

However, no success met the attempt to establish good relations with the Soviet Union. The victor acted toward the vanquished with unusual suspicion, which it is impossible to explain except as stemming from a bad conscience or bad intentions. For example, when the Russian Minister to Helsinki returned to his post after the peace, the first thing he did was to lodge a protest because the city's flags were at half mast on that day. They had been lowered in mourning for the dead. He had considered it perfectly clear that the flags at half mast were a demonstration against him, and did not bother to find out the real explanation.

Yet Russia should have been able to afford magnanimity toward Finland. By the Moscow peace she had grabbed so much at Finland's expense that one would have thought her satisfied. On March 21, 1940, Molotov admitted that all questions with Finland had been settled once and for all, and in his speech in the Supreme Soviet on August 1, he announced that Finland had satisfactorily fulfilled the peace terms.

It has been claimed that the reason for the continuing unsatisfactory relations was Finland's propaganda. The truth is, however, that no propaganda in Finland was directed against the Soviet Union. In fact, there could have been none, since the Soviet Legation filed protests regarding even absolutely insignificant matters, which was enough to make the expression of public opinion exceedingly cautious. The activity of the Soviet government, on the other hand, was the most effective kind of propaganda against itself; specifically, the way it interpreted and applied the peace terms. One chapter of the Finnish Blue-White Book is entitled "Peace without Guaranty of Justice," which aptly characterizes the state of affairs after March, 1940. The oppressive atmosphere which prevailed in Finland in the period after the peace, was surely not created by artificial means. Almost every day seemed to furnish fresh proof for the belief that Russia still continued her war against Finland, although in new forms.

In the first place, the Soviet Union demanded much more than the peace treaty presupposed. It demanded, for example, the return of private property which had been taken out of the areas ceded to Russia, especially factory machinery, and compensation for property damaged during the war in these areas. Even the return of property which had been moved as long ago as 1938 was demanded. Such demands were presented even in regard to civilian and military property taken out by the Finns from the Hanko territory. Furthermore, the Russians demanded a sizable amount of railroad rolling stock, arguing that according to the "rules," the inventories of all larger railroad stations including rolling stock. Such demands as these were unpredictable and seemed unending. In contradiction to the peace terms, and otherwise arbitrary, was the Russian demand that Finland should not ally herself with Sweden.

Also, Russia's demand for the concession to exploit the nickel mines of Petsamo, operated by a Canadian-English combine, or operate them jointly, or to settle the matter in some other fashion was in no way connected with the peace terms. It became clear that in the Petsamo region more than just the mines interested the Russians. Their chief aim was to expel the English concessionaires from Petsamo. Although the Petsamo area was important to Finland both for its nickel and as an outlet to the Arctic Ocean, and after the German occupation of Norway in the spring of 1940, was the only way out of Finland, the threatening Russian demands forced a consideration of the transfer of the nickel mines to a mixed Finnish-

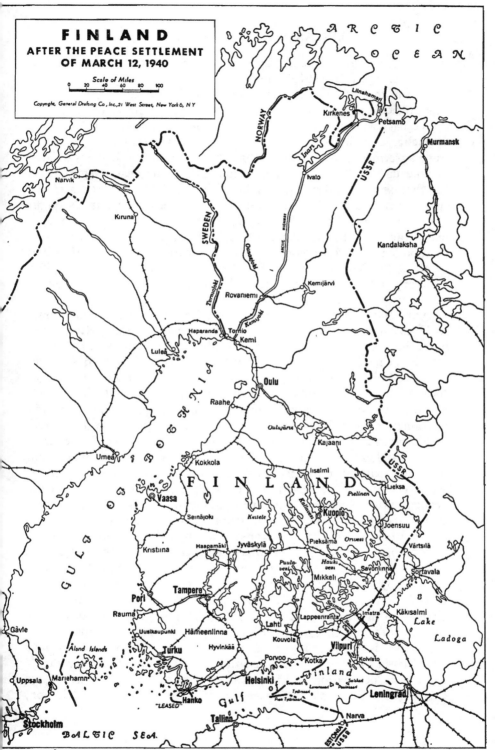

FINLAND
AFTER THE PEACE SETTLEMENT
OF MARCH 12, 1940

Scale of Miles
0   20   40   60   80   100

Copyright, General Drafting Co., Inc., 21 West Street, New York 6, N Y

ARCTIC OCEAN

NORWAY

Liinahamari
Kirkenes
Petsamo
Murmansk

Inari

USSR

Ivalo

Narvik

Kiruna

SWEDEN

Kandalaksha

Ounasjoki

ARCTIC HIGHWAY

Kemijärvi

Kemijoki

Tornijoki

Rovaniemi

Haparanda   Tornio
Kemi
Luleå

USSR

GULF OF BOTHNIA

Oulu

Raahe

Oulujärvi

Kajaani

Umeå

Kokkola

Iisalmi

FINLAND

Lieksa

Pielinen

Vaasa

Seinäjoki   Kestele   Kallavesi   Kuopio

Joensuu

Haapamäki   Jyväskylä   Pieksäma   Orivesi   Värtsilä

Kristiina

Puula-
vesi   Hauki-
vesi   Savonlinna

Sortavala

Mikkeli

Tampere

Pori

Rauma

Uusikaupunki   Hämeenlinna

Hyvinkää

Lahti   Lappeenranta   Imatra   Käkisalmi

Kouvola

Lake
Ladoga

Turku

Porvoo   Kotka   Viipuri   Koivisto

Gävle

Åland Islands

Mariehamn

"LEASED"   Hanko

Helsinki

Gulf   of   Finland   Leningrad

Uppsala

Tallinn   Narva

Stockholm   BALTIC SEA   ESTONIA
USSR

(Courtesy of Mr. Otto G. Lindberg, President, General Drafting Co., Inc.)

83

Russian concern. Impeded by further immoderate demands, the matter was not fully settled when war again broke out in 1941.

Again, the demand for the demilitarization of the Aland Islands was outside the provisions of the treaty, and in direct conflict with the verbal assurances the Soviet government had given in the course of earlier negotiations. Molotov explained, in connection with the trade agreement negotiations on June 27, 1940, that he had not wanted to take up the Aland Island question during the peace negotiations "so that new, fresh demands would not arise." This vague statement suggests the conjecture that interference in the Aland Islands might have run counter to the Ribbentrop pact or would have given Germany the right to demand some compensation. Finland now had to submit to the destruction of her fortifications on the islands and to allow the Russians to verify that the job was done thoroughly. Germany announced frankly that the solution of the Aland Islands question did not interest her at all.

The demand for the right of way on Finnish railroads from Russia to Hanko was also outside the treaty provisions. Since Russia had based her demand for Hanko specifically on the contention that the Red Navy needed a base at the mouth of the Gulf of Finland, it might have seemed that sea transportation would have sufficed. The negotiation for transit rights began on July 9, 1940, and almost two months later, on September 6, the agreement was signed. This right of transit exposed Finland to many dangers. According to the agreement, personnel and weapons were to be transported in separate coaches and cars, but since the chances for Finnish control were well-nigh non-existent, the possibility remained that the Soviet Union, at a convenient moment, could utilize its transit rights to carry out the occupation of Finland. How surprisingly far the Russians went in their exactions is seen in their demand for permission for Soviet agents to use submarines for transportation within Finnish waters.

The instances of Russian interference in Finnish internal affairs are innumerable. In the summer of 1940, dark forebodings were aroused by the activity of the "Finnish-Russian Peace and Friendship Society," which was composed chiefly of communists, and which challenged the forces of law and order. Russia gave this society her full support, and threatened the Finnish government because it had intervened in the activity of the society. This gave rise to the fear that Russia's intention was to use this society as the means for carrying out an occupation of Finland from within, and thus perhaps set the stage for Finland's "voluntary" admission into the Soviet Union, according to the technique perfected in the Baltic States. Furthermore, interference in Finland's presidential election meant clear meddling in the country's internal affairs: on December 6, 1940, Molotov told the Finnish Minister that if any one of four men—Tanner, Kivimäki, Mannerheim or Svinhufvud—were elected President, Russia would conclude that Finland did not want to observe the peace treaty. This extraordinary declaration, it was claimed, meant, however, no Russian interference in Finnish internal questions. Further, Moscow also tried to determine the composition of the Finnish Cabinet. The U.S.S.R. especially objected to Väinö Tanner, who had been Minister for Foreign Affairs during the Winter War and whose resignation Russia demanded in various connections. Even Tanner's resignation, on August 16, 1940, did not satisfy the Russians who argued that Tanner was still working against the Soviet Union behind the scenes. In the same way, they announced that the continuation in the Cabinet of von Born and Fagerholm disturbed Finnish-Russian relations. At Russia's demand, Finland was also compelled to introduce strict censorship for the purpose of seeing to it that nothing displeasing to the Russians could appear in print or be sold in book shops. All literature pertaining to the Winter War was classified as objectionable. In general, it seemed that there were no limits to Soviet interference in Finnish affairs.

Still, in spite of the fact that the granting of many of these demands meant heavy sacrifices for the Finns, they seemed to suggest that Russia would allow Finland to remain independent, at least for the time being. For example, it would have been useless to present many of the demands for restitution and reparations if Finland's speedy conquest was a part of Russia's plans. But on the other hand, attention had also to be fixed on certain other things which indicated that the Soviet Union was preparing for the conquest of Finland. In this class belonged the extensive and intensified Russian espionage which, it was discovered in many cases, was connected with occupation operations planned for the near future. Finnish military circles were disturbed by the knowledge that on the Karelian Isthmus the Red Army, in addition to its regular forces, kept a complete and fully equipped army corps, which could be thrown speedily against the Finnish southeast border at any point. On the other hand, it became known that numerous special forces and weapons intended primarily for land operations, such as mobile railroad artillery, armored cars, etc., were kept in Hanko. Since the defense of Finland's southeastern border had become especially difficult after the loss of the

Karelian Isthmus, the military position of the whole nation was further considerably weakened by the fact that the Red Army now had a strong bridgehead into Finland in Hanko in the southwest.

In such circumstances, Finland had to take very seriously such Russian threats and hints as that of the Russian radio, for example, on January 10, 1941 to the effect that the continuation of the "present exploiters' system" (the use of funds for national defense was being discussed) in Finland for even a year was questionable. Molotov's speech on August 1, 1940, to the Supreme Soviet had to be considered especially ominous. Its main theme was a bombastic survey of the Soviet Union's recent expansion which had added 23 million inhabitants to Russia. Speaking of Finland, Molotov was forced to admit that the peace treaty had been satisfactorily fulfilled. But he uttered a clear threat because "certain elements of Finland's ruling circles" had used force to restrain the communists. If this is not stopped, he said, "it is understandable that Russo-Finnish relations may deteriorate." At the close of his speech he claimed that Japan and the United States threatened to turn the present war into an imperialistic World War. Faced with that prospect, Russia had to strengthen her defenses, economy and productive power. "Then no events can surprise us, and we shall achieve new and even more glorious results for the Soviet Union." It was difficult to interpret the speech in any other way than that Soviet foreign policy aimed at continuing expansion.

It is not surprising, therefore, that especially in the summer of 1940, Finland nervously followed all available indications of the movements of the Red Army and the Red Navy. Soviet military preparations, made prior to the occupation of Bessarabia, Bukovina and the Baltic States, were on a scale large enough to permit more than sufficient observations. Only the course of later events, however, disclosed what particular surprise had been in the making at any given time. During the actual preparations for the surprises, a country as exposed as Finland was naturally had to take into consideration the possibility that the surprise might be Finland's "voluntary" inclusion in the Soviet Union. The Finns were no more ready to submit to inclusion now than before, and they wanted to be prepared to defend their mutilated fatherland. During midsummer, forces had been alerted on the Gulf of Finland coast, but the order could be cancelled immediately. Early in August partial mobilization was ordered because information had been received from several sources, considered both friendly and reliable, of Russia's intention to attack;

this measure, too, was cancelled within a few weeks. Toward the end of January, 1941, Russian troop movements along the Finnish border were observed and led to a consideration of the strengthening of the border units.

It is easy to claim today that these precautionary measures reflected the nervousness prevalent in Finland at that time and were without cause. It is by no means certain, however, that the alerts were useless, let alone without cause. The possibility must also be considered that the demonstration of Finnish preparedness in itself deterred any Russian aggression that might have been intended.

With the documents now available, it is impossible to get a complete picture of Russia's over-all program for Finland in the years 1940 and 1941. It is known definitely, from concrete experience, that the Soviet Union considered Finland as belonging to its own sphere of interest, wanted to isolate her from the rest of the world and eliminate all other foreign influences from the country. To fall into Russia's sphere of interest was looked upon everywhere with apprehension. Even in those Finnish circles which were most conciliatory toward Russia, it was considered that to "remain in the Soviet sphere of interest is death for us, for Russia represents a completely different world which does not suit us and will only exterminate us." But the fate of the Baltic States showed that a still greater danger could confront the country: inclusion in the Soviet Union. Both the leaders of the country and ordinary citizens were animated by the feelings of insecurity and fear. To argue that there were no grounds for such a fear is poor reasoning indeed.

It seemed to be impossible to establish good relations with the big eastern neighbor no matter what was tried. Commercial relations did not become normal, though Finland fulfilled her part of the terms of the trade pact of June 28, 1940. In January, 1941, the Soviet Union stopped the exchange of goods, and one of Russia's leading politicians frankly declared that the beginning of a trade war was implied. Russia was altogether unwilling to establish any cultural relations, unless such relations were in the charge of the communist-led "Finnish-Russian Peace and Friendship Society," and rejected, or by indifference, killed all other initiative from other quarters. In these circumstances, and lacking support from abroad, Finland could do nothing but resist Russian demands cautiously enough so as not to let relations with the Soviet Union deteriorate. Many concessions were made, in the meantime, which weakened the country's political and economic position.

Immediately following the Moscow peace, Finland began to prepare the defenses of the territory still left to her. Entirely new defense lines were built, weapons were procured from various sources abroad, etc. But since it was clear that Finland alone could not long defend herself against giant Russia, it became more urgent than ever to seek support from abroad.

2. RELATIONS WITH THE WESTERN POWERS AND SWEDEN

At the time, the Soviet Union's intentions were suspected everywhere. After the war goodwill toward Finland and desire to aid her continued in the West. After the fall of France in the summer of 1940, however, the western Powers radically changed their attitude toward the Soviet Union and Finland. The reestablishment of a balance of power now became possible only with the help of Russia. The Powers were willing to pay almost any price to get this help. This became clear, for instance, in England's unwillingness to secure her own economic advantages in the Petsamo nickel mines question. Early in November, 1940, a high official of the British Foreign Office revealed this new attitude clearly to the Finnish Minister in London. He said frankly that Great Britain could do nothing for Finland because she could not afford to risk any complications that might lead to Russia's allying herself fully with Germany. He did not deny that the Finnish government's policy, which attempted to establish some sort of a balance against the Soviet Union with German help, was a right one, and quite understandable in any case.[1] It must be admitted, however, that England was prepared to give limited support to Finland. This was especially proven by the permission to allow shipping to continue to the port of Petsamo. Finland's relations with the United States showed the same trend. As late as the summer of 1940 the Americans were still prepared to make certain demarches for Finland; Finland received a moratorium on her debt payments; arms were sold to Finland, etc. Before long, however, the United States became very careful not to offend the potential ally, and finally this attitude became so decisive that the goodwill shown to Finland began to disappear.

The finding of some sort of support seemed so necessary, however, that new Finnish efforts were made. In accepting the Moscow peace terms, Finland had simultaneously asked Sweden and Norway if they would be prepared to consider the possibilities of a joint defense pact

---

[1] This apparently refers to the transit agreement concluded with Germany over a month before the conversation in question (Ed).

after the close of hostilities. Both nations gave affirmative answers the contents of which were published in official press releases on March 14, 1940.

The Soviet Union opposed this plan from the start. As early as March 16, the Swedish Minister to Moscow was informed regarding the poor impression which had been allegedly caused by the statement recently made by Mr. Carl J. Hambro, President of the Norwegian Parliament, to the effect that Finland's new eastern boundary · was only temporary and should be revised; in Moscow that statement was understood as revealing Scandinavian thoughts of revenge. The proposals for a Scandinavian league, news of which had just reached Moscow, were now linked with the alleged revanché attitude. According to the Soviet view such a league was in conflict with Swedish and Norwegian neutrality, and it could only be considered as being directed against Russia. The statements made by Sweden—that a purely defensive league was involved which in no way conflicted with a policy of neutrality, but on the contrary was intended to strengthen neutrality in all directions, and that Sweden would approve no pact directed against Russia—had no effect on the Soviet Union. The official Russian news agency disclosed on March 20 that Molotov remained unbending: the Soviet Union opposed the Scandinavian pact because, it was alleged, the pact was directed against Russia, and on Finland's part was in direct violation of the terms of the Moscow peace. Molotov took the same attitude in his statement on Soviet foreign policy at the meeting of the Supreme Soviet on March 29. He warned against attempts to violate the peace recently made with Finland, which certain Finnish, Swedish and Norwegian circles were allegedly making under the guise of a defensive alliance. Molotov considered the matter so important that he took it up several times at the end of March. He specifically tried to frighten Sweden and Norway by holding that an alliance with Finland would mean the abandonment of their traditional neutrality and the acceptance of a new foreign policy from which Russia could but draw "the obvious conclusions."

In the face of this opposition, the contemplated tri-partite pact was abandoned. Soon afterwards, on April 9, came the German attack on Denmark and Norway, almost as an *argumentum ad hominem* to show the timeliness and need for just such an alliance. In view of the insignificant, small forces with which Germany carried out her Norwegian operations, it is more than probable that Germany would not have made such an attempt if she had known she would be opposed by a Scandinavian alliance which would have made her position in the Baltic also untenable. The only reason Russia could have for opposing this alliance was her desire to hold Finland so firmly in her own sphere of influence as to exclude free Finnish foreign relations. If Russia had still more far-reaching plans regarding Finland at the time, she naturally had even greater reason for preventing the alliance. Thus the Soviet Union as well as Germany must be held guilty of the undeserved fate which befell the Norwegian people for so many years. Whether Russia profited or lost as a result is an open question.

The partial state of alarm, which lasted all summer in Finland, forced a return to the idea of achieving close cooperation with Sweden. The situation of both countries having considerably deteriorated after the German occupation of Norway, negotiations were begun between Finland and Sweden for cooperation in new forms. At the end of September, 1940, the Speaker of Parliament, Väinö Hakkila, and Dr. Henrik Ramsay, discussed the matter on behalf of the Finnish government, with members of the Swedish government. The changed situation had made cooperation more timely than before, as shown, for example, by the joint use by the two countries of the Petsamo harbor and shipping facilities. The Swedes presented the view that a military alliance alone was not sufficient, since one party to the alliance might by itself involve the other party in military complications. Some form of political federation should therefore be considered. Cooperation should thus be closer than previously contemplated. It should include not only defense measures but, as a prerequisite of defense, common action in certain foreign policy and economic matters also. Broadening the alliance idea in this fashion would make it easier, it was believed, to carry through the alliance in the two countries, and outside Scandinavia, especially in Moscow, a readier understanding of the sincere desire for peace, which was the basis of the plan, could be expected. Considering Finland's dangerous situation, the aim was to increase the likelihood of continued peace on the basis of existing treaties. One of the prerequisites was, of course, that assurances could be had that the plan would lead to no difficulties with Russia or Germany. On October 25, Finland assured Sweden that she entertained no plans of revenge and was ready to discuss political union within the framework of her present territory and boundaries.

The Soviet Union considered that these proposals, too, represented some kind of secret conspiracy against the Moscow peace.

Molotov declared on several occasions that he opposed them—immediately following the Moscow peace, and again in September and November, 1940. He issued an especially threatening warning on December 6. Germany, on the other hand, replied that under the circumstances, and considering Finland's delicate relations with Russia, it would not be practical to try to carry out these plans. At the beginning of 1941, therefore, the new Finnish government decided that the practical fulfillment of the plans had to be postponed. Throughout the winter there was no progress beyond the discussion stage. Thus this plan, too, fell through because of Russian opposition which could have had no motive other than shortsighted desire for expansion.

3. THE BEGINNINGS OF COOPERATION WITH GERMANY

After the hopes of support in Scandinavia had failed, Finland was more isolated than ever after the summer of 1940. Then came the Russian demand for transit rights to Hanko, communist-inspired disturbances seemed to threaten the country's position in foreign relations, the armed forces were on the alert, Britain had begun to restrict shipping to Petsamo, and not even the United States supported Finland in that matter. It was expected that the situation would become especially dangerous in the event that Germany continued her attempt to invade Britain. If the invasion materialized, it was to be feared that Russia would continue her expansion and occupy all of Finland. This possibility was apparently seriously weighed in Great Britain, judging from the known fact that at the end of February, 1941, England was considering the recall of her diplomatic representation from Finland and the leaving of British affairs in the hands of the United States Legation. At the end of April, the plan was extended to include Canadian interests also, if Russia were to invade Finland. If such a conception of Finland's position prevailed abroad, it is not surprising that, seen through Finnish eyes, the future did not seem particularly bright.

Some possibility of salvation seemed to be offered by Germany's growing interest in Finland. It is still not clear what changes had occurred in the German plans, but in any event, in the summer of 1940, Germany began to moderate considerably her earlier cool attitude toward Finland. The first concrete evidence of German change was shown in August, 1940, when Ribbentrop, with propagandistic publicity, released Finnish arms shipments which had been confiscated in Norway during the invasion. The new attitude was shown also on August 18, 1940, in connection with the agreement for a very important arms' purchase contract, when permission was asked for the transit of Luftwaffe personnel via Finland to Norway, such as Sweden had granted on July 5, 1940. The bearer of the proposal, Colonel Veltjens, travelled to Finland as a representative for the firm "Veltjens & Aschpurvis, Waffen und Munition," and was thus without official position or official mission. He had requested and received a letter of introduction to the Finnish Commander-in-Chief from the Finnish Minister in Berlin. The Commander-in-Chief referred the matter to the President. Finland could act only favorably on this proposal, for to reject it would have spoiled the chances to procure munitions. To grant it could be expected to ease the country's political and economic position. At that time it also seems to have been decided to leave the practical details of the transit to the military representatives of the two countries. The negotiations of the military representatives began in Berlin; in order to get acquainted with local conditions, they were continued in Helsinki, and were carried out very secretly.

The preliminary agreement was concluded between representatives of the Finnish General Staff and the German Luftwaffe. The result of the discussions was an agreement signed in Helsinki by Lieutenant Colonel Stewen and Major Ochs and dated September 12, 1940. It defined in detail the technical aspects of the troop transit. It presupposed that the Germans themselves would maintain the organization essential for the transports.

The Finnish Minister in Berlin received word of the agreement from Veltjens, who also told him that it had not been made by the Governments of Finland and Germany but by their military, and warned the Minister against discussing it with the German Foreign Office which knew nothing of the matter. However, on September 17, on instructions from his Government, the Finnish Minister demanded that the transit already begun should be covered by an agreement that would satisfactorily meet formal requirements; the agreement should be similar to the Hanko transit agreement granted to the Russians, but less exacting when occasional transportation would be involved. It became clear at the time that the German Foreign Office in fact knew nothing of the matter and was very reluctant to make any agreement "since the matter was too insignificant." It is very probable that the initiative in the transit matter had been Goering's, and that the Foreign Office was reluctant to approve it because of fear that it would cause deterioration in relations with Russia. For the same reason, Germany did not want to have anything to do, officially, with Finland's procurement of arms. Therefore the agreement was not signed in Berlin until September 22, when the transit traffic was already under way, the first transport having arrived at Vaasa on the previous day, to the surprise of that city's and province's officials. The agreement was formulated by the German Foreign Office. It was made in the form of an exchange of notes between the Finnish Minister and the German Foreign Office. It was quite general in phrasing and differed in some important respects from the military's technical agreement. The wording was as follows:

1. At the request of the Reich, the Finnish government permits transit of materiel and necessary personnel from northern Baltic ports, through Rovaniemi, along the Artic road to Kirkenes in northern Norway.

2. The German government will inform the Finnish government, in sufficient time, as to which ports will be involved, the number of transports, their schedules of arrival and departure, as well as intended daily transit routes in northern Finland.

3. The German government will give the Finnish government notification at least twenty-four hours in advance of ship arrivals.

4. Materiel and men will be transported separately in different vehicles. The number of guards and officers who accompany the materiel transports will be fixed by a separate agreement.

Since the Finnish Minister did not know the terms of the agreement reached by the military representatives of the two countries, the Germans were able to interpret the two agreements, which should have coincided in every respect, in markedly different ways. The military agreement spoke of the passage of German materiel and personnel in two stages; the official agreement mentioned, in general terms, only materiel and necessary accompanying personnel. The official agreement was sufficiently indefinite to include almost anything and permit shipments for an indefinite period, although orally it had been declared that it meant at the most the shipment of 5,000 men and necessary supplies; the military agreement had originally been made with the then known requirements of the Luftwaffe in mind. A supplementary agreement providing for continued shipments was made about the middle of October in Helsinki, between the German Minister and the Finnish Minister for Foreign Affairs, in a further exchange of notes. It was expanded by an agreement between the military representatives, Lieutenant Colonels Stewen and Paasonen for Finland, and Captain Berling for Germany, signed on November 22, 1940, to include the travel through Finland of German soldiers on furlough between Germany and northern Norway. According to the agreement, Germany was allowed to send via Finland a maximum of 750 soldiers on furlough, travelling at the same time in both directions. This travel began on December 9, 1940.

This agreement and its various modifications marked the beginning of the infiltration of German forces into Finland and became a factor which later had to be seriously considered in all political plans, and especially in the question of a separate peace. Particularly severe criticism came therefore to be directed against it. At the time, however, conditions were so pressing that no parliamentary government in Finland could or would have dared to refuse to conclude the agreement. It must be realized that Finland was then inside the ring formed by Germany and Russia working hand in glove. If both these great Powers had been given umbrage the partition of Finland was to be feared. By making an agreement with Germany, it was possible to expect that at least some sort of counter-weight to Russia's immoderate demands would be created. This calculation did in fact prove to be correct, for after the beginning of German troop movements through Finland, Soviet pressure on Finland was noticeably lessened. The agreement was considered in Finland, however, simply as an indication that Germany's complete indifference toward Finland had come to an end. The Finnish Minister in Berlin interpreted the significance of the agreement to that effect on September 25, 1940:

> The question is of minor importance, and too far-reaching conclusions should not be drawn from it in Finland. The fact that the troops, which could just as easily be sent to Norway by another route, are being sent by way of Finland, is a demonstration in Finland's favor. Germany has frankly declared that Finland must take care of her own defenses. There is hope, however, that if a new war were to break out between Finland and Russia, Germany would not be as indifferent as before, but a continuing interest toward Finland depends on the future development of German-Russian relations.

At the time it was understood everywhere that Finland could do nothing but accept the agreement with Germany. When it was discussed by the Government on September 24, two ministers (Fagerholm and Salovaara) registered their dissatisfaction only on the grounds that they had not had a chance to participate in the preparation of the agreement, but no criticism of the pact itself was voiced by anyone. Public opinion accepted with satisfaction the news of the beginning of German troop transits through Finland. No one could foresee at the time what complications it was to bring with it. As for the legality of the agreement, no one had anything to say against that, for even the right of transit, granted a few months earlier to the Russians, had not been discussed in Parliament before its approval, since the Russians had demanded it be kept secret. The agreement with Germany did, however, receive tacit approval in Parliament, for it was mentioned in the Government's annual report for 1940, and no objections were raised. The agreement was communicated individually to the members of Parliament as soon as it had been signed, and news of it was received with relief. Foreign Powers also understood the reasons why Finland had had to grant this transit privilege to Germany. Sweden and England were informed of the agreement on September 23. The Soviet Union offered no objections, but Molotov seemed in bad humor. However, even when war broke out again in June, 1941, he did not mention this agreement when he listed Russia's charges against Finland. Official quarters in Scandinavia congratulated Finland on this new agreement. On September 26 the British government lodged a formal protest against it but later privately informed Finland that the making of the agreement had been quite understandable. The United States State Department took an understanding attitude and held that naturally this concession to Germany had been made under duress.

No closer rapprochement with Germany took place, at least not formally. At the time, Germany still considered that a neutral Finland, Sweden and Switzerland best served Germany's interests, and she did not consider it desirable for these countries to join the tri-partite pact. How neutral the relations with Germany were, even after German transit traffic through Finland had begun, is shown by the following. General Falkenhorst requested certain information about military and economic conditions in Finland. President Ryti presided over a discussion in which the request was considered on October 23, 1940, and the possibility was specifically considered that the Germans might pass on the information in question to the Russians.

The German transit agreement was not held to add materially to Finland's security. No attention was focussed on it as a check and balance during the course of the difficult negotiations with the Soviet Union regarding the ownership of the Petsamo nickel resources.

Neither did the battalion of volunteers recruited in Finland for training in Germany, have any definite political significance. The suggestion for it came from Germany in March, 1941, and the recruiting was done by a private Finnish committee, partly made up of men who had actively opposed Tsarism during the first World War. Seen from the Finnish point of view, the sending of volunteers into the German Army might have carried some political meaning, in that German interest toward Finland would be increased by it. To have refused might have affected Finnish-German relations all the more unfavorably, since the formation of such volunteer forces was going on in other European countries as well. At one point in the negotiations Himmler, annoyed at the conditions presented by the Finns, had threatened to "leave Finland completely at Russia's mercy." When the negotiations were completed, however, the Germans promised to give the volunteers instruction in the use of weapons which Finland totally lacked, such as tanks, and in the tactics in blitz-warfare. The volunteers had to enlist for two years. In May and June, 1941, about 1,200 of them left for Germany, followed later by approximately 200 more. The battalion organized from this group was attached to the SS, into which the volunteers of many other countries at that time were incorporated. As a result, the Finnish volunteers received the usual political indoctrination of the SS, but its significance remained nil, since it was too strange for Finnish ways of thought to accept. The fear expressed abroad, that these SS men would form some sort of a fifth column upon their return to Finland, was completely unfounded. The battalion took part in campaigns chiefly in the Ukraine, suffered considerable casualties, and after the term of enlistment returned to Finland in June, 1943, when it was disbanded. The most important fact to note in this connection is that the creation of this battalion was not influenced in the slightest by sympathy for Nazism, nor did the members of the battalion adopt Nazi doctrines.

Late in the autumn of 1940 the relations between Russia and Germany began to get so strained that occasionally indications of it leaked out to the public. That was only to be expected after Russia had eliminated the buffer states separating it from Germany. On November 12-14, Molotov made his famous trip to Berlin. For a long time afterwards, Finland received no word of what had occurred except a few general statements, intended to allay fears, to the effect that no change had occurred in Finland's position, that the visit had not brought about unfavorable results for Finland, and that the

Petsamo nickel question had been touched upon only "incidentally." Information received later was contradictory. The German Minister orally informed the Finnish Minister for Foreign Affairs early in December that Ambassador von der Schulenberg had stated in Moscow late in November that Germany had an interest in the preservation of peace in northern Europe. On the other hand, Germany gave to understand that she wanted to maintain her pact with Russia and was reluctant to do anything in Finland's behalf which might render the continuation of present Russo-German relations more difficult. Not until late in the winter of 1941, when it became obvious that Germany had had to give up her plan to invade England, did Germany presumably begin to consider an attack to eliminate the danger threatening from the east. This meant, of course, that Finland's position in German plans was radically altered. Information of Germany's eastern plans was most indefinite, however, right up to the start of the invasion.

Germany's political representatives insisted that their country's relations with Russia remained unchanged. However, on October 26, 1940, the German military attaché hinted at the possibility that Germany might clash with Russia, but that Hitler was trying to postpone the collision as long as possible. After this hint, however, all German communiques again consistently assured the continuation of peaceful relations with Russia. This propaganda was so effective that diplomats as well as newspapermen, with but few exceptions, generally believed right up to the outbreak of the war that Germany would reach a new agreement with Russia. On May 3 and 8, 1941, German representatives gave assurances to that effect to President Ryti of Finland.

The first hint of any change of policy was given on May 20, 1941 to President Ryti by Hitler's special envoy, Schnurre, who outlined the results of Molotov's November visit to Berlin, and mentioned the many causes of irritation between the two Powers which forced taking into consideration even the possibility of war. In Schnurre's opinion a peaceful solution was quite attainable, but the possibility of Russia's attacking Finland and the Balkans could not be ignored (to secure the advantages which Molotov had demanded, and to gain an advantage in the war between Germany and Russia which then would become unavoidable but which Germany would not begin). With this possibility in mind, Hitler's envoy now proposed that the Finns send one or several of their staff officers to Germany to discuss how military operations could be coordinated in the event of such an

attack against Finland.   In his reply to this proposal, President Ryti
first of all declared that Finland neither wanted to begin offensive
war, nor to become involved in a war between the major Powers.
However, if the country were attacked, Finland would fight, as she
had done before, alone if need be, but naturally pleased if help from the
outside could be received.   The result was a conference of President
Ryti, the Commander-in-Chief, Marshal Mannerheim, the Premier,
Mr. Rangell, the Defense Minister, General Walden, and the Minister
for Foreign Affairs, Mr. Witting, which decided to accept the invitation in the spirit of the President's statement.

Finnish military leaders especially considered negotiations of this
sort indispensable.   A few staff officers, led by General Erik Heinrichs, were sent to Germany, where Marshal Keitel and Generals Jodl
and Halder received them at Salzburg on May 25 and in Berlin on
the following day, and explained the military-political situation in
general terms, giving some indications of their own plans.   The Finns
heard that Russian military concentrations against Germany had
created tension which could be solved peaceably but which might also
lead to a crisis.   Germany had therefore begun preparations, one
phase of which included the exchange of one division, at the time in
northern Norway, for another division to be sent from Germany
to Norway by way of Finland.   The Germans would not expect any
efforts from the Finns, since Finland had just gone through the
exhausting Winter War, and since Germany was not accustomed to
allowing others to spill their blood to achieve Germany's goals.

After the Finns had stated at the beginning of the discussions that
they were not empowered to discuss or to enter into any agreements
and that Finland would not start an aggressive war, the conversations were limited to purely hypothetical operations based on the
premise of an attack initiated by Russia.   Since the Germans indicated that they expected Finland's political and military leaders to
take a stand regarding the considerations presented, it was agreed
that a high-ranking German officer should arrive in Finland on
June 3 to receive the Finnish answer.   The officer in question never
appeared, however, and his failure to show up was never explained.
Considering the later course of events, it seems very probable that the
German High Command wanted to avoid the possibility of a negative
Finnish reply and considered it safest to allow the situation to develop
in such a way that Finland, without any alternative, would be faced
with a *fait accompli*.

At the end of May and the beginning of June, reports began to indicate the possibility of an attack by Germany on Russia. The Finnish Minister in Berlin reported on May 27 that German heavy armor was being shifted from west to east, that railroad equipment was being altered for Russian rails, allegedly because the Germans were supposed to receive transit rights on Russian railroads, a free port in the Far East, etc. Most of the reports pointing to a deterioration in Russo-German relations came from Rumania. The Finnish Minister there sent a long list of news items to that effect: April 6, Rumania's partial mobilization; April 27, strengthening of German forces on the Bessarabian frontier and civilian evacuation of border regions; May 9, Russian evacuations in Bessarabia; June 3, mobilization to fifty per cent of maximum strength; June 19, large Russian concentrations; June 21, that decisive events could be expected in the course of the next few days or hours. It was presumably on the basis of these reports that President Ryti at a meeting of the Government on June 9, stated that he considered it possible that a conflict might break out within two weeks. The official Russian news agency, however, denied on June 13 all rumors of danger of war between the Soviet Union and Germany. This denial, which the Russian Minister Orlov repeated to Minister Witting on June 20, was not considered completely reliable in Finland, since no corresponding statement was made by Germany.

Neither in documents nor in the logic of the events themselves (and this is most important) is there the slightest hint that Germany had revealed to the political leaders of Finland her decision to attack Russia. The Finnish military command, on the other hand, seems to have received a warning a few days in advance to be on the alert on June 22. In general, however, information remained vague to the very end. Finland was urged to be on the alert because of danger of war, but at the same time she was given to understand that a peaceful settlement was possible.

The whole political atmosphere was full of contradictory rumors whose source and purpose it was difficult to explain. Even the Finnish government considered a new German-Soviet agreement to be possible when the President, on May 30, instructed the Finnish Minister to Berlin to try to see to it that the settlement would not take place, as in the autumn of 1939, at Finland's expense. Finland's wishes, which it was hoped Germany would take into consideration in her negotiations with Russia, were very modest: Finland desired a guaranty of her independence; Finland hoped for the restoration of her 1939 boundaries in which case Russia could retain the Karelian Isthmus areas she considered vital to the defense of Leningrad, Finland to be compensated in Eastern Karelia; Russia would send relief supplies to Finland; and twenty trawlers should be obtained for the use of Finnish fishermen in the Arctic.

These desiderata the Finnish Minister presented to the German Foreign Office on May 31. On June 2, he presented the additional suggestion that if the Soviet Union refused to alter the boundaries, at least the Vallinkoski power plant controversy could be justly decided in Finland's favor, and as regards other desires, Finland considered those of guaranties of security and the question of food supplies most important. On June 6 the Minister received further suggestions that in the negotiations he could limit himself, by and large, to requesting the return of Finland's 1939 boundaries. The German Foreign Office kept the Finnish Minister under the impression that the Russo-German negotiations would progress in a normal fashion. On the basis of that impression he informed his Government on June 10 that a satisfactory preliminary reply had been given to Finland's suggestions.

These Finnish suggestions were all useless because the Germans obviously were not carrying on any negotiations with Russia in which questions of this nature were discussed. They have no significance now, except to show that even in June, 1941, the Finnish government believed peace would continue, and that Finland's objectives were as reasonable as could possibly be expected of a country which had recently been the object of an unprovoked attack.

When Hitler, therefore, in his proclamation of June 22 announcing the German attack on Russia, declared that

> Side by side with their Finnish comrades stand the victorious fighters of Narvik on the shores of the Arctic. German divisions, commanded by the conqueror of Norway, together with the heroes of Finnish independence, led by their Marshal, guard Finnish soil,

he was, literally speaking, quite correct. But what he said could only too easily be misinterpreted. Hitler had no authority of any kind to mention the Finns as comrades-in-arms. No agreement of "brotherhood-in-arms" existed. Hitler's speech was, in fact, based on the correct expectation and assumption that the Red Army would attack Finland in any case, whereupon this "brotherhood-in-arms" and joint German-Finnish operations would develop of themselves, without any agreement or pact. In Finland, Hitler's reference to the Finns caused uneasiness and led to diplomatic action. The Finnish government informed—through the Finnish Legations abroad—the Powers, Germany included, that Finland did not consider herself at war with Russia despite Russian bombings and other military attacks against Finnish territory already made before Hitler's speech was delivered, and that Finland's line was neutrality and to keep out of the war. But the situation could not entirely be remedied. There is no doubt that Hitler's speech made Finland's position more difficult in that it provoked misunderstandings and compromised the country, which was in no position to seek a quarrel with the only Power that might help it in case of need. Hitler's speech was a clever chess move which shows how ruthlessly a major Power can treat small nations when its "vital interests" are involved.

CHAPTER 6

FINLAND AND THE WAR, 1941-1942

I. THE OUTBREAK OF WAR

When war breaks out between two nations, one or both are to blame, and in certain cases at least, the responsibility lies with a few leaders of foreign policy. Which nation, or which leaders, were to blame for the renewal of war between Finland and the Soviet Union in 1941?

The question can hardly be answered in a conclusive way on the basis of facts supplied only by Finland, since she was drawn into a game of power politics in which she had hardly anything to say. Only with the aid of foreign source material can the causal relationships between events be fully and satisfactorily determined. From Finland's point of view only the outward course of events can be followed, but at many important points the explanation of the events themselves remain hypothetical.

The course of events was as follows. German-Finnish military conversations had taken place at the end of May in Salzburg and Berlin, dealing with action to be taken in the event of an attack by Russia against Finland.[1] A little later there began, in Finland, a significant transfer of German forces, which seemed to be a normal undertaking covered by the terms of the transit agreement. It was also considered possible that this military movement was a part of a pressure campaign by which the Germans sought to force Russia to accept a peaceful solution of the impending conflict between Germany and Russia. Late in the winter of 1940-1941, when winter weather had cut down much of the transit traffic, the German staff handling the traffic had dwindled (by March 15) to thirty-six officers and 834 men. The size of this force increased in the spring, but not enough to arouse suspicion in Finland. The first infantry unit which

---

[1] In the war guilt trial of ex-President Ryti and others in 1945-1946, both the defendants and several witnesses testified most emphatically that neither in Salzburg nor in Berlin—or in any other place or on any other occasion—had plans been made or agreements been entered into for a common war against Russia. The prosecution was unable to present factual evidence to prove the contrary (Ed.).

was moved through Finland was an SS battalion sent to Kirkenes at the end of April and beginning of May. On June 6, 695 Luftwaffe and 838 Wehrmacht personnel, which could be considered a normal organization essential for handling the details of the transit traffic, were stationed in Finland. Then suddenly the number of Germans in northern Finland greatly increased. The Germans began preparations to transfer to Germany an SS division stationed in Norway. Numerous German ships began to arrive at different Finnish ports, and local harbor officials were unable to get any details of their cargoes in spite of requests for information. Between June 7 and 10, thirty-eight ships arrived, and thirty-six more between June 11 and 21. From the north, the SS division to be transferred began, with all its equipment, its march south toward Rovaniemi, and the division which was to replace it began to proceed north along the Ranua road from the various north Finnish ports.

In the meantime, the political situation abroad had developed in a manner that would have made the Finns feel distinctly relieved even if the two German divisions would not leave Finland too hurriedly. It was remembered clearly how Finland had been unable to defend Petsamo during the Winter War, and how easily the Russians had captured Salla. The Salla sector, where the railroad the Soviet Union had demanded in the Moscow peace was just being completed, appeared to be particularly vulnerable. It was known that the Russian forces facing Finland were numerically strong and fully ready for action. When, in addition, German and Russian troop concentrations against each other suggested an impending storm, it had been felt, as early as May 30, that Commander-in-Chief Mannerheim would have to take precautionary measures, and by June 9 he had more than sufficient cause to call out several reserve groups (partial mobilization). The first steps were taken on the 10th, and on the 17th it was announced that partial mobilization would begin the next day on an expanded scale. The different phases of this activity were explained as resulting from the danger caused by the great number of foreign (German) soldiers within the country. On the 19th, orders were given for manning the Aland Islands, effective on the 22nd. Border units were given strict orders to avoid all activity which might lead to clashes with the Russians. The deployment of forces was so clearly defensive that later, when hostilities began, the forces had to be regrouped.

How defensive these measures taken in June really were is clearly proved by the demand of the Commander-in-Chief for the extensive evacuation of civilians along the southeastern boundary. Some 60,000 people, with their household goods, are not moved needlessly from their homes during the time of their busiest summer chores, and certainly not if an offensive is being planned. A member of the United States State Department claimed, in the fall of 1941, that the decision for a Finnish offensive war had been reached in Helsinki early in April. The proof to the contrary is so weighty, however, that the claim must be considered completely groundless. In addition to other proofs, mention can be made of Germany's attempt to obtain an agreement with Finland as late as the day before the war broke out. The Finnish Minister to Berlin was asked on June 19 to inform President Ryti that Secretary Schnurre, representing the German Foreign Office, would arrive in Stockholm on the 21st, and that Finland could send Colonel Paasonen there for confidential discussions regarding economic, political and military questions. On the following day this invitation was underlined by the information that Schnurre would visit Stockholm to "make Sweden go along."

At the suggestion of President Ryti and the Minister for Foreign Affairs, Dr. Henrik Ramsay went to Stockholm. He had been told that the Germans had requested the Finnish government to send someone to talk with Schnurre. The conversations of Schnurre and Ramsay on the 21st were quite general and did not touch upon political or military questions at all. Both Ramsay and Schnurre remained in Stockholm for a few days on business with the Swedes. Ramsay heard from Schnurre that he was negotiating permission to move one German division from Norway to Finland by rail through Sweden. The Finnish Minister in Stockholm was instructed by his Government to support Schnurre in the matter, and the permission was granted by the Swedes on the 25th. There was no explanation of why Schnurre made no concrete proposals to Ramsay. Schnurre possibly realized that Ramsay had no authorization to make any commitments and therefore considered it useless to lay his cards on the table.

In view of the imminent danger of war, the Finnish High Command on June 15 divided the defense sectors in a manner which assigned the northern front, extending southward to Oulu Lake, to the Germans, and after troop concentrations had been completed, the Finnish forces in that sector were put under the German command for operations and supplies. For a few days the position of these troops was peculiar: the highest German command unit in the area, AOK Norwegen, had issued an order dated June 10, which did not reach the Finnish Third Corps until the 16th, that Finnish troops north of Oulu would be under the command of the German AOK as of the 15th. On June 22, when the war between Russia and Germany began, it was the Finnish Commander, however, who issued orders to his troops to be prepared to make counter measures against Russian attacks but simultaneously declared that they were strictly forbidden to cross the Finnish border for the time being. Not until the 24th did the subordination of the Third Corps to the AOK finally take place, but in spite of that, Colonel Buschenhagen of the German AOK informed the Finnish Third Corps at 5:30 P.M. that same day that permission to cross the border into Russia for reconnaissance did not at that time apply to Finnish troops. Finnish political neutrality during June 22-25 was thus clearly supplemented by military neutrality as well, and was extended even to the Finnish forces which were under German command.

The size of German forces in Finland grew rapidly once the war had begun. In addition to the two German divisions already in Finland, a third German division came from Norway via Sweden in accordance with the special permission granted by Sweden. Units of this division began to arrive on the 27th, and most of them were placed under Finnish command and deployed in the Suojärvi sector and advanced behind Finnish troops to Syväri River. Later two divisions came from Norway to the Petsamo sector, making a total of five German divisions at the end of June. The Germans began their offensive in northern Finland on July 1.

On the Finnish front there was no joint command of German and Finnish forces, either at the outbreak of war or later. Headquarters maintained only normal informational contacts. There were no detailed operational plans, for in this respect, too, the Finns remained independent.

As soon as the German army began its attack against Russia on a wide front, and after Hitler had in general terms proclaimed that the Finns also stood side by side with the Germans, the Soviet Union began military operations against Finland, too, the Russian radio blaring forth that a nation of 200 million could in its anger wipe the "Finnish white guard" from the face of the earth. On the 22nd, Russian planes had already bombed the Alskär fortifications, two Finnish warships in Aland Islands waters, a transport on its way to Aland, as well as the Porsö bastion and other points near Hanko. Porsö was permitted to reply to the fire, but at the same time naval forces were forbidden to open fire or lay mines outside Finnish territorial waters. On the same day the Russians fired at Finnish border patrols in the southeast, and in Petsamo Russian artillery shelled a Finnish ship. The claim advanced later that these attacks were directed against German forces and columns in Finland is ridiculous, because the Russians knew quite well, on the basis of information supplied by the Finnish government itself, that there were no Germans in the areas attacked by the Russians. This argument was not presented at the time, in fact, but much later.

Finnish foreign policy went through a special interim period from the morning of the 22nd to the afternoon of the 25th of June. In spite of its brevity, this interlude is, historically and from a legal point of view, very significant and worthy of attention. During these days Finland tried to remain neutral in the war which had broken out between Germany and Russia. The proofs supporting this statement are many and conclusive. On the day the war began, the Finnish Minister for Foreign Affairs. sent word to all Finnish legations abroad that Finland would remain neutral as long as possible, and would continue diplomatic relations with the Soviet Union, but that Finland would be compelled to defend herself if Russia attacked. The German Minister in Helsinki was given the same statement and as a result of the references to the Finns in Hitler's proclamation, to the effect that the Germans, together with the Finns, were guarding Finnish soil, the Finnish Minister in Berlin was wired the following explanation:

> This corresponds to our view, that at least as far as Finland is concerned only defensive action is involved. It is clear that if Russia attacks we will defend ourselves. The presence of German forces in Finland is to be evaluated independently of the above and can at least for the moment be considered as falling within terms of the transit agreement. Situation from Finland's point of view nevertheless undeniably indefinite.

On the same day an official British statement was released through news agencies in London. It declared that no change in the position of Finland's Legation in London had occurred, for Britain was not at war with Finland. On the following day, the 23rd, a representative of the Finnish Ministry for Foreign Affairs gave a statement to the Swedish newspapers *Social Demokraten* and *Svenska Dagbladet,* that Finland intended to remain neutral and that only a Russian attack would cause her to abandon neutrality. At the same time, Foreign Secretary Eden, in a conversation with the Finnish Minister in London, expressed satisfaction over Finland's neutral position, and the hope that Finland would not take part in the war directed against Russia, since in that case friendly English-Finnish relations of long standing would be jeopardized, and it would be especially dangerous for Finland to get in on the "wrong side" in this war. The German Foreign Office, on the other hand, requested the Finnish Minister to answer to three questions as soon as possible: what was Finland's ideological stand regarding bolshevism? what was Finland's attitude to the Soviet Union? and in what ways had the Soviet Union now violated Finnish neutrality?

Before Finland had time to reply, the changed situation made an answer unnecessary. On the third day of Finnish neutrality, June 24, the Minister for Foreign Affairs sent an announcement to all Finnish legations that it was Finland's intention to continue, as long as possible, the same foreign policy as before. Eden declared in the British Parliament that Finland was neutral, and that no change in Russian-Finnish relations had occurred. As late as June 24, Germany considered Finland a country not at war. That is, when the German radio explained, on that day, the stand of the different countries in the war against Russia, Finland was no longer mentioned as a country fighting with the Germans, as Hitler had in general terms stated on the 22nd; the German Foreign Office explained that this omission resulted from the still uncertain stand of Finland. The British Foreign Office advised its Ministry of Economic Warfare that Finland was to be considered a neutral state. The Finnish Premier had prepared a statement to the Parliament for the 25th on the same basis, but before the evening of that day (the statement was to be presented in the evening session of the legislature), such systematic and numerous Russian violations of Finnish neutrality had occurred, that the speech had to be rewritten completely. Shortly before the Parliament convened on the 25th, Finland was still acting in accordance with her neutrality policy. In the conference in Stockholm which were held regarding the transit of a German division through Sweden to Finland, the Finnish delegate had taken continued Finnish neutrality for granted, which caused the German representative to declare that it made a bad impression in Germany for Finland to appeal to her neutrality in a negotiation as intimate as this one.

This neutrality phase of Finland's foreign policy during the fateful days of June 22-25, 1941, shows that Finland had no commitment or pact to wage war with Germany against Russia. Even Finnish neutrality should have been sufficiently advantageous to satisfy Germany, for it would have meant at the least that Russia would have had to keep considerable forces tied down along the Finnish border. At this stage of the situation Russia herself performed a great service to Germany by forcing Finland into military cooperation with Germany.

Immediately following the first bombings, the Finnish Minister for Foreign Affairs protested to the Russian Minister, but the latter refused to accept the protest and contended—referring to Molotov's speech on the same day—that no such bombings had occurred but that on the contrary, airplanes from Finland had flown over Russian territory. The rejoinder that these flights could only have been made by Russian planes returning from raids on Finland received no answer.

Since the accusation that planes from Finland had carried out flights over Russia and thus broken the peace was politically important, an investigation of possible German flights was made. This investigation disclosed that before dawn on the 22nd, Luftwaffe planes had taken off from the Proveren airport in East Prussia and, approaching from the sea, had laid mines in the waters between Kronstadt and Leningrad, without touching Finnish territory, and that on the following day German planes had flown south of Leningrad, bombing the Stalin Canal and, without landing, had returned to their bases. Not until the 26th did two German planes, part of a force which had raided Russia, land at Finnish airports while the rest of the planes returned to their East Prussian base. Later German air raids on Leningrad also were carried out from airports in Estonia. When the Russian Minister in Helsinki inquired on the 22nd what Finland's attitude in the conflict was, he was informed that Parliament would consider the question on the 25th, and that continuing violations of Finnish territory would hardly improve relations. Another Finnish protest, delivered on the following day, regarding border violations in the southeast, brought no results. Word received at that time that the Russian Consul in the Aland Islands was closing his office seemed to indicate that the Soviet Union was preparing to recall its representation from Finland.

On the evening of June 23, Finland's Minister to Moscow, Hynninen, was asked to visit the Commissariat for Foreign Affairs. Hynninen went. Molotov demanded information regarding the Finnish government's attitude toward the situation created by the war between Germany and the Soviet Union, and insisted again that Russia had been attacked from Finnish territory. The telegram, which the Minister immediately sent his Government asking for the necessary facts, was delayed by the Russian authorities so long that it did not reach Helsinki until the night of the 24th. Thereafter the Soviet Union broke off all communications, although in such circumstances a peace-loving nation's responsibility, in accordance with international usage, is to take special pains to maintain regular communications. Later it was learned that on June 28 Orlov, the Russian Minister to Helsinki, had informed a neutral diplomat in Helsinki that he had recommended several days previously that Russia sever communication between herself and Finland. This Russia did on the 23rd. Hynninen's telegram from Moscow was nevertheless let through to Finland, but no chance was given to communicate a reply to Moscow.

Having made it impossible to reply to Molotov's question, the Soviet Union began, on the morning of the 25th, without any declaration of war, such large-scale air attacks against Finland that there was every reason to consider them the beginning of total air war. A short list of the localities bombed suffices to prove this: Kerimäki, Turku (a whole city block destroyed), Inkeroinen, Anjala, Lahti, Heinola, Selänpää, Malmi, Mikkeli, Pyterlahti, Kotka (several times, severe damage), Eskola near Kymi, Porvoo, Forsby, Loviisa (direct hit on a hospital). Finnish fighter planes assigned to defend the southeastern border, which on the 25th still were forbidden to fly close to the Russian border, shot down twenty-six Russian bombers between 7 A.M. and 1 P.M. on the 25th. The planes which bombed Turku approached the city from the sea, having presumably flown in from bases in Esthonia, and were able to carry out their destruction without being much disturbed by Finnish defense. In addition to the air raids, Russian artillery began firing at many points along the Finnish border. Only after this were units along the border given orders to reply to the Russians' fire and use artillery, but the strict orders were still not to cross the frontier.

In the secret session of the Parliament on the 25th, Premier Rangell reviewed the situation and admitted that Finland, having been attacked, had proceeded to defend herself with all available military means and that the country was, therefore, at war. Having heard the Premier's statement, the Parliament gave the Government a unanimous vote of confidence. During no phase, therefore, was this involvement in the war an idea of a few individuals, or the result of a specific action on the part of Finland.

The cautious and waiting attitude of Finland lasted well into July. Thus, it was only on June 28 that the Headquarters first ordered

Finnish reconnaissance patrols to cross the frontier and that certain positions abandoned by the Russians were to be manned. Since Red Army activity on the Finnish front did not assume such proportions as to mean Finnish position warfare, let alone retreat, plans were made on the 29th at Finnish Headquarters together with representatives of the German command for general operations, and Finnish forces were regrouped for attack. Finally, on July 10, the military operations were begun which one writer labelled as "triumphal war" in his description of the spirit in which the Finns proceeded to reconquer the ancient Finnish territory lost by the Moscow peace of March, 1940. Since the Red Army task force which had earlier been placed on the Karelian Isthmus had been transferred elsewhere, the Russian divisions remaining on the southeast border were forced to retreat comparatively quickly and were partly surrounded. At the time the general impression prevailed that the war would not last long. No matter how long the war between Germany and Russia would last, Finland's role was expected to end shortly, since Finnish military objectives were limited. A similar impression prevailed abroad; in the United States, for example, military circles expected that Russia would collapse in a few weeks and that the whole Russian campaign meant but a short breathing spell for Britain.

The facts presented above show that it is unreasonable to seek in Finland a person or persons guilty for the war thus begun. Undeniably it was human that the Finns gladly saw Russia involved in difficulties, for this helped the Finns' own position. That attitude was shown in President Ryti's statement to the Government on June 9, that Finland ought to hope for the outbreak of war between Russia and Germany, but naturally it was clear Finland ought to hope she could remain outside the conflict. The same thought was still more clearly expressed in Ryti's radio address to the nation on June 26 in which he said, in part:

> We do not hate the Soviet Union's long suffering and long oppressed peoples, but after all that has happened, no one can expect us to wear mourning because Molotov, and with him the circles responsible for Soviet policies, have now become the victims of their own predatory politics.

There were two major factors to both of which, for various reasons, it was not only important but necessary to get Finland involved in the war. One was Germany; the other, the Soviet Union.

The existence of the entire long northern flank of the Germans depended on getting the Finns into the war. The Germans were not accustomed to warfare in northern terrain and climate, but this sector meant such major objectives as the Murmansk railroad, Leningrad, and the elimination of the Red Navy by closing the Gulf of Finland. Without Finnish bases most of these objectives could not be reached. Fighting side by side with the Finns also gave the Germans a definite moral advantage, for by it Germany might share in the glory which Finland had acquired in the opinion of the whole world for her Winter War. Germany could not get Finland to join the war by applying direct force, but she could develop the situation in such a way that Finland would inevitably become involved and would be grateful that she did not now have to fight alone. By arranging the transfer of the division stationed in Norway in such a way that it became in actuality only a march to the front for a new war, and by declaring, in general terms, that the Finns stood side by side with the Germans, those tactical moves were completed which brought Finland to the threshold of war. Without a push from the outside, however, Finland would have remained neutral·just the same. The push was given by the large-scale Russian air raids on June 25, which gave German pressure the arguments it needed. After that Finland had no other alternative but to consider herself at war. The political leadership of Germany was naturally more than satisfied upon receiving the news. Finland's Minister to Berlin reported in a telegram to his Government of the 26th:

> The announcement of Russia's attack and the beginning of Finland's defensive war was received at the Foreign Office with obvious satisfaction as a big tactical advantage the granting of which, by the Soviet Union, is considered surprising.

Events had developed according to the plans of German military leaders, just as if definite procedures had really been agreed upon in the Salzburg-Berlin conversations, even though those conversations had merely been one-sided discussions in which the Germans had presented their own ideas. The events which had now taken place made it possible for the Germans *later* to interpret the conversations in such a way as to claim that something concrete had been agreed upon. That, without a doubt, served as the basis for Hitler's letter which Minister Blücher delivered to President Ryti on June 25, after Finland had recognized the state of war, in which Hitler gave assurances that Germany would never desert Finland and announced that he was confirming what the military had previously decided. However, since no agreement had in fact been made, President Ryti's reply to Hitler of the 27th could not refer to it, and his letter contained only polite generalities.

Thus the transit agreement had turned out to be the first move by which Germany succeeded in developing the situation in Finland in the way she had planned. This connection was understood outside Finland as well. Lord Newton, for example, on hearing that Britain had decided to maintain friendly relations with Finland, declared in the House of Lords on July 22, 1941:

> A lot more is to be said for the Finns than appears at first glance.
>
> Finland is at this moment Europe's most sorely tried country. Finland's entry into the war happened because of her misfortune in having a certain arrangement with Germany. Finland did not design this, neither did she want to become a nation at war. The Russians are aware of their errors and are now negotiating with Yugoslavia, Czechoslovakia, and Poland. Is there any reason, therefore, why they should not approach Finland as well?
>
> The Finns would be only too glad of an opportunity to withdraw from the present war, if they were assured that the peace imposed upon them last year would be reconsidered.[2]

On the other hand, as long as the Soviet Union did not steer its policy in an entirely new direction, it had every reason to draw Finland into the war, particularly on the side of Germany. The Finnish Winter War had added several heavy black marks to the list of Russia's criminal record and it definitely increased the difficulties of a rapprochement with Western Europe, where free public opinion is not directed by government commands into whatever direction is considered expedient at the moment. This disturbing record which had led to an inferiority complex could be erased only if Finland were in some way compromised, in which case Russia's wrong-doing in the Winter War would be forgotten or would come perhaps to seem to have been almost justified. Only in this way could Russia fully rehabilitate herself. In view of the repugnance which the democracies felt toward the Hitler regime, Finland could be most readily compromised if she were forced into military cooperation with Germany. Hitler's declaration of June 22 no doubt was received with jubilation in the Kremlin.

[2] Retranslated from Finnish (Ed.).

The two enemies were unanimous on only one point: Finland had to be dragged into the war. Seen from a purely military point of view, it was of no importance to Russia if Finland did become an enemy, since it could be assumed that Finland's army was weakened as a result of the Winter War, and that the Germans in Finland— two or three divisions—were so few as to have no significance. On the other hand, to make Britain and the Anglo-Saxon world turn against Finland was an advantage worth trying for. At the moment of the outbreak of war, Molotov in fact tried to frighten the Finnish Minister in Moscow with the spectre of English enmity. The advantages which Finnish neutrality would have meant seem not to have been highly valued in Russia because Finland offered no usable routes to the West, and because it was considered that Leningrad and the Murmansk railroad could be defended in any case. The peculiar incident of Stalin's promising Paasikivi, when he was leaving Moscow, to deliver a considerable shipment of grain—which, according to the trade pact, should have been sent long before—does not in any way suffice as an indication of Russian change of policy toward Finland. It was used by Russian propaganda to such an extent that there is every reason to believe it was intended from the start purely as a propaganda measure.

Finland's entry into the war, however, did not take a form which pleased either Germany or Russia. Finland had concluded no political agreement with Germany but stubbornly tried to fight a war of her own, with limited military objectives. Germany lay in wait for an opportunity to get Finland completely tied to herself in the war. Russia, on the other hand, failed to get the satisfaction of seeing Finland ally herself with Germany or join the Axis. Russia and her later allies therefore began to destroy by propaganda the goodwill shown toward Finland and to blacken her as being Nazi, a German "satellite," and so forth. But the propaganda was disturbed by the uncomfortable necessity of having to dress up the facts before they could be used.

These two enemies and external factors in Finnish policy were unanimous, then, only in their determination to pull Finland into the big Power war. Together the two were so powerful that Finland probably had no real chance to avoid getting involved. In the fall of 1939 it would have been possible, theoretically at least, by a submission to Russia's demands—but whether acquiescence would have saved Finland any more than it had saved the Baltic States is another question. In the summer of 1941, on the other hand, Finland had to choose the lesser of two evils: whether to become the battlefield of the big Powers or the support of Germany which, for geographical reasons alone, could not be assumed to become anything like the danger that Russia represented.

The situation in which Finland had to fight her new war was therefore exceedingly complex and difficult to control. Since Allied propaganda was well-planned and very effective, difficulties in internal policy were gradually added to those of foreign policy, for Finland's unified and intact home front began to crack toward the end, and supporters were ultimately found for the view, presented without taking into consideration the difficulties which getting out of the war would bring with it, that the country's entire foreign policy had been wrong and a complete change would have to be made.

2. FINLAND'S SEPARATE WAR AND GERMANY'S ATTITUDE

When the war psychosis has disappeared and the course of events can be judged and evaluated objectively, it will undoubtedly be noted that the achievements of the Finnish people and the Finnish army in 1941 were incomparable. The sacrifices and the countless almost legendary deeds of heroism then recorded would not have been possible if the whole nation had not felt that it had suffered a great injustice at the hands of the Soviet Union and wanted to right the wrong. Nothing else could have made possible the show of strength in 1941: sixteen per cent of the total population were drafted or volunteered for service in the armed forces.

The entire people as well as the leaders understood that the new war was but another phase in the Russian history of expansion directed against Finland. The Winter War had truly been a separate war, in spite of the fact that the World War was already being fought elsewhere. In 1941 Finland's war was still considered a separate war, even though Germany was on the same side. The only difference was that in the first war Germany had been on Russia's side, but now fought Russia, and that in the 1939-1940 war Finland had fought alone, but now others were on her side. Germany had her own goals which were lumped together under the slogan of a "crusade against bolshevism." Finland's military objectives were strictly limited: her own defense and security. At no time during the war did the country want to go, or go, any further than these objectives. It is natural that this difference in objectives should have caused many difficulties for Finnish policy.

Finland's position was unique. The Allies in the West did not always understand it, or they did not want to understand it, but among Germany's allies it was looked upon with envy.

Proofs that the Finnish government as well as the Finnish people really did consider their war a separate war were so many that to mention them often seemed almost a mechanical repetition of the obvious, and the Government had to play them down a bit in its news service because they directly caused, in many instances, difficulties in the relations with Germany. A few examples may be cited. In a conversation with the United States Minister on July 4, 1941, President Ryti explained that Finland was not allied with Germany and did not have any political agreements with Germany or her allies. The Finnish military command, Ryti stated, was in touch with the German military command for coordination of military activities, since Finland was, in fact, a "cobelligerent" of Germany in the war against Russia. Finland considered herself fighting a separate defensive war and did not want to become involved in the major Powers' settling of accounts for which she had neither the means nor the strength. Finland's objectives were to defend her own life and guarantee her existence as an independent nation.

Similar declarations, many of them given publicly, are numerous. The statements of Minister Väinö Tanner commanded considerable attention at home and abroad. In a speech at a labor rally in Tampere on July 30, 1941, he declared:

> We will not take part in the war of the great Powers. We are fighting our own, separate war, which is an aside in the great war. Finland is fighting a defensive war. Her policy is not changed because Germany is also at war with the Soviet Union. . . Now we do not have to fight on our own soil. We are defending our soil now on enemy territory.

In his speech at Vaasa on September 14, 1941, which aroused attention even in the United States, he clearly stated that cooperation with Germany was the result of external, accidental factors:

> Although we happen to be brothers-in-arms of Germany, there is no difference of opinion among us that our war concerns Finland alone. We have no part in the World War, and we do not want to become involved in its battles.

In a radio address on October 28, 1941, answering a speech of R. A. Palmer, the Secretary of England's league of cooperatives, Tanner declared:

We have been fighting our defensive war without having made political agreements with anyone. It has been a war only for Finland's own rights . . . We are continuing that same defensive battle which we waged in hopeless circumstances during our Winter War . . . The only difference now is that Britain is Russia's ally. But, in the name of common sense, that cannot of course change our position.

This position was soon put to a test. On July 19, President Ryti received a letter from Hitler which demanded, on the grounds that the British diplomatic personnel might conduct espionage for Russia's benefit, that Finland break off diplomatic relations with Great Britain, as Germany's allies had already done. When the Government considered the matter on the 22nd, it was decided that the Minister for Foreign Affairs should preferably try to handle the matter by reducing England's commercial and military representation. It is shown in another connection that the matter was not handled tactfully, but in any case Finland had not directly followed Germany's proposal. But Finland gave a firmly negative answer to the German demand to break off relations with the Norwegian government-in-exile.

The principle that Finland must remain neutral with regard to entanglements growing out of the World War with which she had nothing to do, is also shown in the refusal to recognize the Nanking government, as Japan had officially requested of Finland on August 27, 1941. The Manchukuo government, on the other hand, was recognized *de jure* on July 18, 1941, because it was felt that concessions had to be made in some instances, and because the Manchukuo government had functioned for ten years and the request for recognition had already been received in March, 1941. The desire to keep Finland separate even in the war on the German front against Russia is shown by the fact that as early as September, 1941, the Finnish Commander-in-Chief requested the Finnish military attaché in Germany to propose the return to Finland of the Finnish battalion of volunteers.[3] The fulfilling of this request was prevented by the volunteers' two-year period of enlistment, which meant that their return took place only in the summer of 1943. This effort to keep Finland's war separate from Germany's was even more clearly shown by the High Command's decision early in November, 1941, to take steps for withdrawing the Finnish units that were under German command. The Finnish Corps that was under German command had just begun

[3] See page 96.

an attack at Louhi, without the knowledge of Finnish Headquarters. The attack progressed especially well and in all probability would have resulted in the Murmansk railroad being cut at least temporarily. The attack was now halted for the same reason as other similar plans.

In the latter half of August, 1941, the Germans proposed Finnish participation in the battle for Leningrad. The Finnish Commander-in-Chief received a letter from Keitel, in which it was suggested that Finland, having reached the old boundary on the Karelian Isthmus, should continue her attack into Russian territory. The German Army was to push on beyond Leningrad and besiege the city, and the Finns should advance on the eastern end of the Karelian Isthmus where they would then meet the German forces. From Aunus the Finns should push on beyond the Syväri River and clear the southeastern shores of Lake Ladoga. On August 24, the Government rejected this proposal and sent the reply to the Germans on the 26th. The Germans were not willing to drop the matter, however, and proposed on the 31st that the Finns should move southward toward Leningrad; to this the Finns again did not want to agree. The result of the bargaining was the German High Command proposal on September 1 that in the Valkeasaari sector the Finns advance at least as far as Mustapuro, about a mile beyond the old border. Since this involved only a local offensive, and because a refusal would undoubtedly have been interpreted as indicating lack of goodwill, it was felt that this proposal could be accepted. However, this operation fell through, too, because the Germans' own operations did not go according to schedule. In connection with the last-mentioned proposal, but without formally connecting it with the German request, the question of Finland's need for grain was taken up because Germany had rejected the request of the Minister of Supply for 25,000 tons of wheat. On September 4th, the immediate shipment of 15,000 tons was promised.

Some time after this, President Ryti openly announced to Hitler's special envoy that Finland intended to end the war *de facto* as far as her part in it was concerned, because to continue the war involved effort beyond the nation's capacity. The first step would be decreasing the size of the forces in the field. At the same time the question of the use of the Petsamo nickel mines came up. Germany wanted a long-term agreement, and even participation in the ownership. Finland did not approve the suggestion, because she did not want to make long-term commitments or prejudice other (i.e., English) interests.

The first time that Finland obviously made a political agreement with Germany was in joining the Anti-Comintern Pact. The German Minister made a formal proposal about the matter to the Ministry for Foreign Affairs and also spoke directly to President Ryti about it. The President was opposed to the idea, pointing out that public opinion was sensitive because of the war and the casualties suffered, and should not be disturbed unnecessarily by any new issues. The Anti-Comintern agreement was purely declaratory and without practical significance, Ryti held, but to join it would surely be considered as the first step toward joining the Axis, in regard to which no unanimity could be achieved in Finland. Signing the Anti-Comintern Pact would also undoubtedly worsen relations with the western Powers, and there was every reason to avoid that. The German Minister admitted that Germany recognized that Finland was fighting her own separate war and would therefore not suggest that she join the Axis. But if Finland remained outside the Anti-Comintern Pact, the result would be distressing publicity which ought to be avoided.

When this question was discussed in the Finnish Cabinet, it was considered obvious that while the Pact was of only ideological significance, to join it would cause troublesome consequences. On the other hand, to refuse might lead to unforseeable difficulties. Furthermore, to join in the Pact, which in reality meant little, might constitute a kind of guaranty against the danger that Germany would bring up the question of Finland's joining the Axis. For that reason, and after Finland had consulted with Denmark who had also decided to join, Finland decided it was best to do likewise. The Finnish Minister for Foreign Affairs signed the Pact, together with representatives from many other countries, in Berlin on November 25, 1941. His speech delivered on that occasion was in part a declaration against the spirit of dictatorship:

> In the course of generations the Finnish people have cleared the wilderness for civilization by hard labor. The heritage of this labor has formed the economic, social, and political foundation on which the Finnish nation now stands. This heritage of centuries has created a love for liberty and unity and the sense of personal responsibility in our people. The school of hard experience, which the Finnish people have gone through in the course of their history, has given us an instinct of liberty which has always been keenest whenever the things our nation values most highly have been threatened.

The part of the speech which directly referred to the Pact showed that Finland did not join it with any enthusiasm, and that the Finns gave it the most limited significance possible:

> Through this Pact we can obtain information regarding the activity of the Communist International, discuss essential defensive measures, and carry them out in close cooperation.

Taken as a whole, this speech of the Finnish Minister for Foreign Affairs reflected the only independent attitude shown at the signing of the Pact, and as such it served to support the theory of a separate war which Finland had accepted throughout.

This attitude was expressed even more clearly in the Finnish press. For example, *Suomen Sosialidemokraatti* commented on November 26:

> The Pact does not, as becomes obvious from its text, limit Finland's independent freedom of action; it does not alter our relations with other countries; it does not tie us to any foreign ideology; it does not impose any political obligations on us . . . The nature of our war also remains the same as before: our war against Russia is separate from the World War and is waged only for our own freedom and security.

On December 5, the same newspaper, having called attention to the fact that earlier, too, the Pact had been looked upon as merely a theoretical political declaration, stated:

> No changes were made in the Pact, and no new explanations regarding its provisions were given, when Germany and the Soviet Union concluded their well-known friendship pact in August, 1939. The whole time that the Ribbentrop-Molotov pact existed and was observed, the anti-Comintern Pact was also in force. It was not considered to be in any way detrimental to the relations between these two countries, and sometimes it was half jokingly remarked that Russia might worm her way into membership in the Pact.

Actually the Pact remained, as had been expected, without practical significance in all matters except enemy propaganda, which found it useful when it began to arouse public opinion in the western world against Finland.

The possibilities for the Finnish army to continue its attack against certain of Russia's strategically important points were so great, however, that the Germans made a whole series of attempts to get the Finnish army to abandon the war of position which the

Finns had adopted by the end of 1941. In the latter part of January, 1942, Keitel requested the Finnish Commander-in-Chief to undertake an offensive against Sorokka for March, when General Stumpf's air forces, based on the shores of the Arctic, would be able to lend their support.

When Keitel's request was discussed by the President's conference on February 23-24, two considerations were held decisive. In the first place, an attack in this direction would place the center of gravity of the Russian northern front in the Sorokka area. In the second place, it would arouse American enmity.[4] On these two grounds, the proposal was rejected. The Finnish Commander-in-Chief intended instead to release older classes of troops, beginning with about ten battalions. In accordance with the decision of the President's conference, the Commander-in-Chief informed Keitel that the long period of attack had exhausted the Finns and that preparations for an offensive could not be made in the short time available, but that the matter would receive further consideration. The Germans made new proposals in March, 1942. On March 24, the President's conference discussed a German proposal for a limited offensive in the Sorokka sector to extend only as far as Parandova, but this proposal was rejected for almost the same reasons as the earlier, more extensive proposal. Later in the summer the same plan was again presented, but with a still more limited objective. This time General Dietl was planning an offensive in the direction of Kantalahti, and he hoped to be aided by a diversionary offensive of the Finns in the direction of Kotshkoma. The proposal was rejected on July 27 because Finland had to conserve her manpower and because that attack, too, would have caused resentment in the United States.

Hitler's visit to Finland, on June 4, 1942, to congratulate Field Marshal Mannerheim on his 75th birthday, aroused all sorts of interpretations. On June 5, however, the United States Minister was given assurances that the visit was not to be interpreted as meaning anything more than the existence of a "comradeship-in-arms" between Finland and Germany. A Washington newspaper remarked quite correctly that Hitler's visit rather proved that Finland was fighting her own war, for Hitler would not travel to visit a "satellite."

All the more important proofs of Finland's separate position were brought out again in the conversation which the President had on January 21, 1943, with the United States chargé d'affaires. Ryti

---

[4] The State Department had warned Finland against severing the connection between Murmansk and the interior of Russia (Ed.).

then again stressed that Finland had no political agreements with Germany, that the Finns were not Nazis, that they were fighting their own war, that having reached their strategic objectives the Finns had not advanced farther, had not taken part in the offensive against Leningrad, and that in the present world catastrophe they were looking out only for their own interests.

One of the propaganda weapons of the western Powers in the effort to influence public opinion against Finland was the charge that Finland was ideologically inclined to Hitlerism. The Finnish attitude in this matter, too, was therefore clearly brought out in many different connections. Cooperation with Germany in the war could in fact have spread National Socialism in Finland if any of the essential prerequisites for it had existed in the country. In his conversation with the United States Minister on July 4, 1941, President Ryti in fact expressed his fear that National Socialist activity might be increased in Finland; Tanner's return to the Government was intended, according to Ryti, to prevent any such development. The fear proved groundless, however. In an interview at the end of October with the American journalist, Henry J. Taylor, President Ryti answered Taylor's question, "Has Finland adjusted herself to German ideological and totalitarian politics?" with every justification, "No. The Finnish people are interested only in the development of the political and social system of their Republic which is historically their own." Though there was reason to avoid making statements which might insult the Germans, the Finnish press frequently expressed the view that Finland had no common ideological point of contact with the German political system. On September 10, 1941, for example, the *Suomen Sosialidemokraatti* wrote:

> The fact that in our present war the mighty German army is fighting on the same front with us, has not changed in the slightest the Finnish people's conceptions of the nature of political freedom and self-rule by the people. To say that we in Finland might be ready for some sort of a new system, such as Quisling's party, for example, represents in Norway, is to ignore the facts.

President Ryti expressed the same idea on as official an occasion as the opening of Parliament on February 3, 1942. In his speech, in which he discussed the country's position and the nature of the war, he stated the following regarding Finnish relations with Germany:

> Friendly and confidential relations are ... natural in all circumstances. Such relations have not been prevented in the past by the fact

that Germany's political and social system differs from our own, and
that difference must not now either emerge as an obstacle. Every
civilized country has a political and social system based on historical
evolution and its unavoidable consequences, as well as on the people's
education, ways of thought and psychological nature at a given time.
A system which is natural and answers the need in one country can be
unsuitable in another. Our political and social system is the result of
centuries of historical development. It is based on the unique and
socially valuable centuries-old freedom of the peasant . . . Just as we
consider it natural that no one from the outside will interfere in our
internal affairs, and will not try to alter that system which we have
developed for ourselves, and which we want to go on freely developing,
so it is our responsibility to respect the systems other countries have
adopted and found good and to leave every nation free to decide about
such matters as their own affair.

These conceptions were not changed or compromised in the
slightest degree at any time during the war.

When one considers how ruthless and shameless German ways of
doing things were in countries that were occupied by or allied with
Germany, their attitude to Finland was quite exceptional. It must be
frankly admitted that the Germans' behavior in Finland was correct
throughout, and that they respected the Finnish social and legal system and avoided all needless interference. In spite of that, the relations between the Finns and the Germans never became close or
cordial. That was due partly to the general antipathy toward National Socialism, and partly to the helplessness which at the beginning
of the war became obvious in the activity of the German forces. The
Finns seemed to expect too much of their new brothers-in-arms and
felt disappointed when the Germans failed to deliver under the conditions that prevail in the North where individual fitness and initiative, not dependent on technical equipment, decide the issue. The
Finns soon began to treat the Germans with patronizing condescension and the term "brother-in-arms" acquired an ironical implication.
The German army staff in Finland took care of their responsibilities
without interfering with Finnish internal affairs. It must be stated,
for instance, that claims of Gestapo infiltration into Finnish govern-
mental organizations is completely without foundation. Only the
chief of the Finnish political police seems to have been too ready to
agree to some of the proposals made by the German Gestapo. Finally, it must be stated that the position of those Jews who were Finnish citizens did not suffer the slightest change during the war, nor

did the Germans make any demands in this respect because they knew in advance that they would have been firmly refused.[5]

3. FINNISH WAR AIMS

It is obvious that Finland, having fallen victim to an unprovoked attack, could in the beginning have no other "war aims" than to repel the attack and to prevent her territory, already decreased in size by the Winter War, from becoming a battlefield. But as soon as the army was able to change over to the offensive, the question immediately arose of what war aims should now be defined. It was clear that Finland wanted to recapture the Finnish territory which Russia had seized by the terms of the Moscow peace. Almost equally important was the idea that the bases behind the border from which Finland had been threatened, should be made harmless. The Government was cautious in formulating war aims because it was felt that for such a small factor as Finland to announce a program in advance would serve no useful purpose. Thus, in his radio address on June 26, 1941, after having noted that hostilities had begun, President Ryti stated in general terms:

> The past centuries have shown that in the geographical location which hard fate has given our people, we have not attained lasting peace. Pressure from the East has always been against us. We are now fighting to lessen that pressure, to destroy that eternal threat, to secure the happy and peaceful life of the generations to come.

The Commander-in-Chief's order of the day on the eve of offensive operations seemed to point in a different direction. Recalling to his troops his promise of 1918 to the Karelians that he would never sheathe his sword until Finland and East Karelia were free, he expressed the hope that Finland's army could now fulfill that promise to the Karelians. The Order of the Day (July 10, 1941) ended with the exhortation:

> Soldiers! The soil on which you are about to step is sacred soil, saturated with the blood and sufferings of our kinsmen. Your victories will liberate the Karelians, your deeds will create a great, happy future for Finland.

[5] In the fall of 1942, an attempt was made, apparently by some subordinate officials, to expel Jewish refugees who had arrived since the spring of 1938. Before the effort was brought into the open—it aroused a storm of protest when it became known—eight refugees had been expelled from the country. The laborite, V. Tanner, was among those who raised their voices on behalf of the Jews and saw to it that no further deportations occurred (Ed.).

Since the Government had no advance notice of this declaration, and, war aims not having as yet been in any way defined, it naturally caused a great deal of attention. The Commander-in-Chief explained to the Government that he had not meant to interfere in politics with his Order of the Day, but had issued it merely to increase his soldiers' enthusiasm and readiness for battle, and that he had spoken only of the *liberation* of the Karelians, without attempting in any way to define war aims in general. In keeping with this explanation, the Minister for Foreign Affairs, on July 11, sent all Finnish diplomatic representatives abroad, for their information, the statement that the Order of the Day had been meant for the troops and was not a Government declaration, and that the Government's war aims were the repelling of the attack and the guaranteeing of the country's security. With this objective in mind, the Finns considered themselves morally entitled to get some favorable changes in the boundary. On July 4, 1941, the Government's war aims were more exactly defined for the first time in a conversation of President Ryti with the United States Minister: the recovery of the Karelian territory lost in 1940. But the President declared he personally was willing to draw the boundary somewhat farther to the west, in Russia's favor, than the old 1939 boundary had been.[6]

Many private (unofficial) sources aroused hopes and expectations which could be interpreted as more far-reaching. For example, the Speaker of Parliament, Mr. Hakkila—for years one of the leading laborites—in a radio speech on July 20, 1941, considered it obvious that Finland should receive reparations for damages suffered in both wars, and that reparations should be obtained in full measure. In a speech at Tampere on August 6 he stated:

> Our security, the chance to work in peace, and our national unity, demand boundaries that are geographically, militarily and economically right.
>
> We must also receive full compensation for what the enemy has damaged, destroyed or seized. Justice and reason demand it. The sacrifices and heroism of the defenders of our country demand it. We want only freedom for our kinsmen and natural, secure national boundaries for our country.

Minister Tanner, on the other hand, expressed the view which had to be considered as that of the Government. According to Tanner,

---

[6] This obviously refers to the boundary on the Karelian Isthmus and not to the whole eastern boundary of Finland (Ed.).

Finland had no expansionist aims beyond the old political boundaries of 1939. In Vaasa on September 14, 1941, he stated:

> We will not continue the war any further than our own interests demand. This is, for us, solely a war of defense. By it we want to achieve safe boundaries and lasting peace. Whatever is needed to attain secure boundaries and peace must be done, but beyond that we have no reason to strive.
>
> In great part this goal has already been achieved, in fact. Our extensive border with Russia, however, is still insecure, and it seems necessary to render harmless, in a military sense, the areas behind the boundary. Our final boundaries can only be drawn at the future peace congress. Before that time there is no possibility of making peace with anyone.

Tanner's speech in Hämeenlinna on November 19, 1941, in which he discussed the East Karelia question, caused especially widespread comment. He said, in part:

> Much has been said about Finland's war aims. Yarns about a "Greater Finland" have been making the rounds in certain circles. But it is necessary that questions as serious as these be carefully considered and that heads be kept cool. This is no time for building castles in the air. We are fighting a defensive war now, just as we did in our Winter War, and where it has been necessary to go beyond our borders, it has only been to wipe out the bases of the enemy's attacks. The territory conquered will naturally have to be occupied until the war ends. After that the question of to whom the areas will belong, whether they are to become independent, or join us or someone else, is an altogether different problem. It is a question that time will decide.

After military operations had developed to the point where Finland's old territory before 1939 had been almost completely recovered, the view came generally to prevail that Finland should advance no farther. On December 6, 1941, when Parliament decided to reunite with Finland the territory ceded to Russia by the Moscow peace, the decision did not involve any territory which had belonged to Russia for a longer period, although the army's advance and the principle of national self-determination might well have justified the inclusion even of Russian territory.

After this, the question was only of the strategic objectives of the Finnish army. In his interview with the American journalist, Taylor, President Ryti received and answer the following question:

> Is Finland's advance to stop, in spite of Germany's perhaps conflicting goals in her war with Russia, at Finland's old boundaries,

although new fortifications of the Russians beyond the border are seized?

Ryti's answer shows that the decision was considered to rest with the military:

> The Finnish advance will stop at such a strategic line as Finland independently chooses for the purpose of safeguarding her security. Where that line is, is naturally a military secret.

The strategic objectives were reached before the end of 1941. The Commander-in-Chief's Order of the Day for December 6, 1941, stated:

> Our operations having attained Karhumäki and the Maanselkä station, I order that the offensive operation be ended and defensive measures initiated.

On the same day President Ryti stated, in an address delivered at an Independence Day celebration organized by the Veterans' Association:

> For the sake of our security we must attain certain strategic objectives from which we are now, luckily, not far. According to word I have received today from the Commander-in-Chief, the city of Karhumäki is in our hands. A great step has thus been taken toward our goal.

The Germans would very much have liked to see Finnish war aims definitely formulated, and the more ambitiously the better, for then it would have been more certain that Finland would be unable to get out of the war. This desire was understood well enough in Finland, and German proposals were therefore critically appraised and rejected. When the Germans were advancing toward Leningrad in the summer of 1941, a German liaison officer explained to President Ryti that the Germans considered it desirable and advantageous for the Finns that Leningrad and the surrounding area be annexed to Finland, with such boundaries as Finland herself would desire. When he inquired what Finland thought of the idea, the President replied that it had not been considered at all. For his own part he declared the idea was absolutely impossible, since Finland lacked all prerequisites for such an enterprise, and because it would be absolutely dangerous for a small country to concern itself with a huge city belonging to a great Power. It was presumably on the basis of this conversation that General Schörner complained that the Finns did not want

Leningrad even though the city had been offered to them. In conversations after the signing of the Anti-Comintern Pact the question of Finland's future boundaries was also taken up. Hitler delivered a long lecture to Finland's Minister for Foreign Affairs in which he explained that Finland now had a unique opportunity to define for herself any kind of boundaries she wished. The worthy lecturer received no answer. The meaning of these offers was quite obvious. It was to get Finland's army committed to a continued attack at least as far as Leningrad and the Murmansk railroad.

However, having achieved her own war objectives, Finland refused to continue the attack. On August 2, 1943, in an interview with the Danish newspaper *Börsen,* Minister Fagerholm explained these limited war aims quite clearly:

> We are a democracy and do not believe in the permanence of dictatorships. Since December 5, 1941, Finnish military activities have been limited to guarding and patrolling, and Finland has in fact never fought for anything but her independence. We know that bolshevism means physical destruction, but we are not fighting an ideological battle or a war of conquest.

In keeping with these views, Finland began reducing her field army at the earliest possible stage. In a conference in Helsinki on November 28, 1941, at which the Commander-in-Chief was present, various Ministers explained that lack of manpower was beginning to paralyze the economic life of the country, and plans were made for the continuing demobilization of the field forces. According to the plan, 9,000 men were to be released immediately, and thereafter, gradually, 110,000 men. In the event that Leningrad should fall, 250,000 more were to be released. The plan shows clearly that Finland firmly refused to influence the outcome of the conflict between the major Powers. General conditions, however, prevented the plan from being carried out except in part, and relatively late. In a government conference of February 23-24, 1942, the Commander-in-Chief announced he was beginning to demobilize approximately ten battalions of older men.

Since Finland's war aims were strictly limited, no long-term plans for occupied Eastern Karelia were made, for the fate of the area would not depend on Finland's decisions. For example, on August 19, 1942, the President informed the German Minister that the Finnish government considered the Eastern Karelia question altogether hypothetical, and that it was therefore useless to continue discussion on that point. This attitude did not, however, prevent Finland's carrying out humanitarian relief measures in Eastern Karelia.

4. Relations with Great Britain and the United States

When Finland became involved in war with the Soviet Union, Great Britain had no mutual assistance agreement with Russia, at least none that was publicly known, and the United States was not yet at war. Public opinion in both countries was favorable toward Finland, though it could easily change. In Finland, official circles as well as the public in general considered it particularly important that good relations with Britain and the United States be continued. This was clearly shown, for example, in the attempts of Finnish labor organizations to explain the nature of Finland's defensive war to labor groups in England and America. The Social Democratic party and the central organization of Finland's united labor union sent the following appeal to the British trade unions on July 3, 1941:

> Finland has again become involved in war with the Soviet Union. Our people wanted to avoid war in 1941 as in 1939. Russia attacked us now just as she did in 1939. Moscow has declared that Finland must be completely destroyed. This intention is in line with the policy which Russia has followed toward Finland ever since the Moscow peace . . . We have had no alternative but to defend ourselves. Labor has not hesitated in this respect. It is fighting for independence and a free social order based on democratic principles. Those principles are the same now as they were in 1939, when the British labor unions showed great sympathy for our cause in the war which then broke out . . . We hope that you will fully understand our position.

The Chairman of the Central Committee of Finnish Labor Unions, Eero A. Vuori, sent a similar statement, on August 12, to President William Green of the American Federation of Labor:

> The Finnish people's fight in circumstances which as a peace loving nation it sought to avoid to the end, is now as in 1939-1940 a war against Soviet imperialism. It is at the same time a fight against bolshevistic politics the aim of which is to bring our nation into slavery under foreign dictatorship. Our reasons for fighting, therefore, are the same as in 1939-1940, when Finland had to fight alone for her independence. At that time we received a great deal of goodwill from your powerful organization. We sincerely hope that you will fully understand that our fight is for Finnish independence and for the essentials of free labor unions. It is for this reason that our unions and their members support this war.

The leaders of British foreign policy had obviously known rather early that war would break out between Russia and Germany. Advance preparations for this contingency included the cutting off of Finnish shipping to Petsamo, and a warning to Finland against military cooperation with Germany against Russia. The note which the British Minister delivered to the Finnish Minister for Foreign Affairs on June 14, 1941, spoke of these facts very frankly:

> If Finland joins in a Russo-German war on the side of Germany, she will lose Great Britain's aid and sympathy, and we shall be forced to exert all possible economic pressure in our power against Finland. Because of the uncertainty of the present political situation, we are stopping all shipping en route to Petsamo. As soon as the attitude of Finland becomes clear to His Majesty's Government, the latter will be prepared to consider the question in the light of the political and military situation that then prevails.[7]

On the day that Hitler began his campaign in the East, Churchill declared that Britain would aid everyone who fought against Nazism (i.e., Germany), but would consider everyone who cooperated with Germany an enemy. The war against Russia thus sufficed to set even Great Britain against Finland. Because of old friendship, a breaking off of relations would not automatically result, but would be nevertheless difficult to avoid. The closer British cooperation with Russia became, the more untenable became Finland's position with regard to Britain, because Russia made demands which could be postponed but not wholly avoided. For example, in Finland it was not felt possible to agree to England's demand that Finland must not carry her military operations beyond the old boundaries and hence not continue the offensive. On June 28, 1941, the Finnish Minister in London was instructed to call attention to the fact that Finland could not differentiate in military operations between defense and offense, and therefore could not give advance assurances that she would not fight on both sides of the boundary. In the United States, where it was believed at first that Russian resistance would not last long and where Russia was less highly thought of, Finland's position was understood in official and private circles which only hoped that Finland would keep her war a separate one, and would not bind herself to Germany in such a way that she would have to continue fighting against the Allies after Russia had been defeated. This attitude changed relatively slowly, influenced by the course of events and

---

[7] The above quotations are translations from the Finnish version (Ed.).

British propaganda. In Finland itself, the traditional friendly relations with the Western world were considered of prime importance and, looking to the future, especially so; and it was understood that the continuation of friendly relations was one of the cornerstones of the separate war Finland was waging.

Relations with Britain were very delicate and difficult to maintain because Germany demanded that Finland break off relations and Russia demanded the same of Britain. It is natural that in this conflict the weaker party found itself in a difficult position. It is very doubtful if a breaking off of relations could have been long avoided, no matter what was desired or done by either side.

The relations began to get strained as a result of Hitler's demand that Finland break off relations with Britain. Finland had to give way in some measure to Germany's continuing pressure. On June 27, the German Minister had suggested that British-Finnish relations be "clarified," and on July 8 the Councilor of the German Legation, Zechlin, remarked that Britain's Consular representation in Finland should be ended. After Hitler's letter to the President on July 19, the pressure from the German Legation increased. Furthermore, Finland's own army command was disturbed by the possibilities for intelligence activities which the numerically large British representation enjoyed. Some steps had to be taken, therefore, which would give the appearance of acceptance of the German demand. On July 22 the Government decided to authorize the Minister for Foreign Affairs, at his suggestion,

> to take suitable steps to decrease the diplomatic staff of Great Britain in Helsinki and, if necessary, to bring its harmful operations to a close.

Ministers Fagerholm and Tanner, who were in the minority in the voting on this matter in the government, proposed that the British Legation be requested to withdraw only its commercial and military attachés and its information section. The wording of the authority given to the Minister for Foreign Affairs was vague and made possible the ending of the entire activity of the Legation. To bring about the closing of the Legation was understood to be only a last desperate measure, however, as President Ryti's notation in his diary shows:

> Witting received authorization to handle the matter. He is to try to avoid a complete break and to clear up the matter by considerably reducing the commercial and military sections, or possibly closing them

completely. If it should become impossible to settle the matter in this fashion, he would have recourse, as a last resort, to the severance of relations.

The Government thus proceeded on the assumption that reducing the representation of Britain would be tried first, and that only if this attempt failed, would recourse be had to sharper measures. At first, Witting handled his delicate task according to instructions. To inform the Finnish Minister in London of his procedure, Witting explained to him on July 23 that on the following day he would inform the British Minister in Helsinki of the unfortunate impression created in Finland by Lord Snell's statement in Parliament that England could break off relations with Finland at any moment; that Britain's military and consular representation in Finland aroused uneasiness because of the Russo-English alliance; and that it might become necessary to refuse to the British Legation the right to receive and send messages in code. On the 24th, Witting spoke to the British Minister of Britain's hunger blockade against Finland and Finland's readiness to lease 40,000 tons of merchant shipping to England, and then asked if a "suitable temporary solution" might not be that England withdraw her military, commercial, consular and press representatives from Finland. The British Minister was unwilling to make this change, partly because the transfer of the British officials to Stockholm would mean added expense. The question was left open at the time, and it was agreed to take it up again at a later date.

A few days later, however, the question was taken up in a way which was not at all in keeping with the Government's instructions to Witting. On July 28, Witting, the Minister for Foreign Affairs, delivered to the British Minister the following memorandum which was published two days later:

> As a result of measures which Great Britain has put into effect on several occasions since July, 1940, against Finnish shipping and foreign trade and which, in June, 1941, ended with the complete blockade of Finnish overseas trade, diplomatic relations between Finland and Great Britain in the fields of trade and shipping have in fact ended.
>
> Furthermore, by force of circumstances, Finland is a cobelligerent of Germany against Russia, while Great Britain, on the other hand, has concluded a military alliance with the Soviet Union and has declared she will use all available means to aid the Soviet Union.
>
> In the light of these facts, regular diplomatic relations between the two countries can scarcely be maintained without difficulty. This would seem to be the impression of Great Britain's government as well, judg-

ing by certain statements in the British Parliament, according to which relations with Finland can be broken off at any moment.

In estimating the present situation, the Finnish government has concluded that, as a logical consequence of the course of events, Finland's Legation in London should for the time being discontinue its functions.

The Government of Finland would be grateful to learn if the Government of Great Britain is of the same opinion in regard to the functioning of the British Legation in Helsinki.

Upon receipt of this communication, the British Minister said that he interpreted it to mean that he should ask for his passport. Mr. Witting stated that he was unable to deny that the communication should be interpreted in that way.

The question naturally rises why Finland's Minister for Foreign Affairs took the radical step of breaking off diplomatic relations. It is impossible to find any other explanation for his note than to say that it was the result of some outside influence. Whether that influence was Finnish or German will remain unknown for the time being because the Minister himself is now dead. There is no doubt but what Finland's action was ill-founded. Although the end result would surely have been the same no matter what Finland did, to take the first step in breaking relations was neither wise nor advantageous.

Britain soon gave two answers to the memorandum. On July 30, British planes bombed Liinahamari. The British Minister later explained that the bombing had resulted from a mistake. The official answer of the British government was delivered on August 1, after it had already been made public by radio. According to it, Britain would make her action dependent on what Finland did:

> Insofar as the intention expressed in the note of the Finnish government will be carried out and the Finnish Legation in London is closed, the action of the Finnish government will make it necessary for the British government to withdraw its Legation from Helsinki.[8]

In the reply which the Finnish government immediately published, the earlier views were restated and attention was drawn to the statement of the London *Daily Herald* on July 30, to the effect that the real reason why relations with Finland were not broken off immediately after the outbreak of war was that the British Legation in Helsinki served as an exceptionally valuable observation post and news source.

[8] Translated from the Finnish (Ed.).

When diplomatic relations were later broken off, it took place in Finland in friendly fashion. The British Minister paid a farewell visit to President Ryti, and the Minister for Foreign Affairs gave the Legation staff a farewell luncheon, which would have been out of the question if the relations between the two countries had really been those of enemies.

The next phase in the relations between Finland and Britain came in September, 1941. In a memorandum dated September 22, 1941, and delivered for Britain on the 28th by the Norwegian Minister, Britain demanded that Finland withdraw her forces behind the 1939 boundary. The memorandum, which came close to being an ultimatum, argued that so long as Finland attacked Britain's ally in that ally's territory, it was impossible to distinguish Finland's war from the general European war:

> If, therefore, the Finnish government continues the advance into purely Russian territory, a situation will arise which will force Great Britain to consider Finland as an open enemy, not only while the war lasts, but also when the peace is made.

The British government expressed the hope, however, that normal diplomatic relations could soon be restored, with certain conditions:

> But the Finnish government will realize that the first condition which will make this possible is that Finland ends her war against Russia and withdraws all her forces from all territory which lies beyond Finland's 1939 boundary. As soon as this is effected, the Government of Great Britain on its part will be ready to consider favorably all proposals to improve relations between Great Britain and Finland, even though the continued presence of German troops on Finnish soil probably will, in the beginning, make impossible the resumption of full diplomatic relations and the resumption of Finnish overseas trade on the same basis as when Finland was still neutral.[9]

Finland's reply, published on October 8, 1941, attempted to prove that the Soviet Union had been the aggressor ever since 1939, and that Finland continued to be the defensive party. Finnish territory (Hanko and the Shredni peninsula) was still in Russian hands, and the occupied areas across the eastern boundary were not "purely Russian" but primarily Finnish. Most important from the Finnish government's point of view, however, were military considerations:

> An effective defense, to which no one can deny Finland's right, is possible only by establishing the defense in those very areas.

[9] See note 8.

The half measure of Britain in breaking off only diplomatic relations naturally did not satisfy Russia. She demanded, as a news story published on November 3, 1941, indicated, that Britain declare war, not only against Rumania and Hungary but Finland as well. That, however, did not happen immediately, as Premier Rangell noted with satisfaction in his statement to the Parliament on November 29, 1941:

> Finland would deeply deplore it if the Government of Great Britain should feel that its interests demanded acceding to the Soviet demand, and that Finland, whose war is a struggle for her existence and continued security, should be drawn into the World War.

Britain took the decisive step in an ultimatum forwarded on November 28th, 1941, by the United States Minister. It stated that Finland had disregarded Britain's note of September 22, and then presented the ultimatum:

> If Finland does not cease her military operations by the 5th of December, and, in addition, refrain from all active participation in hostilities, His Majesty's Government will have no alternative but to declare the existence of a state of war between the two countries.[10]

Finland's reply, handed to the United States Minister on December 4, again emphasized that Finland was fighting a defensive war to guarantee her own security, and then went on to state that Finnish military objectives had almost been reached:

> In the present situation there is reason to declare that Finland's armed forces are not far from achieving their strategic aims, that is, the liberation of the Finnish territories lost by the Moscow peace, and the neutralizing of those areas from which the enemy prepared to destroy Finland.
>
> It is difficult for the Government of Finland to understand that its attitude should contain anything which could give the Government of Great Britain reason to declare a state of war between these two countries. Finland would deeply deplore it if that should happen.

The day after Britain's ultimatum had been delivered Prime Minister Churchill sent a personal letter, through the United States Minister, to Marshal Mannerheim, the Finnish Commander-in-Chief, giving his Government's ultimatum the interpretation that Finland did not necessarily have to make a public statement, but could simply stop fighting and immediately cease all military operations for which

10 See note 8.

the bitter winter would offer all possible justification, and thus *de facto* get herself out of the war.

The Commander-in-Chief's reply, dated December 2 and handed directly to the United States Minister and not forwarded through the Ministry for Foreign Affairs, stated that Finland would finish up only the operations then under way. The reply was intended to be an acceptance of Churchill's offer,[11] but Britain interpreted it as being a rejection. It is peculiar that in the Government's official reply to Britain's ultimatum, no notice was taken of Churchill's milder interpretation of it. The immediate consequence of the Finnish replies was the British declaration of war on Finland's Independence Day, December 6, 1941. It read in part:

> Since the reply of the Finnish government shows that it has not agreed and does not intend to agree immediately to the conditions mentioned, a state of war exists between the two countries as of December 7, 12:01 o'clock noon Greenwich time.[12]

The general political background of Britain's declaration of war has been interpreted in many ways. The report appears very credible that Russia had demanded a declaration of war on two earlier occasions, but that it had not been made earlier because of the opposition in British Parliamentary circles. Thereupon the United States entered the case, under Russian pressure, demanding the declaration of war in order that the Soviet Union would enter the war which was expected with Japan. Great Britain thereupon gave in and declared war on Finland, but Russia did not join the war against Japan until very much later.

Roughly identical with Britain's policy was the policy of the United States toward Finland; it supported Britain, but was considerably behind it in its development. When Finland became involved in war for the second time, the United States was still at peace, and she was not so dependent on Russia as Britain. Her aim in regard to Finland for the time being—specifically, until the battle of Stalingrad—was to prevent Finland from completely allying herself with Germany against the western Powers and to prevent Finland from continuing her attack deep into Russian territory, in order that the important supplies being sent to Russia would not be endangered. As long as Finland did not clash with the United States on

[11] It appears to have been poorly worded and Mannerheim later testified that, "I believed that Churchill as a soldier . . . would correctly understand the content of my letter." *Sotasyyllisoikeuden asiakirjoja*, I, p. 20.

[12] See note 8.

this point, America understood Finland's position and actions. For example, a high State Department official admitted on July 13, 1941 (privately to be sure), that had he been in the position of the Finns, he would have done exactly as they did, and that the July Order of the Day of the Commander-in-Chief was the deed of a statesman, since it disclosed Finland's own war aims in a manner which accented their difference from those of the Germans. When the Finnish army had recovered the Karelian areas lost by the Moscow peace, Secretary of State Hull himself (on October 3) congratulated the Finnish Minister on this achievement, but he also expressed the hope that Finland would issue a declaration stating that her intention was not to go beyond the boundaries of 1939. This idea was also expressed by the Secretary of State in a press conference, which the United States Legation in Helsinki made public on October 9:

> The United States government is naturally interested in the question whether Finland will go on beyond her own boundaries,—that is, her original boundaries, after having regained her lost territory—to take part in the general war. Because of the interest the United States government felt in this subject, it also well understood why the British government was sufficiently concerned with this question to have sent a note to the Finnish government.[13]

Definite American diplomatic activity in the Finnish question began in the latter half of October. Its tactical devices were two: hints of possibilities of peace, which Finland presumably had not taken advantage of, and demands that the Finnish offensive be discontinued and the forces be withdrawn inside the 1939 boundaries. In the United States Minister's memorandum to President Ryti on October 27, 1941, the following demand regarding the military aspect of the question was presented:

> Insofar as the Finnish government is anxious to preserve the friendship of the United States now and in the future, the United States government must be given satisfactory assurances that the intention of the Finnish government is immediately to cease operations against Russian territory, and that Finnish forces will immediately be withdrawn (in principle) from the Russian territory to a line corresponding to the 1939 boundary between Finland and the Soviet Union.
>
> In the event that attacks are made against shipments of military supplies from the United States en route to Russia via the Arctic Ocean, and such attack is presumably made or may be claimed to be made from

[13] This quotation and those that follow are retranslations from the Finnish (Ed.).

Finnish-controlled territory, it must be assumed that in view of the public opinion now prevailing in the United States, such an incident must be assumed to lead to an immediate crisis in Finnish-American relations.

On October 30, 1941, the United States Minister further amplified this stand in a new memorandum, which the Finnish government, it was stated, should take into consideration in formulating its final answer. It was claimed that Finnish military operations had given especial military support to the Nazis in their aggression against the world, and because of this, the following warning was given:

> Without strengthening Finland's own future security, these military operations have in fact constituted a definite threat to the security of the United States. Therefore it must be made absolutely clear that unless her activity in this direction ceases immediately, Finland must lose the friendly support of the United States in those future difficulties which of necessity will result from such a decision.

Secretary of State Cordell Hull expressed the same attitude still more clearly and bluntly in a press conference on November 3, 1941. As reported in Helsinki by the Minister of the United States, the Secretary of State called attention to the fact that the continuation of Finland's offensive military operations in Russian territory on a larger or smaller scale seemed to reflect Finnish policy. Such a policy, he stated, seriously conflicts with the American policy of giving aid to those countries which opposed Hitler. According to America's view, such a policy does not in the long run guarantee Finnish security. In fact, if Finland continued that policy, it would tend to bring war closer to the United States and would possibly speed Finland's falling into Hitler's hands in degree as she increasingly moved into the sphere of Nazi domination.

Therefore, Mr. Hull went on, since the Government of the United States was convinced that it was acting in the interests not only of America but of Finland as well, the Finnish Minister in the United States was informed on August 18 that the United States government had learned that the Russian government was prepared to discuss peace with Finland on the basis of Finland's being granted territorial compensation. However, the Finnish government had not announced, either at Washington or Helsinki, that there was "any desire to investigate the possibility mentioned of the solution of the Finnish-Russian problems by peaceful means." On the contrary, the

Finnish army had continued military operations against Russian territory.

Having claimed that the continuation of Finnish policy in its present form would prove either Finland's dependence on Germany, or her determination to threaten the independence and security of anti-Nazi nations, the Secretary of State continued:

> The United States Minister in Helsinki has recently been instructed to inform the Finnish government, that if the Finnish government desires to maintain good relations with the United States now and in the future, satisfactory proofs are required of the Finnish government's intentions to cease immediately military operations against Russian territory, and that, in principle, the Finnish army will be withdrawn at once. The United States Minister has at the same time reminded the Government of Finland that the United States Department of State has informed the Finnish Minister in Washington that possiblities of settling the Finnish-Russian conflict by peaceful means exist.

At the time, President Ryti's interview with Taylor was published, including the following question and answer:

> How can the unfortunate circumstance of strained Finnish-American relations, caused by Finland's war against Russia with the aid of Germany, be removed?

> By our present and former difficulty, caused by the renewed Russian attack on Finland, being understood in America, and by understanding that we must try to defend ourselves against these attacks as best we can.

The Finnish question had now become an issue in world politics, and the attention drawn to it was lessened only by the large-scale battles which were fought on the Russian front at the time.

The Finnish government's lengthy reply to the State Department on November 11, 1941, first called attention to the nature of Finland's war, asserting that no peace proposals had been presented to Finland, repudiating the argument that Finnish military activities threatened the security of the United States, and refusing to accept the demand that Finnish forces simply be withdrawn to the 1939 Finnish boundary:

> It cannot be possible that the mighty United States demands that a small nation, who has been again attacked by a neighbor fifty times her size and who is fighting for her existence, should withdraw, while fighting is still continuing, to await a new attack behind boundaries

whose defense, if the advantages hitherto gained are abandoned to the enemy, can, considering the differences in strength, easily become impossible . . . Commitments which mean the endangering of defensive advantages by artificially breaking off or voiding military operations which are completely justified, Finland, who is fighting for her life, cannot give.

This Finnish reply no doubt impressed even those who prejudged Finland's case, and was considered with care, as Secretary of State Hull announced in a press conference on November 28, but it did not, he said, answer one question:

> It did not throw light on the question which most concerns the United States government, namely, how far and to what extent Finnish military policy represents a joint Finnish-German military policy, intended to inflict damage on Great Britain and her Allies, and to threaten the northern lines of communication by way of which Russia now receives supplies and assistance from Great Britain and the United States to aid Russia in the fight against Hitler's aggression, and to what extent this Finnish policy constitutes a threat to all American aims for self-defense.

Finally the Secretary of State declared that every act of the Finnish government, since the receipt of her note, had increased America's fear that Finland completely cooperated with Hitler's forces. There was not the slightest knowledge in Finland of what those acts were, since no change had taken place in the relations with Germany.

When the United States became a nation definitely at war, after the Japanese attack on December 7, 1941, her attitude toward Finland gradually stiffened. This became obvious in the United States Minister's memorandum of February 4, 1942, to the Finnish Minister of Foreign Affairs. It declared that since the entry of the United States into the war, the United States had had to review her relations with countries which were not fighting against her or for her. In the relations of the United States with Finland, the circumstance that the Germans were using Finland as a base for their operations was considered a most important factor. On this point the memorandum declared:

> The United States government has no information which would indicate that the Finnish government, after the German declaration of war or before that date, has given any explanation of its position, or has justified that position, in regard to the continued stay of German armed forces in Finland, and of the use of Finnish territory by those

German forces as a base for operations. It must be understood that the
continued stay of German armed forces and their activity in Finnish
territory in the absence of any opposition on the part of the Finnish
government directly affects Finland's position in the present war situation.

At about the same time, the State Department had informed an
official of the Finnish Legation that if Finland wanted to avoid
fighting against American forces, she should announce, at least before
landings on the continent of Europe occurred, that the Germans were
in Finland against Finland's wishes.

The memorandum which the Minister for Foreign Affairs handed
the United States Minister on February 16, 1942, explained that the
arrival of German forces in Finland stemmed from the transit agreement, and their remaining in Finland resulted from the cobelliger-
ency which Russia's attack had brought into being, and that Finland
in no case wanted to become involved in the war between Germany
and the United States.

At the beginning of 1942, the chief aim of the United States was
to prevent Finland from continuing her offensive, and from definitely
joining the general military offensive of Germany. Russian influence
naturally increased in degree as Russia was seen to play an ever more
decisive role in the war against Germany. In January, 1942, a
United States Senator informed the Finnish Minister Procopé that
the Senate would declare war against Finland if the President requested it; in April the same sources indicated the situation to be
such that if the Soviet Union demanded severance of relations with
Finland and a declaration of war, the United States government
could not refuse because all its prospects in the war depended on
Russia. However, the fact that the Finns had not advanced to the
Murmansk railroad was considered a point in their favor. Still, not
even Molotov's visit to Washington in the spring of 1942 seems to
have precipitated any crisis in the Finnish question, though that could
well have been expected. Of course, expressions of disfavor toward
Finland continued. In the summer, beginning on August 1, the
United States closed the Finnish Consulates in America; the action
was explained on the basis of an administrative measure applicable to
all foreign countries, adopted a year earlier by the Finns because of
the exceptional circumstances that then prevailed. But American
public opinion was not yet ready for more drastic measures and it was
likely, as some American newspapers which were friendly toward
Finland interpreted the matter, that even relatively limited restric-

tions sufficed as concessions to Russia. At the end of 1942 the Finnish Information Service in the United States was banned because Finland had limited the expansion of a similar American service in Finland. Finnish Legation personnel were denied the right to travel freely in the United States.

In the fall of 1942 the United States government presented a warning, the purpose of which clearly was to keep the Finns from participating in the large-scale operations planned at the time by the Germans. Just prior to that, the Finnish Minister in Washington had given the American press a lengthy statement regarding conditions in Finland and had declared that Finland's war would continue until the threat against her existence was removed and guaranties for lasting security had been obtained. Since propagandists used this statement to claim that Finland was prepared to make a separate peace, an official explanation was given in Finland on September 25. It was to the effect that, taking Finland's unchanged policy into consideration, all such explanations and conclusions should be considered as unfounded. On the same day the United States Minister in Finland delivered the following memorandum to President Ryti:

> The Government of the United States is deeply concerned over increasing indications that the Germans are pressing Finland to participate in new military operations. Toward numerous past provocations of the Finnish government toward the Government of the United States, the Government of the United States has shown a tolerance which reflects the residue of the goodwill toward Finland at the time when Finland's partnership-in-arms with America's enemies began. Nevertheless it will become necessary to reconsider the relations already strained between the the United States and Finland, if the Finnish government undertakes any activity which the United States could only consider prejudicial to her own vital interests, without forwarding in any way the legitimate interests of Finland in the future.
>
> Finnish sources have recently indicated that the military objectives of Finland are limited to the territory already gained. Present relations between Finland and the United States, which now hang by a very thin thread, would be immeasurably strengthened if a public statement to this effect were made which would clarify Finland's intentions.

An hour before this memorandum was delivered, Premier Rangell had given a statement in Parliament which at one point touched upon the question presented by the United States:

> Our defensive war also defines the clear path followed by our foreign policy. The logical result of the nature of our war is that no changes

in our foreign policy have occurred since the day, more than fifteen months ago, when the aggressive acts of the Soviet Union forced us to continue the war which Russia had begun by her attack in 1939. Finland is fighting the Soviet Union side by side with the Germans, to whom bonds of brotherhood-in-arms join us. Our own definite stand, the aim of which is the achieving of security for our country, has been stated in many different connections so clearly to various foreign powers that no reason can well exist for "interpreting" it. On November 29 last year I had the honor of defining that stand in a communication to the Parliament. It was unanimously approved by the Parliament. As a definition of our foreign policy it still holds unchanged. For one reason or another, some foreign sources have wanted to draw arbitrary conclusions concerning this stand. Only recently, a statement given to the press by one of our Finnish Ministers abroad, based on the statement of the Government just mentioned, was interpreted in a way which deviates from the actual stand of the Finnish government.

The change which has occurred in the attitude toward Finland of some foreign Powers after the first 1939-1940 phase of Finland's defensive war, which these interpretations partly reflect and whose sharpest indication was the British declaration of war on December 6, 1941, has not enabled us to follow any different foreign policy than the one which, according to the unanimous conviction of our people, is dictated by the prerequisites for our country's survival.

In the reply to the American memorandum, on September 28, 1942, Foreign Minister Witting stated that Premier Rangell had made a statement to Parliament which seemed to correspond to the wish expressed by the United States. The reference to numerous provocations was, the reply stated, hard to understand, the charge concerning outside pressure on Finnish foreign policy was refuted, and it was pointed out that when the Russian attack began in 1941, the United States was not an ally 'of Russia and was not even in the war.

Toward the end of 1942, United States diplomatic activity regarding Finland centered chiefly on the demand that Finland should not attack the Murmansk railroad or Leningrad. When it became clear that Finland would not undertake such attacks, a new demand was advanced. It was that Finland explain what general plans she contemplated. The question naturally arises, what were the objectives of the United States, and why, on the other hand, was it difficult for Finland to formulate an explanation which would have been fully satisfactory?

As long as authentic sources are not available, the objectives of the United States can only be conjectured. In any case, two factors in her foreign policy had to be taken into consideration: the public opinion of the nation as it was reflected in the Senate, the Congress, the press, and among the voters, and the Soviet Union as the other. In the prevailing situation it was necessary to do something to satisfy Russia, but not so much that opposition at home would be aroused. The Government saw the developments lead to a general increase in the significance and importance of Russia, and realized that all obstacles to cooperation had to be removed. Since goodwill toward Finland was one of the obstacles, it had to be uprooted by awakening suspicion toward Finland. In that respect, much was achieved by British, Russian, and anti-isolationist propaganda. The State Department tried to force Finland to furnish material for propaganda, since it was doubtless clearly understood that, being a small factor in the general World War, and being placed in a situation which otherwise also was uncertain, Finland faced well-nigh insurmountable difficulties in clearly defining her objectives without knowing the enemy's demands and without breaking with the only nation able to give military help. Scarcely any warring nation can proclaim in advance which line is the goal of its operations. If that were done, the enemy could easily carry out its concentrations and counter measures in such a way that the objective could be gained, if at all, only at the cost of huge sacrifices. Furthermore, such a declaration would have been disloyal toward Germany, since even the possibility of an attack was of some help to the Germans, and could not easily be denied so long as Finnish-German cooperation itself could not be completely ended.

CHAPTER 7

PEACE FEELERS AND THE PROPAGANDA WAR, 1943-1944

1. DETERIORATION OF GERMANY'S POSITION

The defeat at Stalingrad was the beginning of the end of Germany's eastern drive and of the whole World War. From that time on, Germany could no longer hope for a Russian collapse or that a negotiated peace could be concluded. Because the German forces were scattered over wide fronts, they were either defeated individually or were not in sufficient strength on the scene of the major decisions. The war potential of Germany's enemies, on the other hand, was mounting to its peak, and their overwhelming superiority in the air systematically destroyed Germany's war industry and communications while in technical advance as well Germany was losing ground. The occupied countries were seething and awaited only the opportunity to throw off the hated yoke. Having suffered heavy losses, Germany's allies were paralyzed and began to seek opportunities to get out of the war. A special propaganda attack against them therefore promised the best results. In this respect Finland, whose moral position was the strongest, could be considered the most valuable target.

That Germany was going to lose the war became clear even in Finland. At a conference attended by President Ryti, Premier Rangell, and the Minister for Foreign Affairs, Witting, at Army Headquarters on February 3, 1943, after the Stalingrad disaster, the Commander-in-Chief, Marshal Mannerheim, presented that conclusion properly buttressed. Although the Government also understood this, it was forced, in making practical decisions, to take into consideration many problems difficult to solve.

2. FINLAND'S DIFFICULTIES IN GETTING OUT OF THE WAR

In theory, there was nothing to prevent Finland from making a separate peace. However, the Finnish government had to try to see clearly how the situation would develop after relations with Germany were broken off. When the situation was surveyed in these terms, so many difficulties and dangers presented themselves that it was difficult to determine which would be the worst and therefore should be avoided above all others.

The one-sidedness of Finnish economy has always forced the country to rely on imports. As long as relations with Germany continued, communications with the countries in her sphere of influence were open, and the absolutely necessary foodstuffs and raw materials for industry remained available to Finland. If these sources were cut off, Finland would have been unable to get anything from anywhere, because all communications to the West were controlled by Germany and there was no reason to expect any aid from Russia. Economically, then, Finland was completely at Germany's mercy.

Militarily also, a break was far from a simple matter. All of northern Finland, at least to the latitude of Kemi and Kuusamo, would at once fall into German hands, as later developments so clearly demonstrated. Elsewhere, too, particularly at communication centers, the Germans had supply and anti-aircraft installations which, in altered circumstances, would not have remained inactive. The southern coast and the airports were in German hands. To have brought about unfriendly relations with the Germans might have resulted in the whole country's becoming a battlefield, with Russian occupation as the ultimate result. A single attempt on Finland's part to break away from Germany would have sufficed to put the German war machine, which was still frighteningly strong, into motion. A surprise move would scarcely have succeeded, and for moral reasons could not come into question against brothers-in-arms. Any dishonorable way of getting out of the war would not have been permitted by any Finn. Great Powers may be able to afford dishonorable actions, but small nations are not.

What then would have been the terms under which the Soviet Union would have made peace? No definite information regarding the terms was available. Vague surmises and rumors circulated in the world press, according to which Russia would demand at least the boundaries fixed by the Moscow peace. Finland was not yet prepared to submit to such terms, even though reliable sources reported that Foreign Secretary Eden had promised, on his visit to Moscow late in 1941, to agree to Russia's obtaining the March, 1940, boundaries plus Petsamo. As long as the Finnish army was victorious, and in some sectors far beyond the 1939 boundaries, no Finnish government, ready to accept once again the crying injustice of the Moscow peace, could have remained in office. If peace had been made, would there have been any way of preventing Russian occupation of Fin-

land? What guaranty, furthermore, would there have been that
Russia really would honor a peace once it had been made?

Then, too, there appeared the new formula of the Allies, unconditional surrender.[1] In Finland, at least, unconditional surrender was
considered the equivalent of suicide committed because of fear of
death. As long as any other possibility existed, surrender was to be
avoided. In order that the country might not become a battlefield
and then be occupied by a foreign Power, the avoidance of which had
been the chief aim of Finnish foreign policy all along, an attempt to
make peace should preferably be postponed till later, closer to the
general peace, when Germany would already be weakened and the
forces of the western Powers would be able, on the continent of
Europe, to hold Russian demands within reasonable limits.

These considerations influenced the attitude of the Finnish government and popular opinion up to the armistice in 1944. Even the
so-called "peace offensive," which later appeared in Finland in opposition to the Government's policy, had to take these factors into consideration.

3. Peace Moves During the Early Part of the War

During the first autumn of the war, in 1941, many rumors were
circulated about Russia's desire to make peace with Finland. In September, for example, Vichy claimed to know that Russia had offered
peace on the basis of the 1939 boundaries. According to this story,
Finland had indicated willingness to discuss peace, but not on the
basis proposed, and had suggested that the question be left to the
President of the United States to solve. There was no truth to this
story, of course. This was immediately shown when the Russian
press chief, Losovsky, issued a communication on September 4, 1941,
in which not a word was said about the Soviet Union's desire for
peace but, on the contrary, the impression was given that only Finland was in need of peace and that any initiative in the matter could
be expected only from her.

Already in the summer of 1941, however, the United States released a peace feeler the nature and purpose of which was destined to
remain rather unclear. In a memorandum submitted on October 27,
1941, by the Minister of the United States, and in a statement made
by Cordell Hull at a press conference on November 3, the claim was
made public that Finland allegedly had had an opportunity to make

---

[1] The unconditional surrender formula was accepted by the leaders of the
United Nations at Casablanca in January, 1943 (Ed.).

peace in August, 1941. The Secretary of State's version of this "offer" has already been mentioned. The explanation of the discussion in question, contained in Minister Schoenfeld's memorandum, was more detailed:

> The United States government wants to remind the Finnish government that on August 18, 1941, the Under Secretary of State, Sumner Welles, told the Finnish Minister in Washington, that the United States government had learned that the Soviet Union desired, in the event that the Finnish government was so inclined, to discuss a new peace treaty between Finland and the Soviet Union which would include Russian territorial concessions to Finland. At that time the Finnish Minister [in Washington] presented several obvious views about guaranties and other matters. The Under Secretary of State replied that, in the opinion of the United States government, it would be necessary to discuss the questions raised by the Finnish Minister only in the event that the Finnish government was prepared to explore the possibilities suggested, and that it was essential in the first place to ascertain the Finnish attitude toward these possibilities.
>
> The United States government has received no reply from the Finnish government which would reveal its attitude in this question, nor has the Finnish Minister in later conversations with State Department officials given any direct indication of such possible negotiations with the Soviet Union.
>
> Shortly after this conversation of August 18 between the Minister and the Under Secretary of State, it came to the attention of the United States government that certain high Finnish government officials, as well as the press in Finland and Germany, had emphasized that Finland would not make peace with the Government of the Soviet Union as it is now constituted.[2]

In general the memorandum was doubtless correct, but it put the emphasis, in part, on the wrong things, and it ignored certain issues vital to Finland. These issues were pointed out in the Finnish reply, dated November 11, 1941:

> No clarification has been received from the United States government regarding the considerations pertaining to the essentials of a possible peace which the Finnish government has presented.
>
> Specifically, no guaranties of security have even been proposed to Finland to insure a new peace between Finland and the Soviet Union.
>
> It is the impression of the Finnish government that Mr. Welles' statement to Minister Procopé on August 18 was not intended as a

[2] Translated from the Finnish. The same applies to the quotations on the pages that follow (Ed.).

peace offer, or even as a recommendation by the United States, but simply as an informational item, on the basis of which Finland should have asked for peace.

That being so, the Finnish government, with military operations then at a stage where even Viipuri had not yet been captured, decided to wait for the development of events.

Since no exception was taken to the observations in the Finnish reply, it was concluded that the United States Department of State considered them justified. The question then arises as to what the meaning of this peace feeler was. The initiative was not taken by Russia, as is shown by *The New York Times'* Kuibyshev correspondent's news item of November 12, 1941:

> Litvinov and Losovski have denied that the Soviet Union has initiated any action for a separate peace with Finland. Russia has learned of the American proposal to Finland only from foreign news reports. It seems certain that' the feeler was born as a result of a Finnish suggestion or Washington initiative.

It can hardly be believed, then, that whoever released this trial balloon expected any positive results. There seems to remain only the possibility that the peace feeler was a device of psychological warfare, and that its purpose was to place Finland in an unfavorable light abroad and to divide public opinion in Finland. It was natural, under these circumstances, that the Finnish Ministry for Foreign Affairs should have reacted cautiously to the proposal. In instructions to the Minister in Washington on August 30, 1941, the Ministry for Foreign Affairs considered as decisive the fact that neither the United States nor the Soviet Union had initiated the effort:

> Since no peace proposal has been made, from any quarter, we have had no occasion or reason to define our attitude toward peace in the war begun against us. For your own information: our intention is therefore to ignore Welles' proposal.

In spite of all this, Russian propaganda later argued, no doubt in order to show that the continuation of the war was Finland's fault, that Russia had offered peace in vain to Finland in the autumn of 1941. In April, 1942, for example, the Kuibyshev correspondent of the *Christian Science Monitor* reported that in conversation the Russians frequently called attention to the alleged fact that they had offered Finland peace in the fall of 1941, and had been prepared to return what they had conquered, and that they had even been willing to give Finland a part of Eastern Karelia. All such talk, unfortunately, was invented later for purposes of propaganda which finds any kind of weapon useful.

Nor could a hint from Stockholm to the effect that Mme. Kollontay had stated at Christmas, 1941, that contact should be made with the Finns, be considered proof of Russian desire for peace. In the same connection seemingly reliable reports were received that Stalin had demanded of Eden, during his Moscow visit early in 1942, the return of the Finnish 1940 boundaries, and the cession of Petsamo to Russia. But before peace could be made, however, Finland would have to get rid of her present Government. All in all, the hint from Stockholm indicated only the willingness of its unknown author to do something, but it contained nothing that could at that time be utilized for concluding peace.

The Finnish government stated clearly that it was ready to make peace on one specific condition. Thus President Ryti told the United States Minister on April 27, 1942, that he, for his part, was ready to make peace with the Soviet if only the western Powers would give guaranties that the peace would last. There is no reason to doubt that this information reached the State Department, but it did not result in any action in Washington.

After Britain and the Soviet Union signed the treaty on May 26, 1942, binding themselves not to make a separate peace with Germany or her allies, a pause occurred in these peace efforts. They did not become impossible, however, because Finland was not an ally of Germany's, but was simply fighting alongside Germany, and since the kind of clemency and generosity that unconditional surrender implies is, after all, extended to anyone. After the British-Soviet treaty of May, 1942, newspaper reports began to appear, according to which Russia had been promised, in the future peace, at least the boundaries of March, 1940, and in addition, possibly, bases in Finland. Roundabout news from Russia, to be sure, gave assurance that the Soviet Union would be satisfied with less, but these reports could not be considered worth serious attention. At the end of October, 1942, for example, word was received that a Soviet Legation official in Stockholm, Yartsev, had stated that Russia was prepared to discuss a separate peace at that moment on the basis of 1939 boundaries, but that Hanko would have to be left outside discussions. Yartsev had declared that Ryti and Tanner were obstacles that made any negotiations difficult. Yartsev's statement, however, reached the Finnish government in such jumbled form, and seemed so unreliable in all respects, that it was not really seriously considered. There was definite reason to believe, for example, that the Soviet Union would in no event agree to return the 1939 boundaries to Finland. Clarification could have been received only by establishing direct contact with the Soviet representative. This Finland did not want to do without Germany's knowledge. On November 30, therefore, the Finnish Minister in Berlin was instructed to inquire informally if Germany had anything against Finland's testing the opportunity for negotiations which had thus appeared. On December 8, the German Minister in Helsinki, Blücher, delivered the reply. It stated that a Finnish response to suggestions made by Russia would be considered everywhere as a sign of weakness, and Russian feelers should therefore be ignored. Thereafter the Finnish government did not feel that it could go any further and gave the Finnish Minister in Stockholm permission merely to maintain contact. It is natural that the contact could not be maintained for long without concrete consideration of the chief issue.

The leaders of Finnish foreign policy at this time obviously considered it possible that Germany and Russia might conclude a separate peace, and wanted to be able to make peace for Finland at the same time. Even the mere attempt, on Finland's part, to make a separate peace with Russia could have left Finland at Russia's mercy, or might have led to a German-Russian separate peace at Finland's expense. Such considerations sufficed to counsel caution.

Thus the year 1942 ended without any possibility having appeared for such peace discussions as, in the view of the Finnish government, could have been explored at that time without causing serious difficulties for the country.

4. The United States' Offer of Mediation

On February 3, 1943, at conferences at the Finnish Headquarters, the progressive worsening of the general situation after Stalingrad was discussed, and the conclusion was reached that an attempt to conclude peace with the Soviet Union and Britain should be made. In addition to the indications which had been vaguely suggested by the contact with Yartsev, some further information regarding the Soviet's attitude was obtained when it was learned that Molotov had recently been heard to declare that the peace terms that Finland would get would become more severe in the future. This seemed to suggest that peace was possible, under certain conditions. The conference unanimously decided that Finland should try to get out of the war, but only in such a way that the matter could be straightened out in some way with Germany as well. In coming to terms with the Soviet Union, the question of Eastern Karelia should be no obstacle but it would be well, however, to hold it for bargaining purposes. It was also felt that making peace with Britain would be easier than with Russia.

Shortly thereafter, hints of the possibility of peace became more numerous. On February 8, 1943, information was received from Moscow to the effect that the American Ambassador had told the Swedish Minister that Molotov had declared that the Soviet no longer had any reason to continue the war against Finland. Russia would not, however, take the initiative, but Finland should announce on what basis she was prepared to conclude peace. In conferences on February 8 and 10, President Ryti and Minister Tanner decided that in some way advantage should be taken of this suggestion. It was intended to use, in the first place, the mediation of the Swedish Foreign Minister. Finland's 1939 boundaries were thought of as the basis for negotiations. Eastern Karelia was to remain occupied until its fate should be decided at the general peace conference. Tanner was to try to contact Britain through his friends; relations with that country were to be straightened out first. A separate peace being involved, precautions should be taken not to arouse Germany's enmity too early. The Swedish Foreign Minister was, therefore, to be privately informed that Finland desired to reestablish her earlier relations with Britain, and he was to forward this information to the proper parties. On February 13, Tanner wrote a personal letter to First Lord of the Admiralty Alexander, inquiring whether some way for reestablishing peace existed. This letter was sent via the Swedish Foreign Secretary, but no reply was received. As if to give the support of Finnish public opinion to this effort, the executive committee of the Social Democratic party adopted a resolution on February 15, emphasizing Finland's unique position and her right freely to withdraw from the war:

> Finland's present war, a continuation of the Winter War, is a defensive war, into which our people were forced against their will. Its purpose is solely to safeguard the freedom and independence of our country. It is, therefore, a separate war; we have no part in the war between the great Powers and are not fighting for the objectives of either group of great Powers. The fact that Finland and Germany are

fighting the same enemy, Russia, does not alter this fact. Finland is, therefore, free to decide on withdrawing from the war whenever a favorable moment appears and her freedom and independence are guaranteed.

The political leaders of Germany paid considerable attention to this public statement. On the day after it appeared, Ribbentrop informed the Finnish Minister in Berlin, that he and Hitler deplored it because it made Germany's allies restless and gave the enemy a chance to claim that it indicated Finnish weakness. On February 20 Ribbentrop returned to the same topic and argued that the resolution was not "fair play" on Finland's part, for it put weapons into the enemy's hands at a critical moment. The Finnish Minister replied, according to instructions, that Finland had explained throughout the war that she had no part in the war of the great Powers but was fighting for her own existence, and he further explained that the Finns were to be accepted for what they were, and that fifty per cent of them belonged to the working classes and could not be ignored in the war in which labor, too, was wholeheartedly fighting for the country's independence. Ribbentrop seemed satisfied with this explanation. Economic pressure was not yet used, on this occasion.

At this juncture, the Government received a memorandum from the United States chargé d'affaires, McClintock, on March 20, 1943. It stated that, proceeding on the assumption that Finland had confidence in the United States, America was offering her good offices to bring about peace between Finland and the Soviet Union. The offer was underlined by the observation that it would in all likelihood not be renewed.

In the Government's Foreign Affairs Committee meeting, attended by the Commander-in-Chief, the difficulties which the acceptance of this offer of mediation would cause were taken up first. It was concluded that acceptance would ipso facto mean breaking of relations with Germany. Finland would therefore be at Russia's mercy, no matter what demands she might make, and the United States would not be able to help Finland. It was therefore decided to ask the American chargé d'affaires for information regarding Russia's terms, and also information regarding the guaranties to be given to Finland. The Finns had to act frankly with Germany, it was felt. The Finnish Foreign Minister was therefore to go to Germany, to explain the reasons why Finland could not reject the American offer outright, without trying to find out what it might lead to. It was obviously not taken into consideration at the time that the mere fact of consulting Germany would by itself suffice to decide the fate of the mediation offer.

In accordance with this decision, Foreign Minister Ramsay flew to Berlin. He saw Ribbentrop on March 26, after he had waited six hours to learn whether he would be received or not. Ribbentrop, in his usual fashion, expressed strong disapproval of the American offer, without giving Ramsay a chance to speak. If Finland made a separate peace, "extreme conclusions" would be drawn by Germany. To avoid such "extreme conclusions," Finland must discontinue negotiations and immediately inform the United States government to that effect. Finland should, on the contrary, sign a political alliance with Germany, and the treaty should include a clause to the effect that neither party would make separate peace.

The only result of Finland's correct behavior toward Germany in handling the American suggestion was a new difficulty: Germany now began to demand a political agreement, consideration of which had been avoided up to now. To emphasize the firmness of the German attitude, the German Minister, Blücher, announced on April 4 that he was leaving Helsinki, and on the 6th, just prior to his departure, he announced that the German government thought the Finnish government should give its answer to the United States at the earliest possible moment. The American chargé d'affaires, who apparently had learned of the incident, warned the Government on April 8 that the slightest indication that Finland was making her decision under German pressure, and that she was prepared to make further concessions to Germany, would suffice to cause deterioration in Finland's relations with the United States.

The reply to the American chargé d'affaires continued to be postponed, for both the Government and the Committee on Foreign Affairs of the Parliament wanted to wait and see what information regarding peace terms and guaranties would be received. When information was received on April 10th, it turned out to be only a statement to the effect that the United States could not give the information desired, and that the intention of the United States had been simply to act as an intermediary to get negotiations under way. Thereupon, the reply to Mr. McClintock's memorandum was drafted and forwarded.

The reply regretted that Finland had failed to obtain any information of the basis of the negotiations, or of Russia's willingness to negotiate, and stated that Finland was therefore unable to take

advantage of the American offer of good offices and saw no other possibility but to continue her defensive war. When this reply was presented to the Committee on Foreign Affairs of the Parliament, no
criticism of it was offered by the committee.

The turn these peace moves had taken probably came close to
causing an almost complete breach in diplomatic relations between
the United States and Finland. On April 22, the chargé d'affaires,
McClintock, asked for passports for almost the entire personnel of
the American Legation, and arranged to call on the Foreign Minister.
The visit was cancelled, however, on the 24th. Mr. McClintock undoubtedly already had his Government's note informing him that
relations were to be broken off, but some new development had led
to its being cancelled. Two items in the newspapers just at this time
might have influenced the American decision: one of them was the
German radio's jubilation over the erroneous reports that the United
States had already broken off diplomatic relations with Finland; the
second, the much-publicized Katyn affair which caused Russia to
break off relations with the Polish government-in-exile in London.
It may be assumed that both of these incidents caused restraint in
the United States' Finnish policy.

Germany's Minister to Finland, who returned to Helsinki at this
time, was of the opinion that the matter had been solved in a way
satisfactory to Germany. However, he immediately brought up
Ribbentrop's demand for a political pact, in accordance with which
neither party was to make peace except in cooperation with the other.
During the Easter season the German Minister continually pressed
for an answer. Having received word at the end of April that Finland could do no more than give a statement regarding the matter,
he declared that a statement was not enough. Conversations continued for nearly two months, but the Finnish government did not
accept the idea of a political pact, and suggested merely a declaration
to the effect that Finland had shown by her acts that she was willing
to fight until her independence had been secured. Because Germany
did not consider such a declaration to be sufficient, the question was
left open for the time being. To force Finland to give in, Germany,
presumably at Ribbentrop's suggestion, began to block shipments of
foodstuffs, and in June announced she was going to deliver only half
of the amounts of gasoline and oil that had been promised. Later in
June, when the Government submitted to Ribbentrop a detailed explanation of the reasons why no political pact with Germany could

be concluded—the reasons included, among others, the fact that Parliament refused to approve such a pact—Ribbentrop replied that he was confident that Finland would show her loyalty by her actions, and thus provide a solution for the problem. The blockade of foodstuffs was lifted immediately. Ribbentrop presumably realized that the attitude of the Finnish government would not change, and that further pressure would only force Finland to accent her own special objectives.

In the autumn of 1943, however, Germany raised the question once again. In October, Hitler sent a long letter to President Ryti. It contained criticism of Finland's attitude and a request that Mussolini's new Fascist government be recognized by Finland. The Committee for Foreign Affairs of the Government discussed the letter on October 18th. The answer of the Government, which was submitted to the Foreign Affairs Committee on the 25th, and sent to Hitler on October 27, contained no promises or commitments. At the end of November Ribbentrop discussed the matter with the Finnish Minister in Berlin and early in December gave him a memorandum on the subject. He called attention to the fact that the conversations in the spring regarding the pact had led nowhere, and that the many rumors concerning a Finnish separate peace indicated that talk about such a peace was not without foundation in fact. The question of a pact should therefore be taken up once more. He wanted to know what the Finnish government's actual attitude was. On December 4 the Foreign Affairs Committee of the Government unanimously decided that the answer still could only be negative, but that it was not necessary to hurry in saying so. In a meeting on the 29th, the committee approved Minister Kivimäki's draft for an answer, declaring that relations between Finland and Germany had best be continued on the present basis because the pact Ribbentrop proposed would in no case be approved in the Parliament, and to bring up the question would only cause difficulties. When the reply was delivered to Ribbentrop in mid-January of 1944, he accepted it calmly. The following June, however, when Finland's position had been radically changed, it became obvious that Germany had not abandoned the idea of a pact.

5. THE PEACE OFFENSIVE AT THE END OF 1943

Italy's surrender in the summer of 1943 changed the general situation and naturally made Finland's position more difficult. The propaganda campaign against Finland became stronger and more effective: it now included a public discussion of the terms which Finland would have to accept.

For example, on July 31, 1943, the Stockholm *Aftontidningen* published a report of Russia's peace terms for Finland which had been received from the Soviet Legation. According to this report, Russia demanded the boundaries of 1940 on the Karelian Isthmus, for the security of Leningrad, regardless of whether Finland made a separate peace now or fought until Germany was defeated. If she did make a separate peace, she would be allowed to keep her other territories as fixed by the 1939 boundary, but if she continued to fight the Moscow peace boundaries of March, 1940, would be imposed throughout. The report made no mention of Hanko or the Gulf of Finland islands. The Soviet Information Bureau explained, however, that the report was "the fruit of the active imagination [of the *Aftontidningen*] and completely without foundation."

A few days earlier, a private report received via the Belgian Minister in Stockholm stated that Russia was ready to discuss peace, that Finland should take the initiative by submitting in writing direct to Russia her views regarding the basis of negotiations, and that this should be done quickly.

At a meeting of the Committee for Foreign Affairs of the Government, which was attended by President Ryti and the Commander-in-Chief, Marshal Mannerheim, it was decided, in view of Germany's attitude, to use this "contact" with caution. The reply, given to the "contact" on August 10, stated that in Finland's view the negotiations should be on the basis of the 1939 boundaries, but that Finland was prepared to reconsider the boundaries on the Karelian Isthmus, and to cede to Russia the Gulf of Finland islands of Seiskari, Lavansaari, Tytärsaari and Peninsaari. Finland should receive compensation in Eastern Karelia without, however, thereby endangering the Murmansk railroad. On August 13, Semyonov, councillor of the Russian Legation at Stockholm, who had received the Finnish proposal, announced that he could not transmit the proposal to Moscow. Less than a month later, Finland made a new attempt, and offered some additional concessions. They also were considered insufficient, however. Semyonov stated on September 16 that he could not transmit them to Moscow. The attempt had thus broken down, at least for the time being.

At the time of this peace feeler, the Finnish government received for consideration a query that seemed to promise a possibility of

withdrawing from the war which would not have left the country at
Russia's mercy, with no guaranties. The American Embassy in Lis-
bon had asked the Finnish chargé d'affaires at Lisbon what action
Finland would take in the event that an American expeditionary force
landed in northern Norway : would she fight, how could she free herself of German forces, and what supplies would she then need? The
reply was to be sent directly to Cordell Hull early in September. On
September 3 the Finns answered that Finland would not fight the
Americans, that the Americans should not allow the Russians to enter
Finnish territory, that negotiations would be begun with Germany
for the withdrawal of German troops, and that Finland would need,
in addition to her own harvest, certain monthly deliveries of food
supplies. No more was thereafter heard of this plan with the help of
which Finland could have withdrawn from the war at a relatively
early stage.

All the information about the Soviet peace terms which circulated
in the world press at this time suggested either directly or by implication that the minimum Soviet demands meant a return to the Moscow peace boundaries of March, 1940. In addition, Allied propaganda
began to prepare popular opinion for the acceptance of a future situation in which Russia would include all the border states in her sphere
of influence in which the outside world would have nothing to say,
and in which the small countries directly involved would not have
much to say either. For example, in February, 1943, one of America's
best known and most influential journalists, Walter Lippmann, declared in an article that to apply the principles of the Atlantic Charter to
Finland was frankly a problem, because Finland happened to be a
neighbor of Russia's. According to Lippmann's conception, small
countries had to fit their foreign policy to that of their larger neighbor,
i.e., Russia, since they were unable, by themselves, to oppose Russia
militarily, and Britain and the United States would not interfere to
help them. The former United States Ambassador to Russia, Joseph
E. Davies, explained in an interview in March that it was quite natural
that Russia wanted parts of Finland, and the neighbors of the Soviet
Union must be allowed to join the Soviet "voluntarily," since the
Soviet Union does not threaten American security. In September
the *Stockholms Tidningen* quoted Russian circles in London as saying that Russia's main demands in making peace with Finland would
include the following three points: the Germans must be driven out
of Finland; the present Government must be replaced by a "democratic" Government which would not be "aggressive"; and territorial

demands which would satisfy the strategic security requirements of Russia. An armistice would be granted only after unconditional surrender. When reports of the Moscow conference held at the end of October began to circulate, the impression gradually became general that Russia would have a more or less free hand in defining her western boundaries, and that Finland could not hope for a modification of the boundaries fixed by the peace of March, 1940. Finally, Finland's fate seemed to be clarified in Stalin's speech of November 6, 1943, in which he declared that the moment was approaching when the Karelian-Finnish Republic would be liberated. Since this Soviet Republic, founded after the Winter War, included the territory taken from Finland, with the exception of the southern part of the Karelian Isthmus which had been incorporated in the Leningrad district, Stalin's speech officially confirmed that a Russian minimum demand included the boundaries of March, 1940.

General developments had weakened Finland's position to such a degree that even terms as harsh as these had now to be considered, in spite of the fact that, on the basis of previous experience, it could be expected that additional demands would be presented at the last moment.

6. DIFFICULTIES ON THE HOME FRONT

It is probably not possible, in a democratic country, to maintain the unity created by war except while the need is all-compelling. In addition to differing political viewpoints, personal clashes and opposition make for disunity. In Finland the all-compelling need for unity did not last long. By the early part of 1942, the Finnish army had reached its strategic objectives; the major objective, which was the recapture of the territories lost to Russia through the peace of 1940, had been reached even earlier. After that, the Finnish army simply stood "at rest" on the enemy's soil. The war still continued, but it was not war in the sense which continued, unbroken national unity required. Because even position warfare cost several hundred casualties a month, to say nothing of material sacrifices, and as the general situation only grew worse, public opinion began to raise the question of whether Finland should not get out of the war. The efforts which the Government had made to obtain peace were naturally known to only a very small group. When definite opposition to the policies of the Government began to appear in September, 1943, the chief charge of the opposition was that the Government had achieved nothing in its search for a separate peace. The opposition could make use of two powerful arguments: peace had not been made, and the general situation continued to grow worse.

In addition, the opposition had grounds for other arguments as well. At home, but especially abroad, there was talk of the Government's "blackout" of information. It was claimed that news released to the public was one-sided, and that information which could have opened the eyes of the public to the unknown dangers toward which the nation was headed, was withheld. These arguments contained a considerable amount of truth, of course. In time of war it is necessary to restrict the freedom of the press and to screen the news, and that can never be done without mistakes being committed. When the attempt must be made to prevent enemy propaganda from becoming a "decisive weapon," it is necessary to sift news so thoroughly that even unreasonable things are done. In a situation such as Finland's, the will to win must always be considered of utmost importance; without the will to win defeat would be absolutely certain. In addition, it should be noted that the military interfered with the censorship, even in specific instances, in a way which increased the difficulties in applying censorship impartially. The relations with Germany were especially delicate and frequently led to protests from the Germans which could not altogether be disregarded because the national supply set-up was dependent on Germany or on imports coming by way of Germany. However, one cannot speak of a "blackout" as such. Probably no nation at war published, as did Finland, news reports from both warring sides, and scarcely anywhere was the press so free from a war psychosis as in Finland. Even those foreign newspapers which spoke most loudly about the "blackout" of news in Finland, were freely sold in the country. Still, there were ample reasons for dissatisfaction with the censorship, if one was inclined to look for them. Much was made of the argument that the Government itself had created that state of mind which it used as a reason justifying the conclusion that it was impossible to accept the peace terms that had been proposed. If this really had been the case, then the accusation cannot be made against wartime censorship alone. It must also be directed against the whole development of public opinion during the years long before the war.

The opposition found another cause for criticism in the fact that the Government had not clearly defined its war aims. There is truth in this argument, as has already been made clear, but the difficulties faced by the Government must also be taken into consideration. It must be admitted as a serious fault that the Government's attitude in not annexing Eastern Karelia to Finland was never clearly and generally made known.

Especially useful items in criticising the Government were Britain's declaration of war and the deterioration of relations with the United States. The critics did not have to consider, of course, whether those developments could have been avoided without prejudicing Finland's own interests.

Finally, mention must be made of the charge which was connected with the others already mentioned, namely, that the Government did not maintain sufficient contact with the Parliament, and did not permit Parliament to handle all matters which it had handled in time of peace. There is undoubtedly some justification for this charge, for matters were not discussed in full parliamentary sessions in quite the same way they had been in time of peace, but this resulted either from the absolute necessity, imposed by the war, of deciding matters quickly or of keeping them secret. Parliamentary circles were kept informed of the situation by means of a new procedure, adopted after the Winter War, whereby the Premier reported on the situation and answered questions in meetings to which the Speaker and Vice-Speakers of the Parliament and the chairmen of the party groups in the legislature were invited. The procedure proved satisfactory to everyone concerned. If it had desired to do so, Parliament as a whole would have had many opportunities to take a stand differing from that represented by the Government's policy. By means of interpellations, it could have considered any questions it liked, and it could have overthrown the Government by a vote of lack of confidence. Nothing of the sort happened, however. If Parliament was disregarded, its members could blame nobody but themselves.

In any case, dissatisfaction with the Government's policy became great enough so that the opposition could appear publicly. On August 20, 1943, President Ryti received a letter signed by thirty-three citizens which was soon published abroad and afterwards in Finland also. The letter voiced anxiety over the deterioration of the general political situation of the country, stated that Finnish war objectives had been achieved when the territories lost in the Moscow peace were regained, expressed anxiety over the continued deterioration of relations with the United States, and ended with a demand for action which would take Finland out of the war and would secure, by means of negotiations, the country's freedom, independence and peace.

This letter marked the beginning of the opposition which played a considerable part in the final phases of the war. One can still argue the necessity of the letter of the thirty-three and whether its signers, a considerable number of whom were members of the Parliament, should not have had recourse to regular parliamentary procedures. Sending the letter for publication abroad was certainly no service to the country. The same can probably be said about the peace feelers which certain Finns travelling abroad made on their own responsibility, over the Government's head and without its knowledge, for they could easily be interpreted to mean that Finland was ready for peace on any terms that might be offered.

In contrast to the letter of the thirty-three, the statement of the Social Democrat party council on November 8, 1943, was clear and dignified. The peace program it proposed indicated that the crumbling of the home front did not extend to vital matters:

> The people of Finland have wanted to live in peace. In spite of that desire, the country has twice been drawn into war during the present world conflict. We hope that peace will return as soon as possible and that our country can withdraw from the war. The prerequisite, however, is a peace that will guarantee our country's freedom and independence. We cannot bargain with these. Surrender to the mercy of a foreign Power is out of the question. We hope also that when the war once ends and the fate of nations is decided, it will take place in an atmosphere in which the rights of small nations are respected and their right to live in freedom and independence will be guaranteed.

7. Armistice Negotiations, Winter and Spring of 1944

How difficult it was to reach a point where negotiations with Russia could begin is shown by the peace offensive to which Finland was subjected in the winter of 1943-1944.

On November 13, 1943, the Soviet Minister to Stockholm, Mme. Kollontay, had a conversation with the chief of the chancery of the Swedish Ministry for Foreign Affairs, Mr. Boheman, who expressed the opinion that Finland was prepared to withdraw from the war. Mme. Kollontay reported this to her Government and was advised to continue the conversations. At their next meeting, on November 20, 1943, Mme. Kollontay expressed Moscow's hope that Boheman would forward the following note to the Finnish government:

> 1. If Finland is prepared to discuss peace, her representative would be welcomed in Moscow.
>
> 2. Before that, however, the Soviet Union must have a statement of Finland's observations and proposals. It would be important to keep the

statement brief and general, and territories which had not belonged to Finland should not be demanded. The answer should be friendly and should in no event close the door to further conversations. If an understanding is reached, the peace itself can be worked out later.

3. Moscow has no intention of making Finland a province or of violating Finnish independence, unless forced to do so by future Finnish policy. Absolute secrecy regarding the negotiations is important.

Kollontay herself added that Tanner as a member of the Finnish government was like a red rag in Russia's face, and that she would gladly discuss Finland's answer before it was sent to Moscow.

When this proposal, in connection with which Sweden gave hopes of food supplies, was discussed in Government's Committee on Foreign Affairs on November 26-27, it was decided to pursue the offer and develop it to the utmost through conversations in Stockholm, in order to find out whether this path might lead to official discussions. After this had become clear, the matter would be communicated to the Parliament and Germany. The basis for negotiations, it was felt, should be the boundaries of the Dorpat Peace of 1920—that is, the boundaries of 1939—which might be modified in some respects. Russia would be given no Finnish bases, and Finnish sovereignty would have to be guaranteed. Tanner offered to resign from the Government, but the offer was not accepted because it was feared it would lead to disunity within the Social Democrat party.

When Boheman delivered this answer to Mme. Kollontay, she declared it would not satisfy the Soviet government. The future boundaries should in any case be the boundaries of the Moscow peace of March, 1940. Other matters could be discussed later.

On December 29 the Committee on Foreign Affairs of the Government was of the opinion that for reasons of internal politics and foreign relations peace could not be made on this basis, but that conversations should be continued. The answer, approved on January 1, 1944, expressed the hope that conversations would continue, but declared that Finland could not surrender cities and areas vital to her economy, and requested information of Russia's attitude regarding other problems connected with the peace. Lastly, Finland gave assurance that she would do nothing to endanger future negotiations. When the Swedish Foreign Minister, Günther, communicated this reply to Mme. Kollontay, she refused to telegraph it to Moscow in that form and suggested that the wording be modified so as to read that Finland was anxious about the fate of Viipuri.

The conversations seemed to come to a dead end, for no clarification of Russia's peace terms had been received. The question therefore was raised of sending someone to Stockholm or directly to Moscow to ascertain what Russia really wanted.

The pause in negotiations which now followed was abundantly filled by a propaganda war which was so extensive and effective that there must have been a unified plan behind it. Russian airplanes bombed Helsinki on February 6. On January 30, the United States chargé d'affaires, Gullion, delivered a note to the Government, and on February 8 Cordell Hull gave it to the press. In it Finland was advised, in order to secure peace, to take the first step to approach Russia, and the hope was expressed that that having been done, the United States' good offices could help toward a successful solution of the problem. Finland was simultaneously warned through the newspapers that new Soviet military and diplomatic pressure against Finland was to be expected. No support for Finland would be forthcoming from the United States since "it is impossible to close one's eyes to the fact that the present conflict is a World War, in which no separate war or conflict can be acknowledged to exist, and during which nothing must be allowed to obscure the objective which is victory over Germany and Japan." The English and Swedish press joined in this propaganda attack.

After lengthy discussions, the Government sent Paasikivi to Stockholm on February 12. On the 16th he met Mme. Kollontay who announced that Moscow was prepared to receive a Finnish delegation. Russian airplanes seconded the invitation, as it were, by a heavy air raid on Helsinki on the same day, and Germany's Minister Blücher joined the concert by announcing that Germany would consider it downright treachery if Finland made peace, and that Germany would "draw her own conclusions" therefrom.

After meeting Mme. Kollontay on two more occasions, Paasikivi returned to Helsinki on February 19 with the Russian armistice terms. This remarkable document was divided into two sections:

I. Terms to be accepted immediately:

1. The Soviet Union does not demand that Finland declare war on Germany, but naturally Finland must sever all relations with Germany. If Finland wants to remain neutral, she cannot allow the soldiers of a foreign power to remain within her borders. She must at least intern them. If this task is too difficult for Finland, the Soviet Union is ready to give the necessary support with airplanes and armed forces.

2. Restoration of the 1940 peace treaty. Withdrawal of Finnish forces to the 1940 boundary.

3. The immediate return of Russian prisoners and other Soviet citizens in internment camps and in labor service.

II. Questions which should be discussed:

4. Negotiations involving partial or total demobilization, to be conducted at Moscow.

5. Questions of reparations for damage caused by Finnish military operations and by the conquest of Soviet territory.

6. The question of Petsamo.

The first impression of the Government was that it was physically impossible to carry out some of the terms, such as internment of the Germans, for example. Furthermore, it was uncertain whether the nation would accept the Government's approval of these terms. In any case, it was considered that the question had now developed to the point where it should be submitted to Parliament. Russia speeded the decision with an air raid, the worst to date, on Helsinki on February 26. Mme. Kollontay, on the 27th, also tried to hurry the question along and suggested that the Finnish delegation fly to Moscow.

A report of the negotiations and the armistice terms was given to Parliament in secret session on February 29. Although the terms were harsh, and although they could not be accepted in the form proposed by Russia, the Government did not want to ignore any possibility for continuing discussions that might clarify the problem. The Government, therefore, proposed to Parliament that attempts to seek a peace for Finland on the most advantageous terms possible be continued. A parliamentary majority, 105 to 80, voted to approve the Government's decision and estimate of the situation. The minority of 80 also approved, but with the specific notation that "the terms mentioned in the report are in certain respects impossible to accept; if possibilities appear for us to withdraw from the war with guaranties of our independence, freedom and safety, the Government is to consider and report them to the Parliament." The difference of opinion between the majority and minority was thus only on the question of form.

Having received the Parliament's support, the Government prepared a reply on March 2, altered it slightly on the 6th at the suggestion of the Swedish Foreign Minister, and delivered it on the 8th to Mme. Kollontay. It stated that Finland seriously desired the reestablishment of peace between Finland and Russia, and with that in mind, had carefully weighed the armistice terms which had been received, and proposed that Finland be given an opportunity to present her views regarding the questions connected with the terms; in particular, the question of the German forces in Finland was complicated and required careful consideration and discussion. The Government of Finland thus tried to reach the stage of negotiations without first accepting the preliminary terms.

The Russian reply was given on the 10th of March. It stated that the Finnish answer was completely unsatisfactory, because the Russian terms were "obvious minimum terms," and only after their approval would it be possible to discuss the ending of hostilities. The terms were to be approved by the 18th.

Meanwhile, energetic and varied efforts to influence the attitude of the Government and public opinion continued. The King of Sweden, through his Foreign Minister, expressed the hope to President Ryti, Marshal Mannerheim and the Government, that the contact which Finland now had established with the Soviet Union not be severed. This statement was also brought to the attention of the parliamentary Foreign Affairs Committee and the members of the Parliament. On the 11th, the Stockholm *Morgon-Tidningen* published a London report to the effect that the Government of the United States had announced, through its representative, that it would break off relations with Finland unless the Finns reached an agreement with Russia under which Finland would withdraw from the war. On the 13th the American chargé d'affaires, Gullion, did deliver a memorandum, but it contained only the statement that the United States was informed of Finland's negotiations with the Soviet Union and that she had no reason to change her attitude which had been communicated to Finland on January 30. In a press conference on the 13th, Secretary of State Cordell Hull explained that the United States had received no information indicating that Finland had rejected the Russian terms. He stated that the United States government and people hoped that the negotiations between Finland and Russia would lead to Finland's withdrawing from her military alliance with Germany. On the 16th, President Roosevelt stated that it had seemed strange to him and America that Finland cooperated with Nazi Germany. He felt he was speaking on behalf of all Americans when he hoped that Finland would take advantage of the opportunity to free herself from that cooperation.

In this situation it was naturally important for the Government to obtain complete clarity regarding Finland's military prospects. The

Commander-in-Chief's reply was simply: "If Russia wants to drive into Finland, she is able to do it." The general situation had in fact radically changed: the siege of Leningrad had been broken and Russian forces had crossed the Narva River on March 1.

In a secret session of the Parliament on the 14th, Premier Linkomies explained the proposal made to Russia and Russia's reply. Because the Russian government had not approved Finland's moderate request to begin negotiations before acceptance of the terms, a refusal should be given to the demands:

> We are asked to accept in advance, before discussion, not only what is clear to everyone and which deeply concerns the nation's existence, but also other terms, about the contents of which we know nothing definite, but to which, nevertheless, we are asked to agree in advance. Before Finland will submit to such demands, she will continue her fight against odds, placing her faith in that which has given her courage during these years: the justice of her cause and the purity of her escutcheon.

On the next day, after debating the question, the Parliament gave the Government its vote of confidence. Although several members criticized the Government's undertakings, no one considered the armistice terms that had been offered to be an alternative preferable to a continuation of the war.

Having again received the support of the Parliament, the Government in its reply to the Soviet Union on March 17 emphasized how vital it would have been for the Finnish Parliament to receive more detailed information regarding the interpretation of the various clauses of the terms, as well as regarding their factual content:

> The Finnish government regrets that the Soviet Union did not consider it possible to give Finland an opportunity to present her views on these various questions, and that negotiations have been declared possible only after the Finnish government has accepted the Russian terms. The Finnish government, which earnestly continues to seek to establish peaceful relations, and hopes that negotiations will be begun, cannot, however, accept in advance the terms in question, which deeply affect the existence of the nation, without even knowing definitely their content and meaning.

As a result of this reply Russia urged through an intermediary on March 19-20 that the Finnish government "send one or two delegated to obtain from the Soviet Union an explanation of the armistice terms proposed by Russia." On the 21st, shortly before Russia did the same, the Finnish government released a communique on the progress of the negotiations to date and decided to send two men to Russia:

> Since it has been claimed in certain quarters that Russia's original terms have been modified in some respects, and many sources have assured that a favorable modification of terms was possible, it is important that all this be clarified.

The decision was kept secret from Germany, but Minister Blücher probably received some hints of it and inquired about the matter. The occupation of Hungary, which had just then been carried out, indicated what could be expected from Germany. On the 25th, the Finnish delegates, Ministers Paasikivi and Enckell, left for Moscow.

Immediately after the session of the Parliament on March 14, the Swedish press and Finnish groups influenced by it began to claim that the Finnish government's interpretation of the armistice terms was not correct, and that the Parliament had been misled in that it had not even been informed that Russian circles in Stockholm had given the terms a moderate interpretation. Presumably the Russian Legation in Stockholm had hoped that Moscow's interpretation also would be moderate. The truth turned out to be exactly the reverse: while there was no reason to speak of any scaling down of the terms, there was every reason to speak of harsher terms.

The Finnish delegates met the Commissar for Foreign Affairs Molotov and his aide, Dekanosov, on March 27 and 29. At first, after Molotov had asked if the Finns had come only to receive an interpretation of the terms, or to conclude definite agreements, the discussion turned to the question of the delegates' powers. Paasikivi explained that their authority included the question of the interpretation of the armistice or peace terms, and that they were empowered to present their own points of view regarding an armistice or a final peace, but gave them no authority to conclude a treaty which rested with the Government. Enckell, however, declared that their authority did not extend beyond their representing the powers that be in Finland, and that they could only express their own personal views. This statement surprised Molotov, naturally enough. Regarding the terms themselves, Molotov stated that he considered the most important point to be the severance of relations with Germany and the internment of the Germans. Toward the close of the conversations, he added as an alternative, the ousting of the Germans from Finland within a specified time. The Finns, on the other hand, felt that an adjustment of the 1940 boundaries was the most important matter, and explained that after such adjustment, everything else could be settled satisfactorily. Russia did not agree to scale down the terms she had proposed, except concerning Hanko, regarding which the statement was made that shortening the time during which the lease would run, and reducing the size of the leased area, could be discussed. As for reparations, there was talk only of the theoretical aspects of the problem, but the Finns made no comment on its magnitude except that the amount was "quite terrifying." Molotov explained that the terms presented were minimum demands, and he said several times that they were in a sense a punishment for the fact that Finland had been at war with Russia three times in the course of twenty-five years, and he also repeatedly remarked that Russia had power enough to impose any terms she wanted. At the conclusion of the conversations Molotov gave the Finns the armistice terms in the following final form:

1. Severance of relations with Germany, and either internment or ousting of German forces and vessels in Finland by the end of April at the latest.[3] In either case, Russia could lend Finland military aid.

2. Restoration of the Russo-Finnish treaty of 1940, and withdrawal of Finnish forces to the 1940 boundary, to be completed by several stages during April.

3. Immediate return of Allied and Russian prisoners-of-war, as well as civilians, whether interned or employed by the Finns; if peace instead of armistice is concluded, the return of prisoners-of-war to be mutual.

4. A fifty per cent demobilization of the Finnish army, to be completed by the end of May, and reduction of the entire Finnish army to a peace-time footing during June and July. (To be included in the agreement, or to be made into a separate agreement to be signed simultaneously with the peace or armistice.)

5. For damages caused by Finnish military operations and occupation of Russian areas, reparations to the amount of 600,000,000 American dollars to be paid in five years in commodities (paper, cellulose, ships, various machinery and installations).

6. The return to Russia of Petsamo and the Petsamo region, which Russia voluntarily turned over to Finland in the peace treaties of 1920 and 1940.

[3] The ousting of the Germans was thus to be accomplished in less than a month. After the signing of the armistice in September, 1944, Finland undertook the task of getting rid of the Germans still in the country. The hard fighting that then began lasted till April of 1945 and resulted in the complete devastation by the Germans of nearly all of the northern third of Finland (Ed.).

7. Insofar as Finland approves the above six conditions, Russia will consider it possible to relinquish her lease of Hanko and the surrounding area without any compensation.

After the Finnish delegates returned home on April 1 and reported the demands they had received, the first impression of the Government again was that acceptance was impossible because the terms could not possibly be fulfilled. It was impossible, for example, to intern or expel the Germans in the time specified because the Finnish troops and supplies needed to do the job would first have to be transported from distant fronts to North Finland (where the German troops were); and in the meantime, Finnish demobilization was also supposed to be carried out. When economists were consulted regarding the possibility of fulfilling the reparations demands, it was discovered they could not be met. Thus Professor Br. Suviranta showed that reparations would require the output of forty-five per cent of a maximum possible production of the whole nation over a five year period, which in concrete terms would mean that the Finns would have to learn to live without eating. Professor A. Montgomery declared that the annual reparations would amount to 5,500 million marks (in terms of pre-war value), while the surplus of Finland's foreign balance of payments in 1938 had only been 410 million, and in 1934, when it was the highest, 1,570 million. War-impoverished Finland would have been forced to restrict her imports to almost nothing, which again would have made the payment of reparations absolutely impossible. With this in mind, the Government unanimously decided that the terms could not be accepted.

Premier Linkomies reported these terms to a secret session of the Parliament on April 12, analyzed their contents, and concluded:

> Having considered these terms as a whole, the Government has unanimously reached the conclusion that they are impossible to accept. In reaching this decision the Government has not been influenced by any hope of unexpected political or military changes in the general situation. The Government has not permitted itself any illusions of a change in world policy favorable to Finland. It has discussed these terms objectively and realistically. The Government feels that the acceptance of these terms would expose our freedom and independence to the greatest possible threat, and that it is surely better to choose the alternative which, in the future, offers at least a possibility of saving that which would certainly be lost now by an acceptance of these terms. While no one can say that events will take such a turn that we shall get better terms in the future, the fear that future developments will prove

unfavorable cannot lead us now to accept terms which will destroy the life of our nation.

Parliament gave the Government a unanimous vote of confidence, and on April 18 the Government, having thus been supported, presented its reply to Russia. The reply stated that the proposed terms had been considered by the Government and Parliament:

> This consideration disclosed that the acceptance of these terms, which in part cannot be carried out for purely technical reasons, would actually weaken and destroy the possibilities for Finland to exist as an independent nation and, experts agree, would place a burden on the Finns which is far beyond their ability to bear.
>
> The Finnish government, which earnestly desires the return of peaceful relations and lasting good relations with its eastern neighbor, regrets that the terms now proposed, which it has carefully considered, do not offer possibilities for the achieving of this goal.

On April 22, the Soviet government briefly announced that it had been informed that the Finnish government had rejected the Russian armistice terms as a basis for negotiations and had ended the armistice negotiations. On the same day Vyshinsky gave his Government's report of the final phase of the negotiations, and Finland released her official communique on the 24th.

The publication of the Russian terms sufficed to weaken the propaganda campaign against Finland. It became very difficult to convince anyone that Russia had been moderate in her demands and procedures. Pressure on the part of the United States, for example, decreased for a time, but no change occurred in the general attitude toward Finland. On May 11, when the Allies urged the "Axis satellites" to withdraw from the war, Finland was classified among the satellites, although up to this time she had been considered a "borderline case."

Although the Soviet government had terminated the negotiations, it let it be known in a roundabout way that negotiations would still be possible. Minister Tanner, therefore, while attending the Swedish Social Democrat party council in Stockholm, took up the matter on May 19 with a friend who had contacts with the Soviet Legation. He stated that since the Russian terms were impossible to accept, it was not worth while for Finland to make counter-proposals; a wholly new basis for negotiations should be found, and the negotiations should be carried out privately. Tanner declared his readiness for such a procedure and requested his friend to arrange a contact with Counsellor of the Legation Semyonov. The latter, however, received a negative reply from Moscow, based on the contention that the Soviet Union had decided to refrain from having anything to do with Finland's present Government, and this decision could not be changed because the Soviet government could not meet as a result of its members' presence at the front.

Hitler for his part exerted pressure by sending the Finnish Commander-in-Chief a letter at the end of May, deploring Finland's undertaking negotiations for peace, and announcing that he could not supply Finland with a single weapon until he received assurances that they would be effectively used. Germany's dissatisfaction also became obvious in the failure to send grain to Finland in June as specified in the German-Finnish trade treaty.

In the beginning of the summer of 1944, therefore, Finland was in a worse position than before. The general situation became ever more threatening, in degree as the Germans retreated in the Baltic countries, and no political support for Finland came from anywhere. The Finnish army continued to hold its earlier previous positions. For the time being, that was the only concrete point of support of Finland.

8. The June Offensive and the Ribbentrop Pact

In the spring of 1944 there was every reason to expect a major Red Army attack against Finland. The military as well as the political situation made it necessary to expect it, and ample observations of preparations for it were made at the front. Future research in military history will explain why that attack was not halted more successfully than it was. In all probability, everyone was responsible. The progress of military events themselves showed that there had been great weaknesses in the general planning of the Finns. For example, too much confidence had been placed in the strength of the German siege of Leningrad, and when it cracked, decisions demanded by the changed situation were not made speedily enough. It also seems obvious that the tremendous development which had taken place elsewhere had not been matched in Finland. The Red Army in the summer of 1944 was not the same as in the summer of 1941. Technically, in particular, it was on an entirely different level. The morale of the Finnish army, on the other hand, was no longer the same as it had been in 1941, and the two and a half years of *sitzkrieg*,

with furloughs, garrison details, and recreations, had deteriorated the
morale of the troops. All hopes which had been pinned on the army's
ability to repel an attack, and on the depth of the areas for delaying
operations, were only partly justified. However, it must be taken
into consideration that at the crucial parts of the front, the Finnish
army was faced by an overwhelming superiority of force. Against
this background it becomes understandable that the Red Army offensive on the Karelian Isthmus, begun on June 9, reached Viipuri
already on June 20. The High Command naturally had speedily to
withdraw the forces from Eastern Karelia as well, and even that
withdrawal unfortunately was not carried out completely according
to plan.

The loss of the main line of defense and the enemy's speedy advance forced the Government to take into consideration the possibility of a catastrophe, and to take steps either to bolster the front
with German aid, or to make peace. The Commander-in-Chief demanded speedy action.

On June 15 the Government leaders came to the decision that in
view of the fact that the Russian attitude scarcely offered the present
Finnish government any chance to succeed in making peace, a new
government should be formed. At first the Commander-in-Chief,
Mannerheim, was considered for the post of Premier, with the expectation he would later become President, and then General Walden,
but both refused. Finally Ramsay undertook to form a new government, but then word came that Russia would agree to peace negotiations even with the old government. The resignation of the
Government could therefore be postponed. Abroad, Finland's position was obviously considered hopeless. One indication of this probably was the action of the United States in expelling the Finnish
Minister and three other Legation officials without giving any concrete or personal reason, and justifying the action on the grounds
that they had allegedly engaged in activities inimical to the United
States.

After ten days of the Red Army offensive, the military situation
began to look a little brighter, and the High Command began to
consider another alternative, believing that six or eight German
divisions would suffice to reestablish the balance on the Finnish front.
The German Minister had immediately promised eighty airplanes
which could speedily be brought up from the Baltic countries, and
other aid as well.

The Finnish government, however, felt it would be safest to try to get peace. First, however, it was essential to find out if Russia preferred to negotiate with the present government or a new one. With this purpose in mind, a representative of the Foreign Office went to Stockholm on June 22, to announce to the Soviet Legation, through Mr. Boheman, that Finland was prepared to end the war and sever her relations with Germany. At the same time he inquired about the peace terms. On the same day the Finnish government received word that the German Foreign Minister, Ribbentrop, was to arrive in Helsinki. It was easy to guess in advance that the visit was connected with Finland's peace problem.

On the following day, the 23rd, a reply was received from Stockholm. It stated that Russia was ready to conclude peace but that Finland must first surrender. And in Helsinki Ribbentrop delivered long speeches demanding a "clearly defined attitude" and Finland's remaining in the war alongside Germany to the very end, threatening that otherwise Hitler would have to decide if aid to Finland would have to be stopped immediately. It was also reported that one German division was already on its way from the Baltic area to Finland. However, some government members still opposed the granting of the commitment that Germany demanded, and proposed that one more attempt should be made to get more acceptable terms from Russia.

There were thus two alternatives. The first was to accept German aid which the High Command recommended. The second was to continue the attempt to get peace which the President supported. A condition for the receipt of German aid, however, was the much-talked-about political agreement, which the President felt he could not sign without the consent of Parliament. The United States chargé d'affaires, who somehow had found out about Ribbentrop's proposal, informed the Finnish Foreign Minister that the acceptance of the proposal would mean "definite conclusions," as far as the United States was concerned. On the 26th, when a decision had to be made one way or the other, the Commander-in-Chief told the President that since the Army needed supplies, the agreement with Germany ought to be made. The President, therefore, changed his former stand: in view of the fact that the front could not hold without military assistance, the agreement with Germany would have to be made. It was by no means certain, however, that the Parliament would approve the agreement. Nor would it have been wise for the

Parliament to give its consent, for parliamentary consent would have meant that the pact would remain in force, regardless of possible changes of governments. The President, therefore, announced that he was prepared to conclude the pact on his own responsibility. On the basis of two expert judicial opinions, such a procedure could be considered in accordance with the law.

Thus President Ryti concluded the agreement in the form of a personal letter to the Reich Chancellor, without any countersignatures. The letter stated:

> Referring to conversations which have taken place, I want to express my satisfaction that Germany intends to fulfill the wishes of the Finnish government, concerning military assistance, and that, taking into consideration the Russian offensive in Karelia, Germany will immediately aid the Finnish armed forces by sending German troops and materiel. I have also noted that you have given your promise in the name of the Reich to give Finland all possible aid in the future, in order to defeat, together with Finnish forces, the Russian attack against Finland. In this connection I beg to assure you that Finland has decided to wage war side by side with Germany until the danger which threatens Finland from Russia is removed.
>
> Taking into consideration the aid to a comrade-in-arms which Germany is giving to Finland in her present difficult situation, I declare that as the President of Finland I shall not make peace with the Soviet Union except in agreement with the German Reich, and will not permit the Government of Finland, appointed by me, or any other persons, to take steps toward negotiations concerning peace, or any negotiations that might serve that end, except in agreement with the German Reich.

When this letter was read in the meeting of the Government, a minority which included the Social Democrats and a member of the Progressive Party, opposed the proposal and were of the opinion that it should be submitted to the Parliament.

In the official communique issued on June 28 in regard to Ribbentrop's visit, the result of the negotiations was noted briefly:

> During the course of this visit matters concerning Finland and Germany were discussed, and in particular, the hope expressed by the Finnish government of receiving military assistance. Germany has declared she is prepared to fulfill this request of the Finnish government . . .
>
> In all matters between the Government of Finland and that of Germany, a complete meeting of minds was achieved.

The Social Democrat members of the Government having opposed the agreement, the question of their resignation from the Government now arose. When the question was considered at the party's parliamentary group meeting, Minister Tanner's statement at least partly influenced the decision: "If you want to do us a personal service, you must request our withdrawal from the Government, but if you want to do a service to the country, you will suggest that we remain in the Cabinet." Tanner meant by this that it would be easier to render the Ribbentrop agreement harmless as members of the Government. The meeting voted 36 to 26 for the proposal that the Socialist members remain in the Cabinet. Thus the Ribbentrop agreement resulted in no Cabinet crisis. The Social Democrat parliamentary group issued a statement on July 1, which outlined the party's stand and declared that the party had advised its representatives to remain in the Government for the time being:

> A resignation from the Government could easily have been misinterpreted. The defense of our country against the danger threatening it is the most important responsibility at this time and must be supported by all classes.

The United States government took the step which had been long anticipated and dreaded. On June 30 the American chargé d'affaires, Gullion, called on the Minister for Foreign Affairs, Ramsay, to inform him that his Government had decided to end diplomatic relations with Finland.

When the real nature and extent of Germany's military assistance became revealed, it was soon realized that it could not be long depended upon. Material assistance had been relatively generous and it had helped to stop the Red advance, but of manpower only one under-manned infantry division and one Panzer brigade had been sent. After the middle of July, the German air force was withdrawn from the Finnish front, and at the end of the month the infantry also began to withdraw. In this situation, the first task of the political leadership of Finland was to free itself from the political agreement made with Germany in June. This could only be done by changing the country's President and Cabinet. Now it became clear how advantageous for the country, but disadvantageous for himself, President Ryti's decision to make an agreement with Germany on his personal responsibility had been. On a visit to the Army Headquarters the President succeeded in arranging a "gentleman's agreement" whereby he would resign and the Commander-in-Chief,

General Mannerheim, would become his successor. The President's resignation took place on August 1, and the Premier carried on the duties of the President until the election of the new president. The Parliament elected Mannerheim on August 5 and the new President requested A. Hackzell to form a new government, which was appointed on the 8th. The primary task of the new government was to establish peace with the Soviet Union.

CHAPTER 8

THE ARMISTICE AND THE MOSCOW
PRELIMINARY PEACE

1. THE ARMISTICE OF SEPTEMBER 4, 1944

The last act of the Finnish tragedy can be presented very briefly and with little documentation because full details would only throw light on the actions of Finland's opponents but would hardly clarify the prerequisites of the decisions that Finland herself made. When the curtain rose on this final act, there were only a few alternatives to choose from. Finland's surrender still offered great advantages to the Soviet Union: the divisions thus released from the Finnish front were needed elsewhere, in order that when Germany collapsed, as large areas as possible could be occupied; the free exit of Russia's Baltic fleet from the Gulf of Finland was also important, so that Russia's control of the Baltic could be secured.

In his radio address of September 2, 1944, to the Finnish nation, outlining the procedure approved by the Parliament for the reestablishment of peace between Finland and Russia, the new Premier, A. Hackzell, first outlined the unexpectedly unfavorable changes in the military situation which had taken place since the previous April and which had made a revaluation of the situation necessary. Along their own frontier, the Finns had succeeded in halting the enemy's attack after serious losses of territory, but the developments of the World War in general had left Finland more isolated than ever. During the month of August Germany herself had become so hard pressed that no aid was to be expected from her. In the West she was about to lose occupied France, and in Italy she had only the northern portion in her possession. Russia had regained her 1940 boundaries almost everywhere, and in some sections had advanced beyond them. Germany's ally, Rumania, had surrendered on August 27, and on August 29 Bulgaria had declared her intention to seek neutrality. Neither Finland nor Germany could gain real advantage from continuing their former cooperation. The political agreement made with Germany and under German pressure, born out of the necessity of repelling the offensive in June, was no longer valid after

the change in the presidency, because ex-President Ryti had made
it in his own name and it did not correspond in form to the requirements which the constitution specifies for agreements with foreign
nations. When Marshal Keitel visited President Mannerheim on
August 17, this point had been clearly brought to the knowledge of
the German government.

It is obvious that the same compulsion which had hitherto marked
the path Finland had followed, now again directed the actions of the
new government when it delivered a note, on August 25, to the Russian Minister in Stockholm asking if the Soviet government would
be willing to receive a Finnish delegation to negotiate for an armistice or peace or both. The reply which the Finnish Minister in
Stockholm received on the 29th set forth two preliminary conditions
which the Finnish government was to fulfill before Russia would
be prepared to accept a Finnish delegation: it must publicly declare
that it was severing relations with Germany, and it must demand
that the Germans withdraw their forces from Finnish territory within
two weeks after the date when the Finnish government accepted the
preliminary conditions and in any case by September 15. It was
stated that these conditions were made in the name of Great Britain
also and that they had been approved by the Government of the
United States.

In a secret session of Parliament on September 2, Premier Hackzell presented the Government's view that the preliminary conditions
should be accepted in order that negotiations for an armistice or peace
could be begun. Of the 155 members present, 108 supported the
Government while 45 felt that no guaranties existed that the action
proposed by the Government would lead to a peace which would assure the country's independence, and consequently should not be
taken.

An armistice was obtained on September 4 for the period of the
negotiations, on the basis of the military situation at the moment of
the signing of the armistice. This armistice agreement was unique
in that the Finns were to cease hostilities on September 4, but the
Russians not until September 5. This unchivalrous arrangement
caused considerable Finnish casualties at some sections of the front
which could hardly have given pleasure to any honorable soldier.
The armistice now made was, however, more advantageous and honorable for Finland than the terms previously offered, in that negotiations could be begun without formal surrender, and that the Germans
were given a specific time limit within which to leave Finland, even

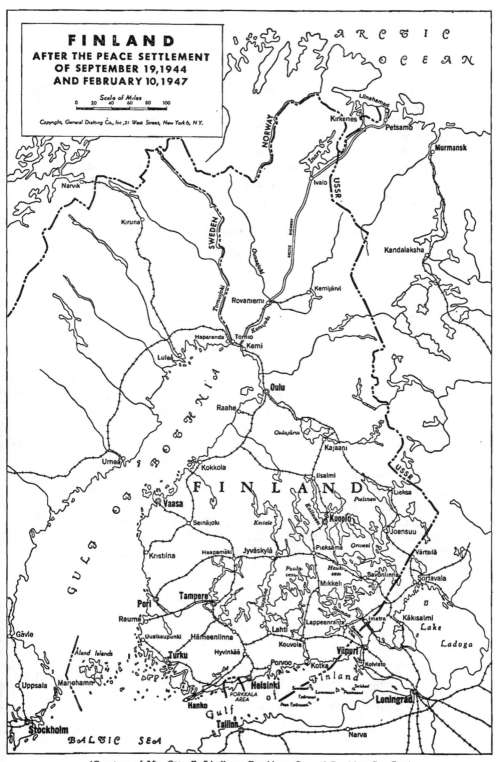

(Courtesy of Mr. Otto G. Lindberg, President, General Drafting Co., Inc.)

though the time had intentionally been made so short that it was impossible to fulfill it in respect to the German forces in northern Finland. When the Germans were requested, on September 2, to remove their forces and no longer use Finnish territory for German military objectives, the Finnish government naturally realized that even with the best will in the world the request could not be met in the time set, but it had reason to believe that the Germans would not intentionally make difficulties since they would gain no advantages thereby.

2. The Preliminary Peace, September 19, 1944[1]

The Finnish delegation, headed by Premier Hackzell, left for Moscow on September 6. The Soviet government had other more urgent matters to deal with just then, and the first discussion was not until the 14th. No negotiations were actually necessary, since the Soviet Union could not be persuaded to change any of the conditions it had set. The preliminary peace agreement was therefore not the result of negotiations. It was a dictated arrangement based on the "right" of the stronger party. On the evening of the 18th Molotov, without permitting any argument to refute him, presented numerous charges against the "bloody and criminal" Government of Finland, and demanded the signing of the preliminary peace agreement by noon of the following day at the latest. He threatened that if this were not done, all of Finland would be occupied by Russia, and hinted that the occupation was already being prepared. The Government, therefore, had at once to obtain from the Parliament the authority for the delegation in Moscow to sign the terms which Russia had dictated. The Parliament was alerted for a secret session at six o'clock in the morning. Sixty-eight representatives out of the total of 200 were unable to arrive in time for the session. The legislature felt that it could do nothing except approve unanimously the Government's suggestion that the necessary powers be granted.

The preliminary peace, signed in Moscow on September 19, is an unusual document in many respects. Immediately after it had been signed, Acting Premier Ernst von Born gave an estimate of it to the Finnish people over the radio. His interpretation revealed that the Government had fully realized that the terms were very close to that limit where the possibility of national existence becomes doubtful.

It is unnecessary here to explain and analyze the details of the

---

[1] See below, Appendix A, pp. 189-200.

document, but a few remarks on their application and implications are not out of place.

When Acting Premier von Born explained the agreement just signed, he considered the following especially worthy of note. First, he mentioned the provision that the withdrawal of the Finnish forces to the 1940 boundary was to begin immediately and that "Finnish Karelia is thus lost, and our hopes that at least the worst economic wrongs caused by this boundary would be corrected have not been fulfilled." Furthermore, Finland had to cede Petsamo and lease the Porkkala peninsula, and also to turn over to the Russians the airports in southern and southwestern Finland for the duration of the war. The Premier felt also that the responsibility of disarming the German forces in Finland, and at the same time, speedily to reduce Finland's own army to a peace-time footing, was a particularly serious matter. Finally von Born emphasized the disastrous consequences, for Finnish peace-time conditions, of the reparations obligation amounting to 300,000,000 American dollars in gold to be paid in goods within six years, which was proportionately heavier than any reparations imposed on any country after the first World War.

Later developments have shown that many provisions of the agreement which von Born did not mention in his discourse, have become more ominous in their implications than those he discussed, and even the points he did outline have been found to involve more than was at first assumed. For example, Finland's responsibility to wipe out all "fascist-minded political, military and semi-militaristic" organizations made it possible (since "fascism" is a term which can be stretched to whatever limits may be considered necessary) to compel Finland to abolish the national guard, which is the cornerstone of the nation's entire defense system, and such voluntary organizations doing social work as the Lotta Svärd and the Veterans' League which have had nothing whatever to do with either Hitlerism or fascism. Finland's obligation to place "war criminals" on trial and to return prisoners-of-war and Russian citizens evacuated to Finland, was not reciprocal. This has made it possible to commit all sorts of crimes against the Finns, without punishment, and has resulted in only a small portion of Finnish prisoners-of-war returning from Russia, half dead from hunger and maltreatment.

The reparations claims, on the other hand, have been hoisted extremely high by means of a supplementary agreement dictated by Russia. It provides that the goods delivered by Finland on the reparations account are valued at 1938 prices, increased by ten or fifteen per cent, and it completely ignores the fact that the present prices of the commodities in question are much higher. Since much of the raw materials for producing the goods that must be delivered to Russia have to be imported, the prompt delivery of such commodities depends on factors which Finland cannot control. Such factors, however, are not taken into consideration in the agreement which specifies a five per cent monthly penalty (in goods) for failure to deliver on time. The Control Commission, in which England is represented in name only, has become the real government of Finland, and the legal government is only its executive arm. Thus, after the armistice, the Soviet Union has repeatedly presented new economic and political demands, just as she did in 1940-1941. Many of these demands are such that if they are met, they endanger the execution of the reparations agreement itself.

Some of the armistice terms have not yet been fully put into effect. For example, the Porkkala area leased to Russia might become, in the hands of the Soviet, the starting point for a whole series of new surprises. That area has been extended by Russia so far inland that one of Finland's most important railroads has been cut, and Helsinki placed within Soviet artillery range. It is ironic that the Soviet Union, which attacked Finland in the name of the security of Leningrad, having gained a free hand, now threatens the security of the capital of its small neighbor, and indeed the national security of that neighbor.

CHAPTER 9

CONCLUSION

Finland lost the war and by the terms imposed on her in 1940 and 1944 she was branded as a war criminal. More than that, the September, 1944, armistice saddled the country with a servitude (slavery would be a better word) that forces the nation's standard of living to the lowest possible level. The reparations obligation is such that it can probably be met only with the aid of the outside world.

The question naturally arises, Is the alleged "war guilt" of Finland such as to justify the punishment meted out to her? The answer is clear and obvious.

Finland's foreign policy before the outbreak of war in 1939 was a policy of strict neutrality. This meant unqualified refusal to become a party to any big Power set-up either by means of direct or masked alliances or commitments, and, as has been noted, an equally firm determination to observe strict and impartial neutrality toward every nation that would become embroiled in war. This neutrality was as absolute with respect, say, to Germany as to Russia. It was fully in keeping with the vital interests of a small nation whose only concern was to remain independent and free from all big Power entanglements.

When Russia proceeded, in the autumn of 1939, to demand that Finland cede parts of her territory to the Soviet Union, the demands were considered wholly unreasonable. They were rejected because the Finns did not want to give up territory to which Russia had no justifiable claim whatever. The Russian contention that territory should be ceded because Leningrad's security demanded it was considered equally unjustified, for Finland did not, in fact, threaten the safety of Leningrad or of any other part of the U.S.S.R. If Finland is branded as a "war criminal," the only possible justification lies in the understandable desire of the republic to protect its territory and to stay clear of the conflict of the great Powers.

The course of the war after June, 1941, definitely proved that Russian seizure of Finnish territory after the Winter War did not add to the security of the Soviet Union. The Kremlin, it was seen, had been guilty of a grave error in interpreting the geographical factors and the military-political situation in general. The fact is that no great Power attack against the Soviet Union can lead through Finland. Because of this fact, and despite the pressure exerted on Finland in the winter of 1940, Finland could not accept the aid offered by Britain and France at the time. Also, as soon as the south coast of the Gulf of Finland fell into German hands in 1941, the Russians at once were forced to abandon Hanko, nor were the islands in the Gulf of Finland of any use in the defense of Leningrad. The undeniable fact is that even after Finland got involved in the war in June, 1941, the only direction from which Leningrad was not threatened was from the direction of Finland. If Russia had had sense enough to honor her treaty obligations and had allowed Finland to remain neutral, Russia would have gained great advantages. In the event that Germany had violated the neutrality of the Finns, they would have resisted. Thus Finnish-Russian military cooperation might well have been spontaneously born. The prerequisite of military cooperation would have involved only one reasonable condition: that Russia was willing to treat her small neighbor in a fair and considerate manner.

After Finland had been drawn into the war—against her will—the primary aim of her military effort was to prevent the country from becoming a theater of war and from being occupied by Russia. The objective was, in other words, the same as in 1939; and the same consideration had led to the acceptance of the harsh peace terms of March, 1940, and the decision not to accept the British and French military assistance which had been offered. For the same reason, the German offer of help was accepted in 1941 when the country was again threatened; for the same reason, the military operations in 1941 were pushed as far beyond Finland's own borders as possible; and for the same reason, President Ryti concluded, in a moment of extreme and pressing need, the political agreement of June, 1944, with Germany which had been consistently avoided up to that time.

Finally, the attempt to keep the country from becoming a theater of war in 1944 compelled the acceptance of the terms of the second (preliminary) peace dictated by Russia in September of that year. To have submitted earlier would not have saved the country, for so long as Germany occupied and controlled the southern coast of the Gulf of Finland and had military forces in various parts of Finland, she could have seized the country as she seized Hungary, or she could have devastated a large part of it. This in fact turned out to be the case when the Finns proceeded to oust the Germans. The under-

taking meant heavy fighting from September, 1944 to April, 1945—
a period during which the Finns were de facto cobelligerents of the
United Nations—and resulted in the Germans' laying waste nearly
all of the northern third of the country.

The course Finland followed after June, 1941, was dictated by
necessity. At each turn of events an attempt was made to avoid the
danger that seemed most threatening at the moment. Judged from
the point of view of the great Powers, such a policy may seem to have
been very shortsighted. A small nation, however, is compelled to
follow such a policy for the simple reason that a given danger which
holds no serious threat to a large nation, may be great enough to
threaten a small nation with catastrophe. In other words, in a world
of great Power aggression, lesser states are forced to contend with
difficulties which compel them to improvise solutions and defensive
measures. In the case of Finland, it is easy to be wise after the event
and to maintain that, in order to avoid a given disaster that threatened, Finland should have acted thus and so. But to merit serious
consideration, such a claim resting on hindsight must be able to prove
that groping for a detour around a given disaster which did occur
would not have led to an unavoidable new and even greater disaster.
And that is something that cannot be proven, hindsight notwithstanding. Only disregard of fact and loose handling of the truth—
both appropriate to politics but not to serious investigation—can lead
to any other conclusion.

Mistakes no doubt were made in Finnish foreign policy. It has
been claimed that the policy was too pig-headed and did not take advantage of the favorable opportunities that came its way. But it can
be asserted that this charge, insofar as it applies at all, holds true only
of questions of secondary importance that did not affect the general
course of policy. And whatever mistakes were made were understandable and defensible. Basically they resulted from Finland's
desire to retain her own territory to which no other nation had the
slightest right. Nor did any part of that territory constitute any
kind of threat to the U.S.S.R. This was so before 1939 and after
and the fact that Russia succeeded in taking large parts of Finland by
force in no way changes the truth of this assertion.

Finland's "war guilt" thus does not grow out of situations or
actions Finland herself deliberately willed. It rests on no more secure basis than the geographical location of the country as a neighbor
of a great Power determined to expand at the expense of others.
And more important, it grew in part from the fact that Finland is

small. Being small, she did not have the resources to resist aggression without help from the outside. Reasons such as these, however, have never sufficed in the past to force civilized men to deny sympathy and good will to the small and the defenseless. Nor do they suffice to rob Finland of the right to her own territories which the hard labor of countless generations has wrested from the wilderness and made fit for the life of civilized man.

Finland's involvement in the war also resulted in part from the fact that the nation continued too long to cherish and embrace ways of looking at things which were not adapted to the age of ruthless aggression and total war. Finland's ideals were the ideals and principles of the nineteenth century which recognized the rights of nationalities and the rights of even small nations. Finland's specific guilt—if guilt there was—lay in not having understood the new age of imperialism which, in its gamble for high stakes, makes use of the mask of democracy and justice but recognizes only the rights of the strong, and which values only strategic considerations and honors agreements solemnly made only so long as direct advantage can be gained thereby. It can safely be left to the future to decide whether Finland has reason to be ashamed of having tried to follow the principles of honor and honesty in her policies. Finland has been compelled because she was defeated in war, to accept in silence the charge that she is guilty of having begun the war but that acceptance, obtained only under the duress of a blackmailer, will not be seriously considered by the ultimate judgment of history.

Finland felt herself to be a very small factor in the gigantic conflict of the war years and did not attempt to influence the outcome of the larger contest. The result was that hesitation and incompleteness of a kind came to characterize Finland's war against Russia. In 1940, the nation hesitated to commit itself to an all-out war by accepting the military aid then offered by Great Britain and France, for to accept the aid would have irrevocably drawn Finland into the World War. In 1941 the Finnish army brilliantly attained the limited goals which had been set for it by its own command. The Finns consistently refused, despite German pressure, to attack Leningrad or to cut the Murmansk railroad, and this at a time when Finland's weight might perhaps have sufficed to decide which way the balance would turn. In thus acting in accordance with the wishes of the West, Finland received no promises of any services in return or any guaranty that the restraint shown would not later be used to her own disadvantage. An official of the United States Department of State summarized the policy of Finland quite correctly in September, 1943, as follows:

> Tactically, Finland has played her cards badly and has not received the thanks of the West, of the Soviet Union or of Germany. An example of this was Finland's refusal to take part in the offensives demanded by Germany. Finland stayed put but failed to give the western Powers any advance guaranties of her stand.

In total war, such a half-and-half attitude is not allowed. In Finland's case, the result of failure to adopt all-out aggression is seen in the armistice terms of September, 1944.

Finland's splendid fight for her territory and rights now seems quite futile and all her sacrifices wasted. But even now, while the country is suffering the consequences of military defeat—a defeat that resulted not from being in the wrong but from being too small— one positive result of the fight to remain independent stands clearly revealed. Finland has proven to the whole world that she wants to remain a free nation. That is a fact that cannot be ignored or erased from the record. Not even an era when "voluntary" national elections can yield whatever electoral results dictatorship may desire, and peoples can be forced to accept any kind of "national" and "democratic" government that the needs of a dictator require, will suffice to obscure this basic fact.

In presenting her case, Finland can appeal only to justice and not to force. A time may yet come when justice and not force will formulate the final verdict. When that time comes the Soviet government, whether as now constituted or possibly changed, will realize and admit that Russia has profoundly wronged her small neighbor and that the wrong must be righted by returning to its rightful owner the areas—of little value to Russia but vital to Finland—that the Soviet Union took by force in 1940 and 1944.

APPENDIX A

ARMISTICE AGREEMENT

Between the Union of Soviet Socialist Republics and the United Kingdom of Great Britain and Northern Ireland, on the one hand, and Finland on the other.

Whereas the Finnish Government has accepted the preliminary condition of the Soviet Government regarding a break with Germany and the removal of German troops from Finland, and whereas the conclusion of a future treaty of peace will be facilitated by the inclusion in an Armistice Agreement of certain conditions of this peace treaty, the Government of the Union of Soviet Socialist Republics and His Majesty's Government in the United Kingdom of Great Britain and Northern Ireland, acting on behalf of all the United Nations at war with Finland, on the one hand, and the Government of Finland, on the other hand, have decided to conclude the present agreement for an armistice, the execution of which will be controlled by the Soviet High Command similarly acting on behalf of the United Nations at war with Finland, hereinafter named the Allied (Soviet) High Command.

On the basis of the foregoing the representative of the Allied (Soviet) High Command, Colonel-General A. A. Zhdanov, and the representatives of the Government of Finland, Mr. Carl Enckell, Minister of Foreign Affairs, General Rudolf Walden, Minister of Defence, General Erik Heinrichs, Chief of General Staff, and Lieutenant-General Oscar Enckell, duly authorised thereto, have signed the following conditions :—

Article 1.

In connexion with the cessation of military activities on the part of Finland on the 4th September, 1944, and on the part of the Soviet Union on the 5th September, 1944, Finland undertakes to withdraw her troops behind the line of the Soviet-Finnish frontier of 1940, in accordance with the procedure laid down in the Annex attached to the present Agreement. (See Annex to Article 1.)

Article 2.

Finland undertakes to disarm the German land, naval and air armed forces which have remained in Finland since the 15th September, 1944, and to hand over their personnel to the Allied (Soviet) High Command as prisoners of war, in which task the Soviet Government will assist the Finnish army.

The Finnish Government also accepts the obligation to intern German and Hungarian nationals in Finnish territory. (See Annex to Article 2.)

Article 3.

Finland undertakes to make available at the request of the Allied (Soviet) High Command the aerodromes on the southern and south-western coast of Finland with all equipment to serve as bases for Soviet aircraft during the period necessary for air operations against German forces in Estonia and against the German navy in the northern part of the Baltic Sea. (See Annex to Article 3.)

Article 4.

Finland undertakes to place her army on a peace footing within two and a half months from the day of signing of the present Agreement. (See Annex to Article 4.)

Article 5.

Finland, having broken off all relations with Germany, also undertakes to break off all relations with Germany's satellite States. (See Annex to Article 5.)

Article 6.

The effect of the Peace Treaty between the Soviet Union and Finland, concluded in Moscow on the 12th of March, 1940, is restored subject to the changes which follow from the present Agreement.

Article 7.

Finland returns to the Soviet Union the oblast of Petsamo (Pechenga), voluntarily ceded to Finland by the Soviet State in accordance with the Peace Treaties of the 14th October, 1920, and the 12th March, 1940, within the boundary indicated in the Annex and on the map attached to the present Agreement. (See Annex to Article 7 and map to scale 1 :500,000.)

Article 8.

The Soviet Union renounces its rights to the lease of the Peninsula of Hangö, accorded to it by the Soviet-Finnish Peace Treaty of 12th

March, 1940, and Finland for her part undertakes to make available to the Soviet Union on lease territory and waters for the establishment of a Soviet naval base in the area of Porkkala-Udd.

The boundaries of the land and water area of the base at Porkkala-Udd are defined in the Annex to the present article and indicated on the map. (See Annex to Article 8 and map to scale 1 :100,000.)

Article 9.

The effect of the Agreement concerning the Aaland Islands, concluded between the Soviet Union and Finland on the 11th October, 1940, is completely restored.

Article 10.

Finland undertakes immediately to transfer to the Allied (Soviet) High Command to be returned to their homeland all Soviet and Allied prisoners of war now in her power and also Soviet and Allied nationals who have been interned in or deported by force to Finland.

From the moment of the signing of the present Agreement and up to the time of repatriation Finland undertakes to provide at her cost for all Soviet and Allied prisoners of war and also nationals who have been deported by force or interned adequate food, clothing and medical service in accordance with hygienic requirements, and also with means of transport for their return to their homeland.

At the same time Finnish prisoners of war and interned persons now located on the territory of Allied States will be transferred to Finland.

Article 11.

Losses caused by Finland to the Soviet Union by military operations and the occupation of Soviet territory will be indemnified by Finland to the Soviet Union to the amount of three hundred million dollars payable over six years, in commodities (timber products, paper, cellulose, sea-going and river craft, sundry machinery).

Provision will also be made for the indemnification in the future by Finland of the losses caused during the war to the property of the other Allied States and their nationals in Finland, the amount of the compensation to be fixed separately. (See Annex to Article 11.)

Article 12.

Finland undertakes to restore all legal rights and interests of the United Nations and their nationals located on Finnish territory as they existed before the war and to return their property in complete good order.

Article 13.

Finland undertakes to collaborate with the Allied powers in the apprehension of persons accused of war crimes and in their trial.

Article 14.

Finland undertakes within the periods fixed by the Allied (Soviet) High Command to return to the Soviet Union in complete good order all valuables and materials removed from Soviet territory to Finland during the war belonging to State, public and cooperative organisations, factories, institutions or individual citizens, such as: equipment for factories and works, locomotives, railway carriages, ships, tractors, motor vehicles, historical monuments, valuables from museums and all other property.

Article 15.

Finland undertakes to transfer as booty to the disposition of the Allied (Soviet) High Command all war material of Germany and her satellites located on Finnish territory, including naval and other ships belonging to these countries in Finnish waters.

Article 16.

Finland undertakes not to permit the export or expropriation of any form of property (including valuables and currency), belonging to Germany or Hungary or to their nationals or to persons resident in their territories or in the territories occupied by them without the permission of the Allied (Soviet) High Command.

Article 17.

Finnish merchant ships other than those already under Allied control shall be placed under the control of the Allied (Soviet) High Command for their use in the general interests of the Allies.

Article 18.

Finland undertakes to transfer to the Allied (Soviet) High Command all ships in Finnish ports belonging to the United Nations, no matter at whose disposal these vessels may be, for the use of the Allied (Soviet) High Command for the duration of the war against Germany in the general interest of the Allies, these vessels subsequently to be returned to their owners.

Article 19.

Finland will make available such materials and products as may be required by the United Nations for purposes connected with the war.

Article 20.

Finland undertakes immediately to release all persons, irrespective of citizenship or nationality, held in prison on account of their activities in favour of the United Nations or because of their sympathies with the cause of the United Nations, or in view of their racial origin, and will also remove all discriminatory legislation and disabilities arising therefrom.

Article 21.

Finland undertakes immediately to dissolve all pro-Hitler organisations (of a Fascist type) situated on Finnish territory, whether political, military or para-military, as well as other organisations conducting propaganda hostile to the United Nations, in particular to the Soviet Union, and will not in future permit the existence of organisations of that nature.

Article 22.

An allied Control Commission will be established which until the conclusion of peace with Finland will undertake the regulation and control of the execution of the present Agreement under the general direction and instructions of the Allied (Soviet) High Command, acting on behalf of the Allied powers. (See Annex to Article 22.)

Article 23.

The present Agreement comes into force as from the moment of signature.

Done in Moscow the nineteenth day of September, 1944, in one copy which will be entrusted to the safekeeping of the Government of the Union of Soviet Socialist Republics, in the Russian, English and Finnish languages, the Russian and English texts being authentic.

Certified copies of the present Agreement, with Annexes and maps, will be transmitted by the Government of the Union of Soviet Socialist Republics to each of the other Governments on whose behalf the present Agreement is being signed.   For
the Governments of the the Union of Soviet Socialist Republics and the United Kingdom

A. Zhdanov
For
the Government of Finland
C. Enckell
R. Walden
E. Heinrichs
O. Enckell

ANNEXES

To the armistice agreement between the Union of Soviet Socialist Republics and the United Kingdom of Great Britain and Northern Ireland on the one hand and Finland on the other, signed in Moscow on the 19th September, 1944.

A. Annex to Article 1.

The procedure for the withdrawal of Finnish troops behind the line of the State frontier between the U.S.S.R. and Finland laid down in the Peace Treaty of the 12th March, 1940, subject to the modifications arising from the Armistice Agreement signed on the 19th September, 1944, on all sectors occupied by Finnish troops, shall be as follows :——

1. In the course of the first day as from the moment of signing of the Armistice Agreement Finnish troops shall be withdrawn to such a distance that there shall be a gap of not less than one kilometre between the forward units of the Red Army and the Finnish troops.

2. Within forty-eight hours (two days), counted as from the same moment, the Finnish troops shall make passages through their mines, barbed wire, and other defences to a width of not less than thirty metres in order thereby to make possible the free movement of battalion columns with their transport, and shall also enclose the remaining mine fields within clearly visible marks.

The above-mentioned passages in the defences and the enclosure of mine fields shall be made throughout the whole territory from which Finnish troops are withdrawn.

The clearance of passages by Finnish troops shall be made on all roads or paths which may serve for movement both in the neutral belt of one kilometre and also throughout the whole depth of the defences.

Towards the end of the second day the Command of the Finnish troops shall hand over to the appropriate Red Army Command exact plans of all types of defences with an indication on these plans of the passages made and to be made by the Finnish troops and also of the enclosures of all mine fields.

3. The Finnish Command shall hand over within a period of five days to the Command of the Red Army and Navy the charts, forms and descriptive maps at its disposal with legends for all mine fields and other defences on land, in rivers, and lakes and in the Baltic and Barents Seas together with data about the courses and channels to be recommended and the rules for navigation along them.

4. The complete removal of mines, barbed wire and other defences throughout the territory from the line occupied by the advanced Finnish units to the line of the State frontier, and also the sweeping and the removal of all defences from the channels on the approaches to Soviet territories, shall be made by the Finnish land and naval forces in the shortest possible time and in not more than forty days from the moment of the signing of the Armistice Agreement.

5. The withdrawal of Finnish troops behind the state frontier and the advance of the troops of the Red Army up to it shall begin as from 9.0 a.m. on the 21st September, 1944, simultaneously along the whole length of the front.

The withdrawal of Finnish troops shall be carried out in daily marches of not less than 15 kilometres a day and the advance of the troops of the Red Army shall take place in such a manner that there shall be a distance of 15 kilometres between the rear units of the Finnish troops and the advanced units of the Red Army.

6. In accordance with paragraph 5 the following limits are set for the withdrawal of Finnish troops on individual sectors behind the line of the State frontier.

On the sector Vuokinsalmi, Riihimäki the 1st October
On the sector Riihimäki, River Koitajoki the 3rd October
On the sector River Koitajoki, Korpiselkä the 24th September
On the sector Korpiselkä, Lake Puhajärvi the 28th September
On the sector Puhajärvi, Koitsanlahti the 26th September
On the sector Koitsanlahti, Station Enso the 28th September
On the sector Station Enso, Virolahti the 24th September.

The retreating Finnish troops shall take with them only such reserves of munitions, food, fodder and fuel and lubricants as they can carry and transport with them. All other stores shall be left on the spot and shall be handed over to the Command of the Red Army.

7. The Finnish Military Command shall hand over on the territories which are being returned or ceded to the Soviet Union in complete good order and repair all inhabited points, means of communication, defence and economic structures including: bridges, dams, aerodromes, barracks, warehouses, railway junctions, station buildings, industrial enterprises,

hydrotechnical buildings, ports and wharves, telegraph offices, telephone exchanges, electric power stations, lines of communication and electric power lines.

The Finnish Military Command shall give instructions for the timely demining of all the installations enumerated above which are to be handed over.

8. When the Finnish troops are being withdrawn behind the line of the State frontier the Government of Finland shall guarantee the personal inviolability and the preservation of the dwelling places of the population of the territory to be abandoned by the Finnish troops together with the preservation of all the property belonging to this population and of the property of public, co-operative, cultural-social services and other organisations.

9. All questions which may arise in connexion with the transfer by the Finnish authorities of the installations enumerated in paragraph 7 of this Annex shall be settled on the spot by representatives of both sides, for which purpose special representatives for the period of the withdrawal of the troops shall be appointed by the Command to each basic route for the movements of the troops of both armies.

10. The advance of Soviet troops to the line of the State frontier on the sectors occupied by German troops shall be made in accordance with the instructions of the Command of the Soviet forces.

B. Annex to Article 2.

1. The Finnish Military Command shall hand over to the Allied (Soviet) High Command within a period fixed by the latter all the information at its disposal regarding the German armed forces and the plans of the German military Command for the development of military operations against the Union of Soviet Socialist Republics and the other United Nations and also the charts and maps and all operations documents relating to the military operations of the German armed forces.

2. The Finnish Government shall instruct its appropriate authorities regularly to supply the Allied (Soviet) High Command with meteorological information.

C. Annex to Article 3.

1. In accordance with Article 3 of the Agreement the Allied (Soviet) High Command will indicate to the Finnish Military Command which aerodromes must be placed at the disposal of the Allied (Soviet) High Command and what equipment must remain on the aerodromes and

equally will lay down the manner in which these aerodromes are to be used.

The Finnish Government shall enable the Soviet Union to make use of the railways, waterways, roads and air routes necessary for the transport of personnel and freight despatched from the Soviet Union to the areas where the abovementioned aerodromes are situated.

2. Henceforth until the end of the war against Germany Allied naval vessels and merchant ships shall have the right to make use of the territorial waters, ports, wharves, and anchorages of Finland. The Finnish Government shall afford the necessary collaboration as regards material and technical services.

D. Annex to Article 4.

1. In accordance with Article 4 of the Agreement the Finnish Military Command shall immediately make available to the Allied (Soviet) High Command full information regarding the composition, armament and location of all the land, sea and air forces of Finland and shall come to an agreement with the Allied (Soviet) High Command regarding the manner or placing the Finnish Army on a peace footing within the period fixed by the Agreement.

2. All Finnish naval vessels, merchant ships and aircraft for the period of the war against Germany must be returned to their bases, ports and aerodromes and must not leave them without obtaining the requisite permission to do so from the Allied (Soviet) High Command.

E. Annex to Article 5.

1. By the rupture referred to in Article 5 of the Agreement by Finland of all relations with Germany and her satellites is meant the rupture of all diplomatic, consular and other relations and also of postal, telegraphic and telephone communications between Finland and Germany and Hungary.

2. The Finnish Government undertakes in future until such time as the withdrawal of German troops from Finland is completed to discontinue postal diplomatic communications and also any radiotelegraphic or telegraphic cypher correspondence and telephone communications with foreign countries by diplomatic missions and consulates located in Finland.

F. Annex to Article 7.

The line of the state frontier between the Union of Soviet Socialist Republics and Finland, in connexion with the return by Finland to the

Soviet Union of the oblast of Petsamo (Pechenga), shall proceed as follows:

From the boundary post No. 859/90 (Korvatunturi), near the Lake Yauriyarvi, the line of the State frontier shall be fixed in a North-westerly direction along the former Russian-Finnish boundary by boundary posts Nos. 91, 92 and 93 to the boundary post No. 94, where formerly the frontiers of Russia, Norway and Finland met.

Thence the line of the frontier shall run in a general North-easterly direction along the former Russian-Norwegian State frontier to Varanger-Fjord (see the attached Russian map, scale 1:500,000).

The line of the frontier, fixed from the boundary post No. 859/90 (Korvatunturi), to the boundary post No. 94, will be demarcated on the spot by a Soviet-Finnish Mixed Commission.

The Commission will establish boundary signs, will make a detailed description of this line and will enter it on a map of the scale of 1:25,000.

The Commission will begin its work on a date to be specified by the Soviet Military Command.

The description of the boundary line and the map of this line made by the abovementioned Commission shall be confirmed by both Governments.

G. Annex to Article 8.

The boundary line of the area of Porkkala-Udd leased by the Union of Soviet Socialist Republics from Finland shall begin at a point of which the map references are: latitude 59° 50′ North; longitude 24° 07′ East. Thence the boundary line shall proceed North along the meridian 24° 07′ to a point of which the map references are: latitude 60° 06′ 12″ North; longitude 24° 07′ East. Thence the boundary line shall proceed along the line indicated in the map in a Northerly direction to a point of which the map references are: latitude 60° 08′ 6″ North; longitude 24° 07′ 36″ East.

Thence the boundary line shall proceed along the line indicated on the map in a general North-easterly by Easterly direction to a point of which the map references are: latitude 60° 10′ 24″ North; longitude 24° 34′ 6″ East. Thence along the line indicated on the map along the bay of Espon-Lahti, and further East of the islands of Smuholmarne, Björken, Medvaste, Heg-holm and Stur-Hamn-holm to a point of which the map references are: latitude 60° 02′ 54″ North; longitude 24° 37′ 42″ East, and thence the boundary line shall proceed South along the meridian 24° 37′ 42″ to the outer boundaries of Finnish territorial waters. (See the map, scale 1:100,000 attached to the present Agreement.)

The boundary line of the leased area of Porkkala-Udd will be demarcated on the spot by a Soviet-Finnish Mixed Commission. The Commission shall establish boundary marks and shall draw up a detailed description of this line and shall enter it upon a topographical map scale 1 :20,000 and a naval map scale 1 :50,000.

The Commission shall begin its work on a date to be specified by the Soviet Naval Command.

The description of the boundary line of the leased area and the map of that line prepared by the abovementioned Commission shall be confirmed by both Governments.

2. In accordance with Article 8 of the Agreement the territory and waters in the area of Porkkala-Udd shall be transferred by Finland to the Soviet Union within ten days from the moment of signature of the Armistice Agreement for the organisation of a Soviet naval base on lease, to be used and controlled for a period of fifty years, the Soviet Union making an annual payment of five million Finnish marks.

3. The Finnish Government undertakes to enable the Soviet Union to make use of the railways, waterways, roads and air routes necessary for the transport of personnel and freight despatched from the Soviet Union to the naval base at Porkkala-Udd.

The Finnish Government shall grant to the Soviet Union the right of unimpeded use of all forms of communication between the U.S.S.R. and the territory leased in the area of Porkkala-Udd.

H. Annex to Article 11.

1. The precise nomenclature and varieties of commodities to be delivered by Finland to the Soviet Union in accordance with Article 11 of the Agreement and also the more precise periods for making these deliveries each year shall be defined in a special agreement between the two Governments.

As the basis for accounts regarding the payment of the indemnity foreseen in Article 11 of the Agreement the American dollar is to be used at its gold parity on the day of signature of the Agreement, i.e. thirty-five dollars to one ounce of gold.

I. Annex to Article 22.

1. The Allied Control Commission is an organ of the Allied (Soviet) High Command to which it is directly subordinated. The Control Commission will be the liaison link between the Allied (Soviet) High Command and the Finnish Government, through which Government the Commission will carry on all its relations with the Finnish authorities.

2. The chief task of the Control Commission is to see to the punctual and accurate fulfilment by the Finnish Government of Articles 2, 3, 4, 10, 12, 13, 14, 15, 16, 17, 18, 20 and 21 of the Armistice Agreement.

3. The Control Commission shall have the right to receive from the Finnish authorities all the information which it requires for the fulfilment of the abovementioned task.

4. In the event of the discovery of any violation of the abovementioned Articles of the Armistice Agreement the Control Commission shall make appropriate representations to the Finnish authorities in order that proper steps may be taken.

5. The Control Commission may establish special organs or sections entrusting them respectively with the execution of various tasks.

Moreover the Control Commission may through its officers make the necessary investigations and the collection of the information which it requires.

6. The Control Commission shall be established in Helsingfors.

7. The members of the Control Commission and equally its officers shall have the right to visit without let or hindrance any institution, enterprise or port and to receive there all the information necessary for their functions.

8. The Control Commission shall enjoy all diplomatic privileges, including inviolability of person, property and archives, and it shall have the right of communication by means of cypher and diplomatic courier.

9. The Control Commission shall have at its disposal a number of aircraft for the use of which the Finnish authorities shall grant all the necessary facilities.

APPENDIX B

TREATY OF PEACE WITH FINLAND

[Signed in Paris, February 10, 1947]

The Union of Soviet Socialist Republics, the United Kingdom of Great Britain and Northern Ireland, Australia, the Byelorussian Soviet Socialist Republic, Canada, Czechoslovakia, India, New Zealand, the Ukrainian Soviet Socialist Republic, and the Union of South Africa, as the States which are at war with Finland and actively waged war against the European enemy states with substantial military forces, hereinafter referred to as "the Allied and Associated Powers," of the one part, and Finland, of the other part;

Whereas Finland, having become an ally of Hitlerite Germany and having participated on her side in the war against the Union of Soviet Socialist Republics, the United Kingdom and other United Nations, bears her share of responsibility for this war;

Whereas, however, Finland on September 4, 1944, entirely ceased military operations against the Union of Soviet Socialist Republics, withdrew from the war against the United Nations, broke off relations with Germany and her satellites, and, having concluded on September 19, 1944, an Armistice with the Governments of the Union of Soviet Socialist Republics and the United Kingdom, acting on behalf of the United Nations at war with Finland, loyally carried out the Armistice terms; and

Whereas the Allied and Associated Powers and Finland are desirous of concluding a treaty of peace which, conforming to the principles of justice, will settle questions still outstanding as a result of the events hereinbefore recited and will form the basis of friendly relations between them, thereby enabling the Allied and Associated Powers to support Finland's application to become a member of the United Nations and also to adhere to any Convention concluded under the auspices of the United Nations;

Have therefore agreed to declare the cessation of the state of war and for this purpose to conclude the present Treaty of Peace, and have accordingly appointed the undersigned Plenipotentiaries who after presentation of their full powers, found in good and due form, have agreed on the following provisions:

Part I

Territorial Clauses

Article 1

The frontiers of Finland, as shown on the map annexed to the present Treaty (Annex I), shall be those which existed on January 1, 1941, except as provided in the following Article.

Article 2

In accordance with the Armistice Agreement of September 19, 1944, Finland confirms the return to the Soviet Union of the province of Petsamo (Pechenga) voluntarily ceded to Finland by the Soviet State under the Peace Treaties of October 14, 1920, and March 12, 1940. The frontiers of the province of Petsamo (Pechenga) are shown on the map annexed to the present Treaty (Annex I).

Part II

Political Clauses

Section I

Article 3

In accordance with the Armistice Agreement, the effect of the Peace Treaty between the Soviet Union and Finland concluded in Moscow on March 12, 1940, is restored, subject to the replacement of Articles 4, 5 and 6 of that Treaty by Articles 2 and 4 of the present Treaty.

Article 4

1. In accordance with the Armistice Agreement, the Soviet Union confirms the renunciation of its right to the lease of the Peninsula of Hangö, accorded to it by the Soviet-Finnish Peace Treaty of March 12, 1940, and Finland for her part confirms having granted to the Soviet Union on the basis of a fifty years lease at an annual rent payable by the Soviet Union of five million Finnish marks the use and administration of territory and waters for the establishment of a Soviet naval base in the area of Porkkala-Udd as shown on the map annexed to the present Treaty (Annex I).

2. Finland confirms having secured to the Soviet Union, in accordance with the Armistice Agreement, the use of the railways, waterways,

roads and air routes necessary for the transport of personnel and freight dispatched from the Soviet Union to the naval base at Porkkala-Udd, and also confirms having granted to the Soviet Union the right of unimpeded use of all forms of communication between the Soviet Union and the territory leased in the area of Porkkala-Udd.

Article 5

The Aaland Islands shall remain demilitarized in accordance with the situation as at present existing.

Section II

Article 6

Finland shall take all measures necessary to secure to all persons under Finnish jurisdiction, without distinction as to race, sex, language or religion, the enjoyment of human rights and of the fundamental freedoms, including freedom of expression, of press and publication, of religious worship, of political opinion and of public meeting.

Article 7

Finland, which in accordance with the Armistice Agreement has taken measures to set free, irrespective of citizenship and nationality, all persons held in confinement on acount of their activities in favor of or because of their sympathies with, the United Nations or because of their racial origin, and to repeal discriminatory legislation and restrictions imposed thereunder, shall complete these measures and shall in future not take any measures or enact any laws which would be incompatible with the purposes set forth in this Article.

Article 8

Finland, which in accordance with the Armistice Agreement has taken measures for dissolving all organisations of a Fascist type on Finnish territory, whether political, military or para-military, as well as other organisations conducting propaganda hostile to the Soviet Union or to any of the other United Nations, shall not permit in future the existence and activities of organisations of that nature which have as their aim denial to the people of their democratic rights.

Article 9

1. Finland shall take all necessary steps to ensure the apprehension and surrender for trial of:

(a) Persons accused of having committed, ordered or abetted war crimes and crimes against peace or humanity;

(b) Nationals of any Allied or Associated Power accused of having violated their national law by treason or collaboration with the enemy during the war.

2. At the request of the United Nations Government concerned, Finland shall likewise make available as witnesses persons within its jurisdiction, whose evidence is required for the trial of the persons referred to in paragraph 1 of this Article.

3. Any disagreement concerning the application of the provisions of paragraphs 1 and 2 of this Article shall be referred by any of the Governments concerned to the Heads of the Diplomatic Missions in Helsinki of the Soviet Union and the United Kingdom, who will reach agreement with regard to the difficulty.

Section III

Article 10

Finland undertakes to recognise the full force of the Treaties of Peace with Italy, Rumania, Bulgaria and Hungary and other agreements or arrangements which have been or will be reached by the Allied and Associated Powers in respect of Austria, Germany and Japan for the restoration of peace.

Article 11

Finland undertakes to accept any arrangements which have been or may be agreed for the liquidation of the League of Nations and the Permanent Court of International Justice.

Article 12

1. Each Allied or Associated Power will notify Finland, within a period of six months from the coming into force of the present Treaty, which of its pre-war bilateral treaties with Finland it desires to keep in force or revive. Any provisions not in conformity with the present Treaty shall, however, be deleted from the abovementioned treaties.

2. All such treaties so notified shall be registered with the Secretariat of the United Nations in accordance with Article 102 of the Charter of the United Nations.

3. All such treaties not so notified shall be regarded as abrogated.

PART III

MILITARY, NAVAL AND AIR CLAUSES

Article 13

The maintenance of land, sea and air armaments and fortifications shall be closely restricted to meeting tasks of an internal character and local defence of frontiers. In accordance with the foregoing, Finland is authorized to have armed forces consisting of not more than:

(a) A land army, including frontier troops and anti-aircraft artillery, with a total strength of 34,400 personnel;

(b) A navy with a personnel strength of 4,500 and a total tonnage of 10,000 tons;

(c) An airforce, including any naval air arm, of 60 aircraft, including reserves, with a total personnel strength of 3,000. Finland shall not possess or acquire any aircraft designed primarily as bombers with internal bomb-carrying facilities.

These strengths shall in each case include combat, service and overhead personnel.

Article 14

The personnel of the Finnish Army, Navy and Airforce in excess of the respective strengths permitted under Article 13 shall be disbanded within six months from the coming into force of the present Treaty.

Article 15

Personnel not included in the Finnish Army, Navy or Airforce shall not receive any form of military training, naval training or military air training as defined in Annex II.

Article 16

1. As from the coming into force of the present Treaty, Finland will be invited to join the Barents, Baltic and Black Sea Zone Board of the International Organisation for Mine Clearance of European Waters and shall maintain at the disposal of the Central Mine Clearance Board all Finnish minesweeping forces until the end of the post-war mine clearance period, as determined by the Central Board.

2. During this post-war mine clearance period, Finland may retain additional naval units employed only for the specific purpose of minesweeping over and above the tonnage permitted in Article 13.

Within two months of the end of the said period, such of these vessels as are on loan to the Finnish Navy from other Powers shall be returned to those Powers, and all other additional units shall be disarmed and converted to civilian use.

3. Finland is also authorized to employ 1,500 additional officers and men for minesweeping over and above the numbers permitted in Article 13. Two months after the completion of minesweeping by the Finnish Navy, the excess personnel shall be disbanded or absorbed within the numbers permitted in the said Article.

Article 17

Finland shall not possess, construct or experiment with any atomic weapon, any self-propelled or guided missiles or apparatus connected with their discharge (other than torpedoes and torpedo launching gear comprising the normal armament of naval vessels permitted by the present Treaty), sea mines or torpedoes of non-contact types actuated by influence mechanisms, torpedoes capable of being manned, submarines or other submersible craft, motor torpedo boats, or specialized types of assault craft.

Article 18

Finland shall not retain, produce or otherwise acquire, or maintain facilities for the manufacture of, war material in excess of that required for the maintenance of the armed forces permitted under Article 13 of the present Treaty.

Article 19

1. Excess war material of Allied origin shall be placed at the disposal of the Allied Power concerned according to the instructions given by that Power. Excess Finnish war material shall be placed at the disposal of the Governments of the Soviet Union and the United Kingdom. Finland shall renounce all rights to this material.

2. War material of German origin or design in excess of that required for the armed forces permitted under the present Treaty shall be placed at the disposal of the two Governments. Finland shall not acquire or manufacture any war material of German origin or design, or employ or train any technicians, including military and civil aviation personnel, who are or have been nationals of Germany.

3. Excess war material mentioned in paragraphs 1 and 2 of this Article shall be handed over or destroyed within one year from the coming into force of the present Treaty.

4. A definition and list of war material for the purposes of the present Treaty are contained in Annex III.

Article 20

Finland shall co-operate fully with the Allied and Associated Powers with a view to ensuring that Germany may not be able to take steps outside German territory toward rearmament.

Article 21

Finland shall not acquire or manufacture civil aircraft which are of German or Japanese design or which embody major assemblies of German or Japanese manufacture or design.

Article 22

Each of the military, naval and air clauses of the present Treaty shall remain in force until modified in whole or in part by agreement between the Allied and Associated Powers and Finland or, after Finland becomes a member of the United Nations, by agreement between the Security Council and Finland.

PART IV

REPARATION AND RESTITUTION

Article 23

1. Losses caused to the Soviet Union by military operations and by the occupation by Finland of Soviet territory shall be made good by Finland to the Soviet Union, but, taking into consideration that Finland has not only withdrawn from the war against the United Nations, but has also declared war on Germany and assisted with her forces in driving German troops out of Finland, the Parties agree that compensation for the above losses will be made by Finland not in full, but only in part, namely in the amount of $300,000,000 payable over eight years from September 19, 1944, in commodities (timber products, paper, cellulose, sea-going and river craft, sundry machinery, and other commodities).

2. The basis of calculation for the settlement provided in this article shall be the United States dollar at its gold parity on the day of the signing of the Armistice Agreement, i.e. $35 for one ounce of gold.

Article 24

Finland, in so far as she has not yet done so, undertakes within the time-limits indicated by the Government of the Soviet Union to return to the Soviet Union in complete good order all valuables and materials removed from its territory during the war, and belonging to State, public or co-operative organisations, enterprises or institutions or to individual citizens, such as: factory and works equipment, locomotives, rolling stock, tractors, motor vehicles, historic monuments, museum valuables and any other property.

Part V

Economic Clauses

Article 25

1. In so far as Finland has not already done so, Finland shall restore all legal rights and interests in Finland of the United Nations and their nationals as they existed on June 22, 1941, and shall return all property in Finland of the United Nations and their nationals as it now exists.

2. The Finnish Government undertakes that all property, rights and interests passing under this Article shall be restored free of all encumbrances and charges of any kind to which they may have become subject as a result of the war and without the imposition of any charges by the Finnish Government in connexion with their return. The Finnish Government shall nullify all measures, including seizures, sequestration or control, taken by it against United Nations property between June 22, 1941, and the coming into force of the present Treaty. In cases where the property has not been returned within six months from the coming into force of the present Treaty, application shall be made to the Finnish authorities not later than twelve months from the coming into force of the Treaty, except in cases in which the claimant is able to show that he could not file his application within this period.

3. The Finnish Government shall invalidate transfers involving property, rights and interests of any description belonging to United Nations nationals, where such transfers resulted from force or duress exerted by Axis Governments or their agencies during the war.

4. (a) The Finnish Government shall be responsible for the restoration to complete good order of the property returned to United Nations nationals under paragraph 1 of this Article. In cases where property cannot be returned or where, as a result of the war, a United Nations national has suffered a loss by reason of injury or damage to property in Finland, he shall receive from the Finnish Government compensation in Finnish marks to the extent of two thirds of the sum necessary, at the date of payment, to purchase similar property or to make good the loss

suffered. In no event shall United Nations nationals receive less favorable treatment with respect to compensation than that accorded to Finnish nationals.

(b) United Nations nationals who hold, directly or indirectly, ownership interests in corporations or associations which are not United Nations nationals within the meaning of paragraph 8 (a) of this Article, but which have suffered a loss by reason of injury or damage to property in Finland, shall receive compensation in accordance with sub-paragraph (a) above. This compensation shall be calculated on the basis of the total loss or damage suffered by the corporation or association and shall bear the same proportion to such loss or damage as the beneficial interests of such nationals in the corporation or association bear to the total capital thereof.

(c) Compensation shall be paid free of any levies, taxes or other charges. It shall be freely usable in Finland but shall be subject to the foreign exchange control regulations which may be in force in Finland from time to time.

(d) The Finnish Government shall accord to United Nations nationals the same treatment in the allocation of materials for the repair or rehabilitation of their property in Finland and in the allocation of foreign exchange for the importation of such materials as applies to Finnish nationals.

(e) The Finnish Government shall grant United Nations nationals an indemnity in Finnish marks at the same rate as provided in sub-paragraph (a) above to compensate them for the loss or damage due to special measures applied to their property during the war, and which were not applicable to Finnish property. This sub-paragraph does not apply to a loss of profit.

5. All reasonable expenses incurred in Finland in establishing claims, including the assessment of loss or damage, shall be borne by the Finnish Government.

6. United Nations nationals and their property shall be exempted from any exceptional taxes, levies or imposts imposed on their capital assets in Finland by the Finnish Government or any Finnish authority between the date of the Armistice and the coming into force of the present Treaty for the specific purpose of meeting charges arising out of the war or of meeting the costs of reparation payable to any of the United Nations. Any sums which have been so paid shall be refunded.

7. The owner of the property concerned and the Finnish Government may agree upon arrangements in lieu of the provisions of this Article.

8. As used in this Article:

(a) "United Nations nationals" means individuals who are nationals of any of the United Nations, or corporations or associations organised under the laws of any of the United Nations, at the coming into force of the present Treaty, provided that the said individuals, corporations or associations also had this status at the date of the Armistice with Finland.

The term "United Nations nationals" also includes all individuals, corporations or associations which, under the laws in force in Finland during the war, have been treated as enemy;

(b) "Owner" means the United Nations national, as defined in sub-paragraph (a) above, who is entitled to the property in question, and includes a successor of the owner, provided that the successor is also a United Nations national as defined in sub-paragraph (a). If the successor has purchased the property in its damaged state, the transferor shall retain his rights to compensation under this Article, without prejudice to obligations between the transferor and the purchaser under domestic law;

(c) "Property" means all movable or immovable property, whether tangible or intangible, including industrial, literary and artistic property, as well as all rights or interests of any kind in property.

Article 26

Finland recognises that the Soviet Union is entitled to all German assets in Finland transferred to the Soviet Union by the Control Council for Germany and undertakes to take all necessary measures to facilitate such transfers.

Article 27

In so far as any such rights were restricted on account of Finland's participation in the war on Germany's side, the rights of the Finnish Government and of any Finnish nationals, including juridical persons, relating to Finnish property or other Finnish assets on the territories of the Allied and Associated Powers shall be restored after the coming into force of the present Treaty.

Article 28

1. From the coming into force of the present Treaty, property in Germany of Finland and of Finnish nationals shall no longer be treated as enemy property and all restrictions based on such treatment shall be removed.

2. Identifiable property of Finland and of Finnish nationals removed by force or duress from Finnish territory to Germany by German forces or authorities after September 19, 1944, shall be eligible for restitution.

3. The restoration and restitution of Finnish property in Germany shall be effected in accordance with measures which will be determined by the Powers in occupation of Germany.

Article 29

1. Finland waives all claims of any description against the Allied and Associated Powers on behalf of the Finnish Government or Finnish nationals arising directly out of the war or out of actions taken because of the existence of a state of war in Europe after September 1, 1939, whether or not the Allied or Associated Power was at war with Finland at the time, including the following:

(a) Claims for losses or damages sustained as a consequence of acts of forces or authorities of Allied or Associated Powers;

(b) Claims arising from the presence, operations or actions of forces or authorities of Allied or Associated Powers in Finnish territory;

(c) Claims with respect to the decrees or orders of Prize Courts of Allied or Associated Powers, Finland agreeing to accept as valid and binding all decrees and orders of such Prize Courts on or after September 1, 1939, concerning Finnish ships or Finnish goods or the payment of costs;

(d) Claims arising out of the exercise or purported exercise of belligerent rights.

2. The provisions of this Article shall bar, completely and finally, all claims of the nature referred to herein, which will be henceforward extinguished, whoever may be the parties in interest.

3. Finland likewise waives all claims of the nature covered by paragraph 1 of this Article on behalf of the Finnish Government or Finnish nationals against any of the United Nations whose diplomatic relations with Finland were broken off during the war and which took action in co-operation with the Allied and Associated Powers.

4. The waiver of claims by Finland under paragraph 1 of this Article includes any claims arising out of actions taken by any of the Allied and Associated Powers with respect to Finnish ships between September 1, 1939, and the coming into force of the present Treaty, as well as any claims and debts arising out of the Convention on prisoners of war now in force.

Article 30

1. Pending the conclusion of commercial treaties or agreements between individual United Nations and Finland, the Finnish Government shall, during a period of eighteen months from the coming into force of the present Treaty, grant the following treatment to each of the United Nations which, in fact, reciprocally grants similar treatment in like matters to Finland:

(a) In all that concerns duties and charges on importation or exportation, the internal taxation of imported goods and all regulations pertaining thereto, the United Nations shall be granted unconditional most-favoured-nation treatment;

(b) In all other respects, Finland shall make no arbitrary discrimination against goods originating in or destined for any territory of any of the United Nations as compared with like goods originating in or destined for territory of any other of the United Nations or of any other foreign country;

(c) United Nations nationals, including juridical persons, shall be granted national and most-favoured-nation treatment in all matters pertaining to commerce, industry, shipping and other forms of business activity within Finland. These provisions shall not apply to commercial aviation;

(d) Finland shall grant no exclusive or discriminatory right to any country with regard to the operation of commercial aircraft in international traffic, shall afford all the United Nations equality of opportunity in obtaining international commercial aviation rights in Finnish territory, including the right to land for refueling and repair, and, with regard to the operation of commercial aircraft in international traffic, shall grant on a reciprocal and non-discriminatory basis to all United Nations the right to fly over Finnish territory without landing. These provisions shall not affect the interests of the national defence of Finland.

2. The foregoing undertakings by Finland shall be understood to be subject to the exceptions customarily included in commercial treaties concluded by Finland before the war; and the provisions with respect to reciprocity granted by each of the United Nations shall be understood to be subject to the exceptions customarily included in the commercial treaties concluded by that State.

Article 31

1. Any disputes which may arise in connexion with Articles 24 and 25 and Annexes IV, V and VI, part B, of the present Treaty shall be

referred to a Conciliation Commission composed of an equal number of representatives of the United Nations Government concerned and of the Finnish Government. If agreement has not been reached within three months of the dispute having been referred to the Conciliation Commission, either Government may require the addition of a third member to the Commission, and, failing agreement between the two Governments on the selection of this member, the Secretary-General of the United Nations may be requested by either party to make the appointment.

2. The decision of the majority of the members of the Commission shall be the decision of the Commission and shall be accepted by the parties as definitive and binding.

Article 32

Articles 24, 25, 30 and Annex VI of the present Treaty shall apply to the Allied and Associated Powers and France and to those of the United Nations whose diplomatic relations with Finland have been broken off during the war.

Article 33

The provisions of Annexes IV, V and VI shall, as in the case of the other Annexes, have force and effect as integral parts of the present Treaty.

Part VI

Final Clauses

Article 34

1. For a period not to exceed eighteen months from the coming into force of the present Treaty, the Heads of the Diplomatic Missions in Helsinki of the Soviet Union and the United Kingdom, acting in concert, will represent the Allied and Associated Powers in dealing with the Finnish Government in all matters concerning the execution and interpretation of the present Treaty.

2. The Two Heads of Mission will give the Finnish Government such guidance, technical advice and clarification as may be necessary to ensure the rapid and efficient execution of the present Treaty both in letter and in spirit.

3. The Finnish Government shall afford the said Two Heads of Mission all necessary information and any assistance which they may require for the fulfilment of the tasks devolving on them under the present Treaty.

Article 35

1. Except where another procedure is specifically provided under any Article of the present Treaty, any dispute concerning the interpretation or execution of the Treaty, which is not settled by direct diplomatic negotiations, shall be referred to the Two Heads of Mission acting under Article 34, except that in this case the Heads of Mission will not be restricted by the time limit provided in that Article. Any such dispute not resolved by them within a period of two months shall, unless the parties to the dispute mutually agree upon another means of settlement, be referred at the request of either party to the dispute to a Commission composed of one representative of each party and a third member selected by mutual agreement of the two parties from nationals of a third country. Should the two parties fail to agree within a period of one month upon the appointment of the third member, the Secretary-General of the United Nations may be requested by either party to make the appointment.

2. The decision of the majority of the members of the Commission shall be the decision of the Commission, and shall be accepted by the parties as definitive and binding.

Article 36

The present Treaty, of which the Russian and English texts are authentic, shall be ratified by the Allied and Associated Powers. It shall also be ratified by Finland. It shall come into force immediately upon the deposit of ratifications by the Union of Soviet Socialist Republics and the United Kingdom of Great Britain and Northern Ireland. The instruments of ratification shall, in the shortest time possible, be deposited with the Government of the Union of Soviet Socialist Republics.

With respect to each Allied or Associated Power whose instrument of ratification is thereafter deposited, the Treaty shall come into force upon the date of deposit. The present Treaty shall be deposited in the archives of the Government of the Union of Soviet Socialist Republics, which shall furnish certified copies to each of the signatory States.

LIST OF ANNEXES

I. Map of the Frontiers of Finland and the Areas mentioned in Articles 2 and 4
II. Definition of Military, Military Air and Naval Training
III. Definition and list of war material

IV. Special provisions relating to certain kinds of property:
   A. Industrial, Literary and Artistic Property
   B. Insurance
V. Contracts, Prescription and Negotiable Instruments
VI. Prize Courts and Judgments

ANNEX I

(See Articles 1, 2 and 4)

Map of the Frontiers of Finland and the Areas Mentioned in Articles 2 and 4

ANNEX II

(See Article 15)

Definition of Military, Military Air and Naval Training

1. Military training is defined as: the study of and practice in the use of war material specially designed or adapted for army purposes, and training devices relative thereto; the study and carrying out of all drill or movements which teach or practice evolutions performed by fighting forces in battle; and the organised study of tactics, strategy and staff work.

2. Military air training is defined as: the study of and practice in the use of war material specially designed or adapted for air force purposes, and training devices relative thereto; the study and practice of all specialised evolutions, including formation flying, performed by aircraft in the accomplishment of an air force mission, and the organised study of air tactics, strategy and staff work.

3. Naval training is defined as: the study, administration or practice in the use of warships or naval establishments as well as the study or employment of all apparatus and training devices relative thereto, which are used in the prosecution of naval warfare, except for those which are also normally used for civilian purposes; also the teaching, practice or organised study of naval tactics, strategy and staff work including the execution of all operations and manoeuvres not required in the peaceful employment of ships.

ANNEX III

(See Article 19)

Definition and List of War Material

The term "war material" as used in the present Treaty shall include all arms, ammunition and implements specially designed or adapted for use in war as listed below.

The Allied and Associated Powers reserve the right to amend the list periodically by modification or addition in the light of subsequent scientific development.

Category I.

1. Military rifles, carbines, revolvers and pistols; barrels for these weapons and other spare parts not readily adaptable for civilian use.

2. Machine guns, military automatic or autoloading rifles, and machine pistols; barrels for these weapons and other spare parts not readily adaptable for civilian use; machine gun mounts.

3. Guns, howitzers, mortars, cannon special to aircraft; breechless or recoil-less guns and flamethrowers, barrels and other spare parts not readily adaptable for civilian use; carriages and mountings for the foregoing.

4. Rocket projectors; launching and control mechanisms for self-propelling and guided missiles; mountings for same.

5. Self-propelling and guided missiles, projectiles, rockets, fixed ammunition and cartridges, filled or unfilled, for the arms listed in sub-paragraphs 1-4 above and fuses, tubes or contrivances to explode or operate them. Fuses required for civilian use are not included.

6. Grenades, bombs, torpedoes, mines, depth charges and incendiary materials or charges, filled or unfilled; all means for exploding or operating them. Fuses required for civilian use are not included.

7. Bayonets.

Category II.

1. Armoured fighting vehicles; armoured trains, not technically convertible to civilian use.

2. Mechanical and self-propelled carriages for any of the weapons listed in Category I; special type military chassis or bodies other than those enumerated in sub-paragraph 1 above.

3. Armour plate, greater than three inches in thickness, used for protective purposes in warfare.

Category III.

1. Aiming and computing devices, including predictors and plotting apparatus, for fire control; direction of fire instruments; gun sights; bomb sights; fuse setters; equipment for the calibration of guns and fire control instruments.

2. Assault bridging, assault boats and storm boats.

3. Deceptive warfare, dazzle and decoy devices.

4. Personal war equipment of a specialised nature not readily adaptable to civilian use.

Category IV.

1. Warships of all kinds, including converted vessels and craft designed or intended for their attendance or support, which cannot be technically reconverted to civilian use, as well as weapons, armour, ammunition, aircraft and all other equipment, material, machines and installations not used in peace time on ships other than warships.

2. Landing craft and amphibious vehicles or equipment of any kind; assault boats or devices of any type as well as catapults or other apparatus for launching or throwing aircraft, rockets, propelled weapons or any other missile, instrument or device whether manned or unmanned, guided or uncontrolled.

3. Submersible or semi-submersible ships, craft, weapons, devices or apparatus of any kind, including specially designed harbour defence booms, except as required by salvage, rescue or other civilian uses, as well as all equipment, accessories, spare parts, experimental or training aids, instruments or installations as may be especially designed for the construction, testing, maintenance or housing of the same.

Category V.

1. Aircraft, assembled or unassembled, both heavier and lighter than air, which are designed or adapted for aerial combat by the use of machine guns, rocket projectors or artillery or for the carrying and dropping of bombs, or which are equipped with, or which by reason of their design or construction are prepared for, any of the appliances referred to in sub-paragraph 2 below.

2. Aerial gun mounts and frames, bomb racks, torpedo carriers and bomb release or torpedo release mechanisms; gun turrets and blisters.

3. Equipment specially designed for and used solely by airborne troops.

4. Catapults or launching apparatus for ship-borne, land- or sea-based aircraft; apparatus for launching aircraft weapons.

5. Barrage balloons.

Category VI.

Asphyxiating, lethal, toxic or incapacitating substances intended for war purposes, or manufactured in excess of civilian requirements.

Category VII.

Propellants, explosives, pyrotechnics or liquefied gases destined for the propulsion, explosion, charging or filling of, or for use in connection with, the war material in the present categories, not capable of civilian use or manufactured in excess of civilian requirements.

Category VIII.

Factory and tool equipment specially designed for the production and maintenance of the material enumerated above and not technically convertible to civilian use.

ANNEX IV

Special Provisions Relating to Certain Kinds of Property

A. Industrial, Literary and Artistic Property

1. (a) A period of one year from the coming into force of the present Treaty shall be accorded to the Allied and Associated Powers and their nationals without extension fees or other penalty of any sort in order to enable them to accomplish all necessary acts for the obtaining or preserving in Finland of rights in industrial, literary and artistic property which were not capable of accomplishment owing to the existence of a state of war.

(b) Allied and Associated Powers or their nationals who had duly applied in the territory of any Allied or Associated Power for a patent or registration of a utility model not earlier than twelve months before the outbreak of the war with Finland or during the war, or for the registration of an industrial design or model or trade mark not earlier than six months before the outbreak of the war with Finland or during the war, shall be entitled within twelve months after the coming into force of the present Treaty to apply for corresponding rights in Finland, with a right of priority based upon the previous filing of the application in the territory of that Allied or Associated Power.

(c) Each of the Allied and Associated Powers and its nationals shall be accorded a period of one year from the coming into force of the present Treaty during which they may institute proceedings in Finland against those natural or juridical persons who are alleged illegally to have infringed their rights in industrial, literary or artistic property between the date of the outbreak of the war and the coming into force of the Treaty.

2. A period from the outbreak of the war until a date eighteen months after the coming into force of the present Treaty shall be excluded in determining the time within which a patent must be worked or a design or trade mark used.

3. The period from the outbreak of the war until the coming into force of the present Treaty shall be excluded from the normal term of rights in industrial, literary and artistic property which were in force in Finland at the outbreak of the war or which are recognised or established under part A of this Annex and belong to any of the Allied and Associated Powers or their nationals. Consequently, the normal duration of such rights shall be deemed to be automatically extended in Finland for a further term corresponding to the period so excluded.

4. The foregoing provisions concerning the rights in Finland of the Allied and Associated Powers and their nationals shall apply equally to the rights in the territories of the Allied and Associated Powers of Finland and its nationals. Nothing, however, in these provisions shall entitle Finland or its nationals to more favourable treatment in the territory of any of the Allied and Associated Powers than is accorded by such Power in like cases to other United Nations or their nationals, nor shall Finland be thereby required to accord to any of the Allied and Associated Powers or its nationals more favourable treatment than Finland or its nationals receive in the territory of such Power in regard to the matters dealt with in the foregoing provisions.

5. Third parties in the territories of any of the Allied and Associated Powers or Finland who, before the coming into force of the present Treaty, had bona fide acquired industrial, literary or artistic property rights conflicting with rights restored under part A of this Annex or with rights obtained with the priority provided thereunder, or had bona fide manufactured, published, reproduced, used or sold the subject matter of such rights, shall be permitted, without any liability for infringement, to continue to exercise such rights and to continue or to resume such manufacture, publication, reproduction, use or sale which had been bona fide acquired or commenced. In Finland, such permission shall take the form of a non-exclusive licence granted on terms and conditions to be mutu-

ally agreed by the parties thereto or, in default of agreement, to be fixed by the Conciliation Commission established under Article 31 of the present Treaty. In the territories of each of the Allied and Associated Powers, however, bona fide third parties shall receive such protection as is accorded under similar circumstances to bona fide third parties whose rights are in conflict with those of the nationals of other Allied and Associated Powers.

6. Nothing in part A of this Annex shall be construed to entitle Finland or its nationals to any patent or utility model rights in the territory of any of the Allied and Associated Powers with respect to inventions, relating to any article listed by name in Annex III of the present Treaty, made, or upon which applications were filed, by Finland, or any of its nationals, in Finland or in the territory of any other of the Axis Powers, or in any territory occupied by the Axis forces, during the time when such territory was under the control of the forces or authorities of the Axis Powers.

7. Finland shall likewise extend the benefits of the foregoing provisions of this Annex to France, and to other United Nations, which are not Allied or Associated Powers, whose diplomatic relations with Finland have been broken off during the war and which undertake to extend to Finland the benefits accorded to Finland under the said provisions.

8. Nothing in part A of this Annex shall be understood to conflict with Articles 25 and 27 of the present Treaty.

B. Insurance

1. No obstacles, other than any applicable to insurers generally, shall be placed in the way of the resumption by insurers who are United Nations nationals of their former portfolios of business.

2. Should an insurer, who is a national of any of the United Nations, wish to resume his professional activities in Finland, and should the value of the guarantee deposits or reserves required to be held as a condition of carrying on business in Finland be found to have decreased as a result of the loss or depreciation of the securities which constituted such deposits or reserves, the Finnish Government undertakes to accept, for a period of eighteen months, such securities as still remain as fulfilling any legal requirements in respect of deposits and reserves.

ANNEX V

Contracts, Prescription and Negotiable Instruments

A. Contracts

1. Any contract which required for its execution intercourse between any of the parties thereto having become enemies as defined in part D of this Annex, shall, subject to the exceptions set out in paragraphs 2 and 3 below, be deemed to have been dissolved as from the time when any of the parties thereto became enemies. Such dissolution, however, shall not relieve any party to the contract from the obligation to repay amounts received as advances or as payments on account and in respect of which such party has not rendered performance in return.

2. Notwithstanding the provisions of paragraph 1 above, there shall be excepted from dissolution and there shall remain in force such parts of any contract as are severable and did not require for their execution intercourse between any of the parties thereto, having become enemies as defined in part D of this Annex. Where the provisions of any contract are not so severable, the contract shall be deemed to have been dissolved in its entirety. The foregoing shall be subject to the application of domestic laws, orders or regulations made by any of the Allied and Associated Powers having jurisdiction over the contract or over any of the parties thereto and shall be subject to the terms of the contract.

3. Nothing in part A of this Annex shall be deemed to invalidate transactions lawfully carried out in accordance with a contract between enemies if they have been carried out with the authorization of the Government of one of the Allied and Associated Powers.

4. Notwithstanding the foregoing provisions, contracts of insurance and re-insurance shall be subject to separate agreements between the Government of the Allied or Associated Power concerned and the Government of Finland.

B. Periods of Prescription

1. All periods of prescription of limitation of right of action or of the right to take conservatory measures in respect of relations, affecting persons or property, involving United Nations nationals and Finnish nationals who, by reason of the state of war, were unable to take judicial action or to comply with the formalities necessary to safeguard their rights, irrespective of whether these periods commenced before or after the outbreak of war, shall be regarded as having been suspended, for the duration of the war, in Finnish territory on the one hand, and on the

other hand in the territory of those United Nations which grant to Finland, on a reciprocal basis, the benefit of the provisions of this paragraph. These periods shall begin to run again on the coming into force of the present Treaty. The provisions of this paragraph shall be applicable in regard to the periods fixed for the presentation of interest or dividend coupons or for the presentation for payment of securities drawn for repayment or repayable on any other ground.

2. Where, on account of failure to perform any act or to comply with any formality during the war, measures of execution have been taken in Finnish territory to the prejudice of a national of one of the United Nations, the Finnish Government shall restore the rights which have been detrimentally affected. If such restoration is impossible or would be inequitable, the Finnish Government shall provide that the United Nations national shall be afforded such relief as may be just and equitable in the circumstances.

C. Negotiable Instruments

1. As between enemies, no negotiable instrument made before the war shall be deemed to have become invalid by reason only of failure within the required time to present the instrument for acceptance or for payment, or within which notice of non-acceptance or non-payment should have been given to the drawer or endorser, or within which the instrument should have been protested, has elapsed during the war, and the party who should have presented or protested the instrument or have given notice of non-acceptance or non-payment, has failed to do so during the war, a period of not less than three months from the coming into force of the present Treaty shall be allowed within which presentation, notice of non-acceptance or non-payment, or protest may be made.

3. If a person has, either before or during the war, incurred obligations under a negotiable instrument in consequence of an undertaking given to him by a person who has subsequently become an enemy, the latter shall remain liable to indemnify the former in respect of these obligations, notwithstanding the outbreak of war.

D. General Provision

For the purposes of this Annex, natural or juridical persons shall be regarded as enemies from the date when trading between them shall have become unlawful under laws, orders or regulations to which such persons or the contracts were subject.

ANNEX VI
Prize Courts and Judgments

A. Prize Courts

Each of the Allied and Associated Powers reserves the right to examine, according to a procedure to be established by it, all decisions and orders of the Finnish Prize Courts in cases involving ownership rights of its nationals, and to recommend to the Finnish Government that revision shall be undertaken of such of those decisions or orders as may not be in conformity with international law.

The Finnish Government undertakes to supply copies of all documents comprising the records of these cases, including the decisions taken and orders issued, and to accept all recommendations made as a result of the examination of the said cases, and to give effect to such recommendations.

B. Judgments

The Finnish Government shall take the necessary measures to enable nationals of any of the United Nations at any time within one year from the coming into force of the present Treaty to submit to the appropriate Finnish authorities for review any judgment given by a Finnish court between June 22, 1941, and the coming into force of the present Treaty in any proceeding in which the United Nations national was unable to make adequate presentation of his case either as plaintiff or defendant. The Finnish Government shall provide that, where the United Nations national has suffered injury by reason of any such judgment, he shall be restored in the position in which he was before the judgment was given or shall be afforded such relief as may be just and equitable in the circumstances. The term "United Nations nationals" includes corporations or associations organised or constituted under the laws of any of the United Nations.

INDEX

CPSIA information can be obtained
at www.ICGtesting.com
Printed in the USA
BVHW081052180421
605248BV00023B/2518

9 781258 491215